ENJOY SELF-PUBLISHING
HAVE FUN, MAKE MONEY, QUIT WORRYING

PATTY JANSEN

GET FREE EBOOKS

JOIN MY NEWSLETTER

RECEIVE THIS STARTER PACK FOR FREE

Visit pattyjansen.com
to sign up for Patty's mailing list. You get four series starter ebooks for free!

SELF-PUBLISHING HAS CHANGED

I wrote the first iteration of the Self-publishing Unboxed series in 2017.

At the time, the self-publishing community was steeped in boundless optimism about the industry.

I revised the first two books slightly in 2019 and again in 2022, because some businesses I mentioned in the first edition stopped existing.

I recently read through the books and cringed with the tone set in those books. Do this and do that, and the world is your oyster.

After a time when authors flooded into the industry (and are still coming), a pandemic and tough economic times, it's fair to say that the landscape has changed somewhat.

There are barnacles in the oyster farm! And just like the real thing (just ask the Hawkesbury oyster farmers) a disease has taken hold of the crop.

The disease is called FOMO (Fear Of Missing Out) and it eats at the minds and wallets of unsuspecting victims.

There is also the new ~~shopfront~~ farm nextdoor that lures larvae in with shiny new ~~managed services~~ roosts but that asks an ever-increasing proportion of ~~your sales~~ the harvest.

Costs for services and subscriptions have increased a lot, while not delivering a corresponding increase in sales.

The big companies and other service providers are proving every day that they are not our friends.

And yet, it is still possible to sell your writing and make some money. You may just have to be sharper at determining where your readers are, or look at out-of-the box (or shell?) ways of marketing.

Yes, the world is still your oyster, even if the shell is a bit malformed and overgrown with barnacles. The inside tastes the same.

(Yes, yes, I know I've taken the oyster metaphor far enough. I'll shut up now).

Creative freedom is more important than ever.

Independence is more important than ever.

Knowing who your readers are is more important than ever.

Hence, this new edition.

That is not to say that this edition will remain definitive for many years. It won't. If I look back on these words in 2028, I will probably cringe again.

That is the nature of the industry: it changes.

So what has changed?

Well, in recent years, especially since the pandemic, a lot of shine has gone out of the industry.

The original 2017 version of this book was written in a "you can do it" vibe. To do the same today would be ignoring the reality of many authors: that they can be doing everything right and still struggle.

I have no doubt whatsoever that back in 2017 those people also existed and there were far more of them than the industry acknowledges.

In this book, I'm talking to those people: the silent majority who feels shamed into remaining silent because their books don't sell huge numbers.

Of course I was always talking to these people.

This is why the original phrasing of the series premise included the words "no bestseller".

But right now, I'm talking to them even more than I was before. And I'm now going to give away the basic principles of what I strongly believe in:

SELF-PUBLISHING HAS CHANGED

- Don't believe the hype. You're not a failure
- It's about catalogue, not flash-in-the-pan success
- Spend less than you earn
- Never do something (especially spend money) because someone says so

If you take nothing else away from this book I want you to understand those things.

About this collected edition:

The original series had four volumes.

In this edition, I will be keeping the material covered in those four books together and will add to or amend the original structure.

Self-publishing Unboxed covers starting in self-publishing. It will concentrate on organisation issues and mindset about the start of your career.

Mailing Lists Unboxed remains the most current book. It shows you how to sell through your mailing list and covers mindset issues in relation to mailing lists.

Going Wide Unboxed is a small volume that discusses all the different places where you can sell and the mindset required to sell across a wide range of platforms.

Indie Author Unboxed takes a couple of fictional writers and follows them through their struggles.

Rather than break the books up, I've elected to update them and add interludes relating to the current state of publishing.

So here it is *Enjoy self publishing have fun, make money and quit worrying.* Or as I would say but that would make the book hard to advertise because of language: how to self-publish and not lose your shi(r)t.

SELFPUBLISHING UNBOXED

CHAPTER 1
THIS IS A BOOK ABOUT MAKING MONEY FROM YOUR WRITING

Gasp, I know. How dare I talk about *money*?

Writers are supposed to be precious and exclusive creatures who need no food and clothing and have no kids who need education and no rent that needs paying. They live off thin air. They have no lives because they can't afford lives, begging from friends, couch-surfing, slaving away in exploitative, backbreaking jobs, all the while banging away at their typewriters in the attic at night.

Because, art.

Every now and then, you will come across much-hyped articles in lauded, old-fashioned newspapers, or even websites (but writers can't afford the Internet, remember?) that perpetuate the myth of a poor suffering writer by trotting out just one of these writers.

They signed a book deal, got a $3000 advance. The book never earned out, and the publisher didn't want the second book. They wrote another book that sold even less and now earn a pittance from their writing and supplement their writing income from speaking gigs and teaching writing classes. Because, obviously, the world needs more starving writers who can't sell their books.

I know, right?

Of course, on the other side we find the other myth, that of the writer selling their soul to the devil called commerce, writing vast quantities of pulp books, churning them out, even contracting other people to write for them, because they write books that readers gobble up like cheap candy. This soulless writing (or so the literati say) thrives on churn; one book is like every other. But, hey, at least these writers can afford to pay for their own attic.

Stereotypes. Who doesn't love them? As soon as you say you're a writer, people will mentally put you in either of those two boxes.

This book is not about either of those extremes, although both definitely exist. It is also not about the soulless grind of finding an agent and selling your book to publishers who pay next to nothing, make you sign restrictive contracts, give you a poor cover and publish the book two years after they acquired it, barely market it and then hog your rights until the end of time.

It's about writing what you love, writing it well, positioning it well in today's market, and building a long term career through taking control of your own publication and your own audience.

It's a book about making an income through self-publishing.

A lot of writers are doing this already. They are not writers you will find mentioned in articles in *The Guardian*, because they don't have spectacular multi-million bestseller success. They are not the Amanda Hockings and Hugh Howeys and Andy Weirs of the world, although all of those saw fame from self-published books. But many of the writers I'm talking about never have any books in any top 100 anywhere.

They are writers who have been empowered by the ability to upload their own books to retailers and cut out the necessity of a middleman, a.k.a. a publisher. They have done this by putting out quality books that enough readers wanted to read that they, the authors, could lead the lives they have always dreamed of.

Not the riches as much as freedom. If you want riches, go back out that door and find a salaried job, because that's a far easier path. This book holds no promises about the size of your payout.

This is still a hard industry and a good deal of luck is involved: luck of writing the right thing at the right time and finding the right audience.

But with patience and a bit of savvy, you can absolutely still make more money than you spend, supplement your income and pay for little extras. It is also still possible to give up your day job, but I don't advocate that you start out expecting this to happen.

Self-publishing has changed the lives of many. It has enabled carers to look after their sick partners, parents to be there for their kids, retirees to travel around the world or simply live comfortably. It's allowed people to leave toxic marriages, leave bad jobs, provide for disabled family members, pay off mortgages, or even obtain mortgages.

It involves nothing except yourself, your sense of savvy and your computer.

It's self-publishing, but self-publishing with a plan. Give it three years. The three-year plan.

But first...

CHAPTER 2
SELF-PUBLISHING UNBOXED

FIRST WE NEED TO PUT A FEW MYTHS TO SLEEP THAT STILL CIRCULATE ABOUT self-publishing, myths that have proven very hard to kill.

THE MYTH THAT ALL SELF-PUBLISHED BOOKS ARE CRAP

There is certainly a lot of crap out there. Self-published authors are not helping by putting out poorly written books with zero editing. And by poorly written, I don't mean books that don't conform to some literati's self-imposed high standard of crafted prose, I mean books with such poor and twisted sentences that they are barely readable. Books with so many demonstrable grammar and spelling errors that a primary school kid with a decent grasp of language could do better. Unedited books by people who obviously don't write a lot in English, or books that have been hauled through Google Translate. Books with extremely badly made pixelated covers. Books with formatting that renders them unreadable.

I mean books that fail the absolute minimum standards of publication.

And the fact that this myth exists is because there are still far too many people out there putting out books just like that. So maybe "self-published books are crap" is not a myth, but it's definitely a myth when you want to apply it to *all* self-published books.

The thing is, there are also a lot of books that look great, contain fewer editing oopsies than books from big publishers, and have awesome covers. Books that look indistinguishable from trade-published books. Books that have been through a thorough editing process, have beautiful cover and are properly formatted.

If you're still doubtful that such books exist, go to the Science Fiction > Space Opera category on Amazon US, and look at the publishers of the bestselling books. If it says "Amazon Digital Editions" or the book is in Kindle Unlimited, then it's self-published. On non-Amazon retailers, it will often say Smashwords Edition, or the publisher may be listed as Draft2Digital. At the time of writing, trade publishers appear to have withdrawn from publishing Space Opera. Self-published writers OWN this category on all platforms.

These quality books are the books we're talking about. These are the books we want to emulate.

THE MYTH THAT SELF-PUBLISHED BOOKS COULDN'T FIND A PUBLISHER

This goes hand in hand with the previous myth.

Yet, the thought that self-publishing is somehow second rate to traditional publishing will not die.

But here is the truth: most of the self-published books you will see in online retail stores have never been submitted to a publisher.

Self-publishing is a lifestyle choice, not something you do after all your options are exhausted. Well—you can do that, of course, but in that case the book has probably exhausted you, and, having searched for a publisher, you have no real interest in publishing it yourself and making a business out of it, but are doing it out of frustration, and probably have no energy left to market it.

That's not a great place to be in when you publish.

Self-publishing is a business decision.

THE MYTH THAT SELF-PUBLISHED AUTHORS HAVE BOOKS IN THEIR GARAGE

It was not until I ventured onto the new social media app Threads that I saw how common the assumption is that you must do a print run, and that, by extension, book sales are all about print and getting books into stores.

No.

Emphatically and categorically, NO.

Self-published book sales are foremost digital. Well, they aren't always, for reasons we'll get to later, but when starting out, digital sales require little up-front cost. If you want printed books, print-on-demand requires no up-front investment either.

No print runs unless you can justify the cost and you know you can definitely sell the books.

Brick & mortar bookstores are not the venues you target most.

THE MYTH THAT SELF-PUBLISHING IS EXPENSIVE

Again on Threads, it is surprising how common this attitude is. It's mainly perpetuated by people who wail loudly and publicly that they don't have money and therefore they could never publish.

No, no and NO.

At its very roots, self-publishing is FREE. It costs *nothing* to put up a book.

Of course, to do a decent job, you will need some processes I will file under "quality control" and some may cost money and even quite a bit of money. The operative in that sentence is *may*. Authors who sell well and shell out big for quality control processes do so *because they can*. Not because spending big is absolutely imperative for getting sales.

Yes, quality control is imperative. How much you pay for it, however, is not. Don't let anyone tell you otherwise.

There will be a section in this book that shows you how to bootstrap these things. How to put out a book that passes general quality control parameters without the need to win a lottery or rob a bank.

Honestly, I cry when I see people goaded into spending thousands or tens of thousands on their first book, with no guarantees that it will sell.

And they spend this money while they've done no market testing and have NO SKILLS to actually sell the book.

It's money down the drain.

THE MYTH THAT ALL SELF-PUBLISHED AUTHORS SPEND A LOT OF TIME AND MONEY MARKETING

Again, no.

You cannot market a book into a success. The book needs to have appeal first and then you can spend more on marketing.

It is also possible to do very little marketing of the ad type at all. You're reading this book because that statement is true. I do very little marketing.

All book sales stand or fall with the book.

The success of your publishing career stands or falls with the business decisions you make and (yawn) how you handle your money.

There will be no career without some attractive books.

Obviously, putting out a well-produced book and placing it in the right genres is the holy grail. This book is about that. But first...

CHAPTER 3
PUT ON YOUR SNARK AND DISTRUST

When you have decided to self-publish, your wallet becomes a battleground.

Sharks start circling the moment you utter the word "self-publishing". Self-publishing means that you'll likely need to contract out some tasks, notably those you can't do yourself. These are tasks like editing, because it's extremely hard to spot your own errors, and cover design, because you don't have an artistic bone in your body. Don't get me wrong, these are *good* expenses. But there are also many potential pitfalls, money-wasters and outright scams.

THE BIG SHARKS

Start by googling "self-publishing" for example. What comes up? A whole page of vanity presses!

These "companies" (I prefer to use the word scammers) prey on the insecurity of hopeful writers. Those people want to self-publish, but have no idea how. Mostly, they have a long list of rejections from traditional publishers (and, sadly, often with reason), have been worn out by the grind and have decided to do it themselves. They start by doing the one thing that would normally give you some pretty decent answers: googling.

Nope! The vanity presses have hijacked the google search results. Not only that, but these results will keep following you around the Internet for the next few months in the Google Ads boxes. Just waiting for you to say: I looked at all the advice, but all this talk about formatting and finding an editor and marketing is too hard, why don't I pay someone $10,000 and be done with it all. Why wouldn't you? Because you're retired, and you *have* $10,000, and you understand and accept that everything costs money. It's rather a bit more than you expected to pay, but hey, you get to see your book published, and look! They offer publicity packages as well!

All of this would be fine, if all these "publishers" did was provide you with the services, and did a decent job. But no—the services I've seen rendered by them are second-rate, overpriced and sometimes unnecessary or ineffective. I've even seen press releases and book launches included in the pricing models!

For those who think a book launch party is vital, understand that the book launch is usually put on by a big publisher. The customers of Big Publishing are bookshops, and bookshop managers like coming to these after-work shindigs so that they can socialise. It has little to do with selling books to readers.

But, worse than all of this, the vanity presses sell you hope. They sell you the idea that everything will be taken care of, and that their expensive "publicity" package actually includes things that work. They sell you the idea that they will take care of the publishing (which they do, overpriced and second-rate though it usually is) *and* that they will deal with the marketing. Because it's the thought of marketing that will give many writers nightmares. They don't want to do the marketing. But, get this: every writer needs to do marketing. Even if you get a traditional publishing deal with a big publisher, you will have to do marketing. If you don't, the publisher won't sign your next book, because you won't sell very many. Marketing is a thing that you do every day.

The days that publishers did this all for you and all you needed to do was write in your attic are over. Done. Finished. Dead as a dodo.

So, get used to it: market or die.

YOU do the marketing. Not some company. Definitely not some company you paid $10,000 to publish your book, because here is another thing about these scammers: once your book is out the door, they're done with you. They've delivered what they said they would: editing (that leaves much to be desired), a cover (which is usually acceptable) and marketing package (that consists of press releases and other crap that doesn't work but sounds really nice).

They're done with you, and you have boxes of books in your garage with no idea how to sell them, and they have gone in search of the next sucker to milk.

If you're still dubious, it is worth noting that people who publish through vanity presses are often attached to the "old ways". They want to get into bookshops and see their books on the shelves. How ironic it is, then, that bookshops are more likely to stock a book openly self-published through Ingram Spark than one published through one of these predatory companies. And while we're at it, promotional sites are not going to want your book either. Don't. Just don't waste your money. Spend it on learning to write engaging stories.

Not having $10,000 to spend can be a blessing in disguise. Money is definitely no substitute for a bit of common sense, and "having more money than brains" is a real thing. Don't be one of those people.

THE LITTLE SHARKS

Say you've managed to avoid the vanity presses and you have found the real self-publishing crowd. Know that sharks are still common.

There are contractors who will take your money and won't deliver, promotional sites that will use shady tactics to promote your book (click-farms, incentivised buys, buy circles) that can get you into trouble with the retailers and can get your accounts on those retailers suspended. Others will simply try to sell you things you don't need or charge you a lot of money for promotions that don't work.

So you must develop a strong sense of distrust. But, I can hear you say, I know little, how do I find out whether a service is legit, whether I need that service or if it's any good?

Google is *usually* your friend here, especially in terms of reviews of business services, but the best method I recommend is to become part of a self-publishing community. At the moment, authors hang out in Facebook groups (I know, I know, but Facebook is actually forum software and does this relatively well, seeing as half the planet has an account). I would recommend Wide For The Win, Learn Self-publishing or Kickstarter For Authors, because any unethical providers or shady behaviour that inevitably enters these communities gets weeded out and exposed.

The groups can be a bit snarky if members feel a certain service or reply doesn't pass muster, but developing a good sense of distrust and snark is vital in this business.

Also check Writer Beware and the attached blog.

WHAT ABOUT THE PLETHORA OF COURSES?

It has become extremely popular for everyone who is in the writing/teaching business to bring out an online course. Are these the real deal or not?

You need to know two things about these courses:

1. These courses contain nothing that you can't find out online. If the course teacher claims there is, don't take the course. It's highly likely to be against someone's terms of service.
2. These courses help you to find this material quickly, and they connect you with a community. Especially the latter can be extremely valuable if you're not already part of a community. A course can be a shortcut.

Before you sign up for a course, determine what it teaches. The more specific, the better. Determine that this is a subject that you need to learn about and, more importantly, that you're willing to invest time and money into learning. There is no point in taking a course and then being hesitant to invest in buying and using the software, memberships, ad platforms or other things that were taught in the course.

Don't forget to evaluate the credentials of the people giving the course. Don't just look at testimonials, but look at the course provider's style and whether that suits your own style. Often these course providers put out a plethora of free webinars, where you can get a glimpse of the type of person giving the course. Don't buy a course unless you can get a glimpse into what it looks like. The best course providers give out a lot of material for free so that you can judge their style before parting with money.

On the subject of money, make sure there is a refund policy.

And decide whether you want to fork out the money and fast-track your learning or whether you have the time to learn organically online. I'm not advocating one over the other. It's up to you to decide. You're going to hear this line a lot in this book. It's not called *self*-publishing for nothing.

SHARK-REPELLENT

Unfortunately, when it comes to paid services, you need to be vigilant. If you adhere to these few guidelines, you'll potentially save yourself a lot of heartache and money.

- When something sounds too good to be true, it always is. Not just that, but Amazon is likely to ban your seller's account over it.
- In relation to the above, if someone tells you about a magic promotion and won't be up-front about how it is done, show you where the book will be promoted and how readers can sign up, then RUN! Chances are high that something shady is being done.
- NOBODY can guarantee a certain number of sales or downloads. If they do, they're using clickfarms to artificially boost your rankings. RUN!
- When someone cold-contacts you and wants to offer something that you need to pay for, it's never something you want.
- When someone gives you advice about how to sell and they don't actually, you know, appear sell a decent number of books or have a history of selling in the genre you want to write in, then what is that advice worth? Repeat with any other service that deals with the production or selling of books.
- On the flip side of the above, if someone sells really well, how much of that is going to be a product of their unique history, a history you don't share? Maybe they got a special opportunity years ago that is not applicable for you now. In particular, the advice of people who "made it" years ago may be outdated, because they are not familiar with what it's like to start as a new author now. They are also likely to give you marketing advice that's in line with their much larger budget and tolerance for risk.

You should always evaluate marketing advice given against your situation and make your own decisions. It doesn't mean the other person is *wrong*, but their marketing advice might not be right for you.

- On the other hand, if someone who sells well gives you advice about your *product*, then do listen carefully.
- No one will care more about your books than you will. Don't believe anyone who makes wonderful promises, for example a certain number of sales. People look after number one. Fact of life.

- And with all the above rules, remember this: never, ever leave your brain at home, and always carry a bullshit meter. Your gut is always right. If it smells like a fart that is because is it a fart.
- And if in doubt, ask your writing community. Ask on social media. And here is a hack: google this: "is [insert name of service] a scam".

There's sharks in them thar waters. This book is your harpoon. (Sorry, I love bad metaphors.)

With this said, we will now move into the most important part of the plan. No, grasshopper, this is not the nuts and bolts of how to set up your mailing list. It's about more stuff you don't want to read.

CHAPTER 4
WHY YOU DON'T WANT TO READ THIS BOOK

IF THIS WERE A BOOK OF THE HOW-TO VARIETY, THIS WOULD BE THE PART where the cheery recommendations go.

You know the shtick. So-and-so big name writer tried my method and had instant success, increasing sales by fifty percent.

Except this book is not about that. Not that people don't do well following the three-year plan mindset, and many others like it. To the contrary. There is a whole host of writers having found success following methods like these.

It's just that the three-year plan is not a box of tricks. This book is not about the glamour or the magic pill. It's about putting the many moving parts of your author business together.

The three-year plan is a philosophy that serves both as sales vehicle and as attitude check to keep you happy and avoid burnout. The three-year plan relies on consistency and persistence more than quote-worthy immediate success. This is not a paint-by-numbers book. It is about writing what you want to write and marketing it.

Massive success is fickle. It frequently comes when you're not ready for it. For a host of reasons, it is rarely sustainable. It's certainly not wise to suggest that it's a right to be earned and kept forever.

What goes up must come down, nothing lasts forever, and other bad clichés. They're clichés because they are true.

Writing income needs to be managed, the troughs ironed out, the peaks savoured, money squirrelled away, because income is neither regular nor secure. It's the nature of the beast.

Rather than telling you all kinds of wonderful things about this book and why you have to read it, I will tell you that you shouldn't read it. You shouldn't read it because it won't tell you what you want to hear: that publishing is easy, that you will make a million dollars in your first year or that your books will be an instant success if only you follow these easy steps.

Make no mistake, having a career as a writer is hard.

But having a career in writing is also much more achievable than it has ever been before. There are many writers making decent money selling ebooks, people you will never have heard of. People selling enough books to pay some or all of their bills.

This book will show you how to give yourself the best possible chance at setting up a career that will build your reader base. This book will show you how to sustain sales in between releases and promotions and other slow periods. This book will show you how to be independent of sales platforms and algorithms and how to spend more of your time doing what you enjoy: writing.

CHAPTER 5
THE PLAN ON STEROIDS

For those keen to get into it, here is the plan in the form in which it was originally published as post on the Kindleboards forum. For a number of years, the Kindleboards was the best place to find out about self-publishing. Then it got bought by a company that wants to wring out money from selling ad space. Every time I go to the site, it's less user-friendly. But the original posts are still up.

The post is quoted here because it still gets a lot of visits. People will read this and will recognise it. Many people have asked me to expand on the different aspects that make up the plan.

THE THREE-YEAR, NO-BESTSELLER PLAN TO MAKING A SUSTAINABLE INCOME FROM YOUR WRITING

I. The Product

1. Write a series of three books in a genre you like. It's best if the books are full-length of 70-80k words at least. There are people who can get away with novellas, but selling well gets harder the shorter your books are. Unless, maybe, your genre is erotica or romance. Maybe. Just make the books full length, OK? It makes life so much easier (insert whisper that sounds like Bookbub: many advertising sites don't accept short books).
2. Make the first book free.

3. Play around a bit with advertising if you feel so inclined (I mean—why the hell not?), but don't worry about stuff that takes you away from writing too much.
4. Make sure you have the following in all your books: a link to your mailing list sign-up form, and, at the end, a live link to the next book in the series.
5. When you finish the series, or even while you're writing it, start the next series. Make it a slightly different subgenre, or use a different setting and characters. Make sure that people don't need to have read the other series in order to follow it. Write three books. Make the first book free.
6. Repeat 5. Twice, if you can. Three years @ 4 novels a year = 12 books = 4 trilogies.
7. Advertise your freebies, but don't fall down any rabbit holes that take you away from writing for major chunks of time (insert snort that sounds like Facebook advertising).

II. The Marketing

1. After a while, your mailing list will start to build up a bit (see point 4 above). Get a paid account at MailChimp or wherever you are. If you are not at a list provider that allows automation and segmentation, and most importantly, automation *based on* automatic segmentation, move your list.
2. Set up mailing automation. When people join your list, send them an email with the freebies, even though they're already free. Don't email the freebies to them, but include download links in the email. Then booby-trap those links so that you can track who downloads what. You'll be using this later.
3. Next, send your subscribers to an automated program that sends them something at regular intervals (Amazon genre newsletters arrive every two weeks, that's good enough for me). What do you write about? About you, about your fiction, free short stories, you ask them questions, tell them about tidbits of research you've done, or places you travelled for your writing. Tell them about box sets you're in, and even plug your friends with similar books. Anything. Booby-trap any links to your books so your MailChimp/AWeber/whatever account knows who clicked what.
4. Siphon people who clicked all the links to series 1 (and downloaded the freebie!) off to a side list, and say three months

later send them an email saying: hey, this is book 2 in the series. Do this with all books 2 in all your series.
5. Repeat steps 3 and 4. Create new emails, use the links and who clicks them to segment your list and send them further information based on who clicked what.
6. Pronto! You have now created your own marketing machine that crawls like a giant slug over your subscriber list.

III. Your Tasks

It's now really clear what you need to do:

1. Keep writing new books that people want to read, continuing your most popular series, starting new series maybe (make book 1 free again). Add new emails about those books to your mailing sequence.
2. Keep feeding people into your giant mailing slug.

Note that there are certain things I don't do anymore, for example, my automation is much simplified. If you move your list to another mailing list provider, or the provider changes their automation process—two things that happened to me in close succession—this badly stuffs up your process. Much better to have a simple sequence that you can quickly rebuild from scratch.

Also, I quite enjoy manually emailing people every two weeks and including recent news. These emails have taken the place of blog posts.

My books are also no longer free on the retailer sites. Instead people can download them for free from Bookfunnel in exchange for their email address. Bookfunnel feeds them directly into my automation sequence. Or they can get them from my web store, which I didn't have at the time when I wrote the post.

Don't worry if the above paragraph went over your head. In the rest of the book, we go into details about how to set all this up.

But first: none of this will work without some more stuff you don't want to hear about.

CHAPTER 6
THIS IS THE PART YOU REALLY DON'T WANT TO READ

None of the plan outlined in this book will work if you don't have a book people want to read.

Let's just repeat that:

You must have a book people want to read.

Sorry to put a damper on your enthusiasm, but you need to learn to write well before you can learn to sell.

This is not a writing craft book, and most of this book is written under the assumption that you have done this, that you have read about story structure and plot and have done a class or two, or spent some time in writing workshops or have otherwise honed your craft.

Some people are natural learners and absorb craft through reading in the genre they want to write in.

But the truth is, just like you can't pick up an instrument and get a gig in a professional orchestra, everyone has to learn to write.

On top of that, once you have written well, everyone needs to learn how to present their book and make it the best possible product before you can start marketing it. Otherwise there is absolutely no point in doing all the other work.

CHAPTER 7
IT STARTS AND ENDS WITH THE BOOK

It shouldn't need to be said, but the most important thing you can do as writer is to write a good book.

Really.

In the marketing hype, this simple fact sometimes gets lost, or it gets confused with the erroneous assumption that all books are equal.

We all know they are not. We all know of good books and bad books. If pressured, most of us will even realise that our good books are not the same as someone else's good books. There is a name for people who don't realise this: it's "literary snobs".

Another truth is that every book will find someone who loves it, even if it's only the writer's mother.

The trick is writing a book that appeals to enough people for it to be marketable. It doesn't need to be a mega-bestseller. The key is *enough* people.

HOW DO YOU KNOW IF YOUR BOOK IS MARKETABLE?

If you have published your book, and people buy it who are not your friends and family, and if people regularly continue to buy it when you promote, you probably have a marketable book or at least the seeds of a marketable book.

If you run promotions or make your book free, and many people download it, but you're having trouble selling book 2, you might have a problem.

I'm not of the type that I'll tell you that a series *should* see a certain percentage of people who buy book 1 also buy book 2. This will depend on many things: the size of the promotion you have done, the size of your book, whether your audience are fast readers, whether book 1 ends in a cliffhanger, whether you can read book 2 independently and a whole bunch of other factors. It also varies over time.

But if you're unhappy with the sell-through, you can probably improve it. And you probably should improve it before you spend too much time and money on marketing.

HOW DO YOU DO THIS?

Apart from the lack of sell-through, problems in the book may manifest in the reviews. If a decent number of reviews mention that the book is slow, hard to understand, or has other problems like poor editing, then this is probably true.

In that case, fix the problems before you go any further. Definitely fix them before you spend huge amounts of money on marketing. The copies you sell or give out will be in circulation forever, and reviews about problems may turn up years after the sale of the book.

The best thing to do of course is not to publish a book with major problems in the first place.

HOW DO YOU AVOID PUBLISHING A BOOK WITH PROBLEMS?

In the first place: learn to write. I cannot stress this enough, even if it is something people seem to want to hear the least.

Spend time doing this. Not months, years. Take some courses, read some books. Join some writing communities and then submit to agents and publishers. No, not because self-publishing is second best, only to be considered if you can't get a traditional deal. It is because for all the supposed ills of the publishing industry, it is still full of people who love books and who see a lot of books pass their desk and who can spot a book that's well-written—even if it may not be up their alley. They will tell you so in their rejection letters: "This is well-written, but doesn't fit our catalogue."

Submit books to them until you get these types of personal replies. Submit shorter works to magazines. Publish a few. Get a sense of confidence that you can write a decent story with a beginning, middle and end in language that a lot of people find pleasant to read.

Seriously: learn to write.

As a caution, don't confuse "quality" with spelling and grammar issues, or with adherence to the many self-imposed "writing rules" that circulate around the learn-to-write community. Some writers genuinely believe their manuscript will be publishable, if only they eradicate every instance of "that" from their manuscripts. Or if they use no "passive voice" (and then they get confused about what passive voice actually is). Remember that there is only one thing worse than a piece of fiction where the word "was" is used multiple times in a sentence: one that has been contorted so that it doesn't occur at all.

If someone says your fiction has a stylistic issue, like the over-use of certain words or constructions, then (presuming the construction you used is grammatically correct), removing and fixing half of them is sufficient to get rid of the problem.

The writing rules are not silly and stupid, as some say. Religious adherence to them, is.

The rules were created with the purpose of making your book more readable. Ultimately, all of them serve the following purposes:

- Don't bore the reader
- Don't confuse the reader
- Don't annoy the reader.

All the rules are mere crutches to aid those points. Don't be boring, don't be confusing, don't be annoying. That's it.

But much more important than all this nitty-gritty is the story. This is why you will see books which are stylistically poor, and some that even have many avoidable grammatical errors, do well: because they tell an engaging story to an audience that's looking for those stories.

Hone your craft of storytelling more than your prose-craft. This can be really *hard*. It can lead to having to completely change your writing process. It may require help from outside.

When you have finished writing, you're not done. Once you have written, you must edit. However you do this is up to you. If you can't afford to pay for editing, at the very least get a nitpicky friend or two to read it for you. The only problem is that you are likely to have to do something for your friend in return. Or you may be able to buy their favour in cases of beer. At any rate, editing will cost you something. It could be money, or time, it could be something else, but you need a process in place to get rid of errors.

EDITING

Once you decide to pay for editing—and I think it's one of the first things you should pay for as soon as you can afford it—you need to know that there are many different kinds of editing.

Developmental Editor. When you're just starting out, it may be a good idea, at least once, to get a developmental editor. This is someone who will comment on storyline, character and plot. This person will look at the flow of the story and make suggestions to have it flow better. A developmental editor is not cheap, but will absolutely make you a better writer. They may not fix *that* book, but will have taught you skills for future books. See it as an investment in your craft.

Content Editor. A content editor will look at the data in the book: the setting if it exists, the science if there is any, the believability and consistency of the setting. The content editor and developmental editor are often the same.

Copyeditor. A copyeditor will look at paragraphs and sentence flow.

Proofreader. This person will pick out the typos, the missed punctuation and wrongly used words. Proofreading and copyediting are the absolute bare minimum of editing you should get.

It is possible to get someone who does more than one type of editing. Definitely ask your potential editor what sort of editing they provide and what other services you should consider hiring that they don't cover.

But remember that editing enhances a work. An editor doesn't exist to fix all your problems. In fact, if a book has so many problems that it needs serious fixing, any editor worth their reputation will not take it on. If you're asking for proofreading, but what you need is extensive developmental and style editing, they will tell you so. Listen to them.

Once you have done all this, have confidence in your abilities. Even if you have edited extensively, there will almost always be some errors.

Some people will complain loudly about them, and many times these people will be wrong. If you are like me and write in Commonwealth English, readers will complain of errors, even if they mean that there is a u in colour and they're not expecting one.

People will complain. That's a fact of life. When you put something out in the world, some people will hate it. But if you've done your job, there will only be a few of these people. Don't give readers any more reason to complain than necessary. But also accept that nothing will ever be to everyone's liking.

HOW DO YOU FIND AN EDITOR?

First, establish what kind of editing you want and look around with that in mind.

The best way is to ask for recommendations in places where self-published writers you respect hang out. You don't know any self-published writers? Get to know some already! Being part of the community is very important, I would say absolutely vital, to your career. Your author friend circle is a great place for the purpose of finding good, reasonably-priced and reliable service providers.

I've often used two editors: first I use someone who reads the books and makes suggestions regarding characters, logic and storyline. She points out the saggy bits, the rushed bits, and the parts that are unclear. We will talk about characters and whether their motivations are clear and whether or not it was clear why the characters decided to do as they did in the book.

She often tells me nothing I didn't already know or suspected, but the value in our interactions is in discussing what to do about those issues.

After this process is completed and I have done an edit, the book will go to a traditional editor who does a line-editing pass and a proofreading pass.

While you don't have to do exactly the same thing, it is a very good idea to have someone read the book for strange jumps of logic or things that may trip readers up, such as a character doing something that people would perceive as unsympathetic or dumb.

Then the copy editing step puts the final touches on the work.

WHAT ABOUT EDITING SOFTWARE OR AI?

There is some really good AI-driven software. Use it, because it will point out things that a good editor will also tell you about: word repetition, missing words, too much passive language, sentences starting with the same word, filter words, all that kind of stuff.

You can even read up on the reasons why the software is flagging the word or phrase and you can learn more by googling it.

It will, however, sometimes make nonsensical suggestions, which you obviously shouldn't accept.

CAN YOU SELF-EDIT?

This is a contentious subject, but here is my feeling about it:

Absolutely, you can. I prefer to say "a book must be edited" and leave who is doing the editing up for people to decide.

BUT (you know there was a but, right?) at the very start of your career, with your very first work of fiction, is probably the worst time to do it.

At that point in your career, you're still learning. You pick up all kinds of bad habits, and many of them will harm your prospects of selling well.

I advise people to get an developmental editor at least once to learn from them, not to fix the book in question. If you can't afford this, being part of a critique group can be a slow but cheap substitute.

Some people have no funds to pay for an editor, especially since prices have skyrocketed since the pandemic. This is a valid standpoint. There is NO need to shame people into thinking they're not good enough because they don't have much money. I also very strongly believe that you should never feel you are forced into paying for things you cannot afford just because someone says so.

If you can't afford an editor, use software and then ask a friend whose language skills you judge good and ask them to answer these questions:

- Do you understand what is happening and why the characters are doing what they're doing?
- Are there parts of the book you find boring?
- Do you spot any writing tics?

And then, when your friend is done and you attended to what they said, run the book through some editing software.

If your book starts selling reasonably well (like, a few copies a day), fix typos by hiring a proofreader, but don't touch the rest. It obviously works.

You do NOT mess with a winning horse. Seriously, don't.

HERE IS THE THING ABOUT EDITING

(Editors, put your hands over your ears, because you will hate what I'm about to say)

Editing is a sliding scale.

If you view editing as "fixing typos", the sort of stuff that a proofreader does, then there is a right and wrong. Wellllll, that is if you discount regional variations and comma placement, some of which are subject to prescribed style guides or personal preferences.

But once you start to take editing into the clarity and storytelling realms, then personal preference takes over from existing rules and a decent amount of this type of editing comes down to experience, some guesswork, gut feelings and pet peeves.

In this space, editors can absolutely make a book easier to read. But, here is the thing, they can also be very wrong.

A big-name editor once told me: if someone tells me your work has an issue, they're always right (insofar as that it's an issue *for them*). When they tell you how to fix it, they're almost always wrong.

So when someone whose opinion you value points to an issue with storytelling or plot, you need to change something. What the thing is you should change... no one can tell you that with certainty.

When a reader says "needs editing" they mean one of a few things:

- There are typos

- There are things they think are typos but they're wrong (either because of regional variation or because they're just, you know, *wrong*)
- They don't understand what's going on
- There are continuity errors, like objects or people that mysteriously appear or go missing in between two sections of the text

These are things that need to be looked at and fixed if the readers are right. These are demonstrable errors that a proofreading pass can fix.

Everything else in the book is a matter of opinion. An editor can help you guide to what is the most likely path to a book people will enjoy. But there is no one right path.

So there you have it. This is as much as I'm going to say about editing.

But even before you get to this stage…

CHAPTER 8
DON'T HATE THE PIGEONHOLES

A VERY IMPORTANT STEP IN THE PUBLISHING PROCESS, PREFERABLY DONE BEFORE you even start writing, is to determine what genre you want to market the book in.

At this point, a lot of inexperienced writers will complain that they don't like being pigeonholed. They don't like to be confined to a certain genre, or they haven't even thought about it. They wrote a mishmash of science fiction with fantasy elements, but it's set in medieval times and oh, the main character is ten, but it's definitely not a book for children. It defies classification.

This was why they got into self-publishing in the first place, right?

Well, no.

Genres are not about pigeonholes or conformity. They are about reader expectations.

How?

Think about what you read and why you read what you read. Chances are that you read only a couple of genres. You are attracted to certain elements—or tropes—common to those genres. I like science fiction and fantasy. Tropes common to these genres are: worldbuilding, usually some sort of adventure, magic or technology that doesn't yet exist. The story is usually, but not always, told in a setting that is not today's world, or if the setting is today's world, there is usually a kind of shadow secret society.

All science fiction and fantasy includes elements that are not real and those elements are important in the story. That is the very essence of those genres. I'd be annoyed if I read a book that was just about characters in a family and might be set in the future but the setting sounds just like today and the characters don't interact with the setting. Because it wouldn't be science fiction.

Similarly, all romances include a couple, and they have a happy ending. That is the very essence of the genre. The couple can be rich, poor, from all corners of the world including the past, including the future, but the relationship between them is central and is the main driver of the plot.

In mystery and crime, the protagonist solves a problem. It could be a murder, a missing-person case, a jewel theft or something strange that happened in the local history museum. But something needs to be solved. A mystery is not about the romance between two of the characters.

These are broad expectations of genre, and as writer, you ignore them at your peril.

Consider your book in terms of these genres, so that you can give the readers what they expect to get. It is best to do this before you start writing so that you can gear your book towards those expectations. It is best to build it into the blurb—which I also recommend you write before the story.

Sure, there are books that can comfortably fit into more than one genre. In that case, you choose the one you think is most attractive to readers. Genre classification is not static and you can change it later.

If you have no idea how to classify your book, I would suggest that you read some of the bestselling books in the genres the book might fall in. And then read the blurbs of a good many more. Make notes of tone, subject matter and types of characters that you might find in titles that sell well today.

I'm afraid I'd have to say that in at least half the cases where writers aren't sure what genre to put their book in, it means they are unfamiliar with the recent publications in that genre. It often means that they've been writing on an island, with little knowledge of what's hot and what's not. It's a mark of inexperience and does not usually bode very well for the book. Sadly, Chosen One fantasy went out of fashion thirty years ago, and the readers are not terribly fond of Mary Sues either. Yet we have all innocently written those types of books—present company included. Educate yourself so that you can see that those types of stories should remain where they are: in your bottom drawer. At least until you gut the plot and turn it into a book that's more in line with what readers want today.

Yes, you can publish—that's the freedom of self-publishing—but the premise of this book was that you want to make money with your writing, so that's what I'm going to assume you want to do.

Now here is a small new section I'm adding in 2024.

I still believe genre is hugely important. If your book clearly falls within the parameters of a genre, it will be so much easier to market.

But these days we have Kickstarter and direct sales.

Kickstarter in particular is a very good place for out-of-the-box genres. I mean—I sold an art book with images of humanoid greyhounds in 1920's style.

So I want to add that it is possible to sell cross-genre stuff, but being solidly in genre makes everything easier.

To sum up, the foremost issue is to determine what genre your book is. It doesn't matter so much that it's not a perfect fit. In fact most books can be classified in more than one way. But classified they must be, so that a reader wanting a romance gets a romance and a reader wanting a mystery gets a mystery.

Genre classification is also very important for cover design. Your cover must reflect the correct genre.

Which brings me to...

CHAPTER 9
EVERYONE JUDGES A BOOK BY THE COVER

BECAUSE EVERYONE DOES. DON'T LET ANYONE TELL YOU OTHERWISE. PEOPLE judge books by their covers all the time.

If you saw a book in a bookstore with an embarrassingly hideous cover, you'd think twice about buying it. You would not want to be seen dead reading a book with that cover on public transport. Why do you think erotic fiction took off with the advent of ereaders? Because no one can see what you're reading!

That's right. People judge people by the books they're reading. People judge themselves by the covers of the books they read.

Before you upload your homemade cover, be honest about it. Do you have any graphic skills? Have you studied book covers in your genre and do you understand what makes them work?

If the answer to both is yes, go ahead and design your own cover. It is entirely possible to produce a cover that sells.

However, unless you have graphic and artistic skills, and you're aware of genre conventions and know about fonts and text placement, and have an artistic eye, and some experience, it's highly unlikely that you can design a cover that's even remotely adequate.

So, be honest: does the cover you've designed—and that looks pretty to you—look anywhere near the covers of books in your genre that sell well?

If in doubt, ask some people who read a lot of books. After all, they won't want to be seen dead with a book that has an ugly cover. Don't take their "it's not too bad" replies as encouragement. The cover you made for your first ever book is terrible. You know it.

Get a cover designer. You'll be glad that you did.

HOW DO YOU FIND A COVER DESIGNER?

The same place you find an editor: recommendations from friends and forums. There are a number of very good cover designers out there who do very nice work for not very much. You can get a good pre-made cover for a very reasonable price. In case you don't know what it is, a pre-made cover is a fully designed cover where the only thing you get to change is the title and your name. This is a very good and affordable way of getting an attractive cover. No, it won't fit the book to a T, but this is much less important than authors think. The function of the book cover is to be attractive, to make people curious and inform them what *sort* of book they're going to get.

If you have zero graphic skills and not much money, get a pre-made cover. Don't be precious about how well it reflects the exact content of your book. Don't let an ugly or ineffective cover stand in the way of people buying your book.

If you want to move up-market, a custom-made photomanipulated cover from a reputable designer would start at a few hundred dollars. If you're really lucky, you can find a good designer who does it for less, but if such a person is a professional, they will be forced to charge the going rate unless design is a hobby for them.

Top-end covers should cost anywhere from $1000 for photo-manipulation and up.

In the last few years, since the pandemic, prices have gone up a lot.

But there are a couple of important things to know when commissioning a book cover.

A cover is an image that represents the content of the book.

Above all, the cover should make it clear what genre and subgenre the book is. How do you know what this looks like? Well, go to the website of any book retailer and look at the covers of recently published books in that genre. At the moment, you will usually find dark blue covers with purples and reds with a woman in dark clothing on Urban Fantasy; you will often find a cloaked figure in a mountainous landscape in Epic Fantasy, space ships in Space Opera, a couple or just a woman with pretty colours in Romance. You'll often find an image with bold type for crime and a cover showing some object in Mystery.

Not sure about your book's genre? Go back to the previous section. You will now see that this is really important.

Apart from indicating subgenre, a good cover illustrates mood and elements from the book. Are there werewolves? Put a wolf on the cover. Does the book contain a crime? Put someone holding a gun on the cover. Add elements of setting—urban vs. country—or climate—make sure people wear thick coats.

One thing that usually does NOT make a good cover is an illustration of a scene from the book. In the vast majority of cases this is because book scenes don't convey genre, and they are often too complex and difficult to get right. For the designer—whose job it is to design your cover, not to read your book—these types of scenes and authors who insist on them are a royal pain in the butt. Authors can get way too precious about it, insist on changes that ruin the design and are outside the skill set of the designer, and the chance that whole thing ends in tears, with a poor cover, is high. A good designer will have a point where they are forced to ditch a client who is too demanding. A good designer has the reputation because their covers are good. It means they're busy. They need to deliver the goods on time. Be clear in what you want, and be reasonable. Give a designer a general brief with the sort of book it is, the elements that are in it, and a few examples of covers that you like. Especially the latter is very helpful for the designer.

And then, for Pete's sake, let the designer do their job. It's your job to write the book. It's their job to produce a cover that sells. You wouldn't want them to do your job, so don't try to do theirs.

COULD YOU DO IT YOURSELF?

Absolutely.

You can learn to design your own covers to an acceptable standard.

The operative in that sentence is *learn*.

You have to study book cover design, perhaps do some courses on using the software if you don't already know this, and, most importantly, learn typography.

Good book cover design is 50% image and 50% typography.

You need to learn about font hierarchy and focus points and font treatment, kerning and more.

Does this type of stuff float your boat? Great! Go for it. Otherwise it's best to let someone else handle it for now. Or just grab a cheap premade.

WHAT ABOUT AI?

I probably cannot get away with rewriting this book without mentioning the waves made by AI, so I might as well do it here.

I'm not a hater.

I'm also not a fanboi.

If it's useful, I will use it. I'd unpack *useful* as having one or both of these qualities:

- It's faster
- It's better

I also adhere to the following: if a layperson can clearly see you've used a tool, then you're using it wrong. This applies to the complete gamut of tools we have, including writing and spelling tools, but also things like 3d models used for book covers, and yes, AI for covers. If someone with no knowledge about design or about AI can clearly tell, it's not done properly and deserves the scorn it may get.

Whether or not you use AI for a range of purposes will depend on your process. However, none of the AI tools are good enough (yet, if ever) to use entirely without editing, and definitely not without extensive checking.

AI can't make book covers, even if its ability to handle text is getting better all the time. It introduces a lot of AI-isms, like hyper-saturation and the tendency to put the subject smack-bang in the middle and this is if you can get a flawless image in the first place. Likely (and probably best practice), you would compose your cover of a combination of AI output and stock photos. You need to fix these images. You need to colour-balance the ensemble. Then you need to do typography that is so super important.

In short: you need to actually *design* the cover, and know how to do this, and how to place text, so that it's not obvious you've used AI-generated elements (for example, you generated a space ship because you are sick to death of the very limited options offered by stock photo agencies with cool space ships).

At that point, we're back to this: learning to design covers is a big task, and if you're just starting out, you've got a lot of other work to do…

CHAPTER 10
THE MOST IMPORTANT 100 WORDS YOU'LL WRITE

THE BLURB, OR SALES COPY, IS THE MOST IMPORTANT PIECE OF TEXT YOU WILL write for your book. The blurb is the bit that goes on the back of a print book and in the description on retailer sites. To many writers, the blurb comes as an afterthought, but it's a vital piece of text.

In the space of a hundred words, you have to convince someone that your book is worth reading. You have to tell them about the characters and the story and make them interested in what happens.

Yet many blurbs are boring or confusing. They try to cram too much information into a small piece of text, and the end result is a paragraph or two of indigestible, confusing mush.

What goes into a good blurb?

As with most things, simple is better. A good blurb needs to be easy to understand and needs to be an engaging piece of text.

Typically it will set the scene for the story; it will introduce a main character and his or her main problems; it will state what gets in the character's way and will leave off there. The blurb is a teaser. It's meant to make you excited or curious so that you have to buy the book to find out what happens. Or it has to make you want to read about this really cool world, or it confirms that yes, this book is a proper murder mystery and therefore you'll like it if you read murder mysteries.

A typical blurb conveys genre and gives a concept, it gives an interesting problem and confirms that the problem fits within the genre, and it brings something that is unique to the book.

Make no mistake, writing a blurb is extremely hard and many writers take a long time to master it.

Some hire someone to do it for them.

There are many different styles of successful blurbs. If you want to know more about blurbs, do the one thing I have now told you to do a few times already: go to the retailer pages of your favourite genre and pull up some of the books that are similar to yours. Look at their blurbs.

A very basic example:

Johnny is an orc, but he's a smart orc and he wants to go to university. Unfortunately, the university admission criteria does not admit orcs, and the evil Dean, Dr Foster, will not make an exception. He hates orcs. But there is that science show competition that allows the winner to be accepted in the course of their choice…

- The *concept* is: orcs going to university. This alone may make you think "Cool!"
- The *character* is Johnny, who is clearly a sympathetic orc.
- The *conflict* is between Johnny and Dr Foster.
- The *plot* is obviously going to be about winning the science competition. At this point the reader may guess that the evil Dr Foster is going to rig the competition.

(Silly aside: yes, the acronym reads CCCP. That was an honest accident and not engineered by some communist plot. People born after 1989 may not get it.)

This is the very basic structure for a blurb. From this basic blurb, I would put the book in Urban Fantasy as it's set in a contemporary world, unless the blurb says that the whole book is set in a fantasy land, or the university teaches magic, in which case I would probably put it in Epic Fantasy, or Comedic Fantasy, if it's meant to be funny. Use your judgement.

In the case of Urban Fantasy, I would put a dark cover on it if the book included dark elements (murder, serious threats to life and dark magic) or a cartoonish cover if it was for younger readers or if the book was funny.

If Epic Fantasy, I would get an artist to draw a cover with orcs and elves and a stately building and I would get the artist to use dark colours if the tone of the book was dark and lighter colours if the book was funny. I would use a different artist for a dark book than I would for a funny book.

This, then, is how the complete presentation package comes together. The title, cover and blurb reflect what's inside. They all point in the same direction so that your potential reader can get a good feel for what type of book it is.

But before we continue, there are a few other important things…

CHAPTER 11
THE UGLY STEPCHILD

...OF SELF-PUBLISHING IS FORMATTING.

For those who say formatting doesn't matter, a single look at a poorly formatted book is enough to dispel this notion.

Try reading a book that hits you in the face with a "wall of text" because of paragraphs that are too large and too densely spaced, or where paragraphs don't have indents (fiction) or an empty line between them (non-fiction) to space them out. Or where the indents are strangely wide, or the chapters mushed together, or... the list is endless.

People click away from books because the text looks "wrong", even if they can't formulate what "wrong" is.

Formatting is not hard. You can do it yourself. At the very basic level, formatting uses HTML code. An ebook is a web document.

But, you say, who still knows how to write code?

(It's an extremely useful skill both to fight bloat and to understand how things actually work, but that aside)

These days, we have a lot of options to format our books.

Fortunately, for the very beginners, most sales platforms allow you to upload DOC files. Amazon does this, Kobo does this, and the aggregator Draft2Digital does this.

Although you can upload Word files and let the retailer sites convert them for you, their formatting output is really basic and sometimes errors creep in, especially if your Word file is messy and contains a lot of invisible character format codes. In this case, you may need to nuke the file by importing it into a super-basic text editor like Notepad and exporting it again.

Of course, doing that stuffs up any formatting and will often also turn your curly quotes into straight quotes.

If you want to get a bit more hands-on, you could use a program like Jutoh or Sigil to guide you in producing the code.

Using the above options, you can, relatively successfully, format a basic text, which is fine for fiction.

But what if you want to add formatting elements such as flourishes with chapter headings, and different fonts for specific purposes? For example if you have an AI speak, you may want to put those lines in monospace Courier font. Or if you write non-fiction, you may want to add bullet points or tables. And any book needs a nice title page, of course, because this highly enhances the free sample that people are going to see on retailer sites.

Sadly, you cannot control how a device will display your text. A reader can choose font, font size, background colour. Features like dropcaps don't display on all readers, especially the older or simpler models, or, for that matter, phones. Ereaders are rather long-lived devices, so it's likely that a significant proportion of your readers will use these.

No, please don't come up with the "those are just the older readers" canned casual ageism line. People whose devices can't handle special features will include:

- Old devices that still work after many years. I'm all about reducing waste so why replace something unless it's broken? Also, please remember the age and model of the device says nothing about the age of the user. Just can it with the ageism about technology users, mK?
- People using simple apps on phones that can't handle complex graphics
- People buying at the Nook store

Formatting emergencies have a habit of sneaking up on you. Readers will not hesitate to let you know about problems you were not aware of, and of course when something like this crops up, it needs to be fixed yesterday.

You may not know how to fix it or where the problem lies. You may need to call in someone who makes formatting their specialty.

In short, there are a number of formatting options:

- DIY, with your own coding. Time-intensive, and it takes a bit of research and knowledge to make files that look pretty.
- You can upload DOC files to various sites, and some of those sites will allow you to use the files they generate elsewhere. This requires a clean DOC file and you may need to manually produce your own Table of Contents.
- You can buy or download software that generates ebook files. Some of the options are fairly basic, but others are sophisticated. If you have a Mac, I absolutely recommend that you buy a piece of software called Vellum, which you can also use to format your print books. An unlimited licence costs $250 at the time of writing, but it formats your files in minutes, the files look extremely nice, are optimised for each sales platform and each device and the Vellum people are extremely on the ball about changes in requirements. This and a program called Scrivener, and the fact that you used to need a Mac to upload files directly to Apple, is the reason that most established writers own a Mac. For completeness the writing app Scrivener (Mac or PC but the Mac version is so much better) can also format books and some people use it but for my money the less said about Scrivener's export functions the better because I may start using some French words.
- For users of either PC or Mac, there is a program called Atticus that's web-based and works on all platforms.
- There is also a free program called Sigil and another program called Jutoh. It is about $40.
- Or you can pay someone to do it for you at $25-100 per file. I used to recommend this, but with the advent of Vellum and Atticus, and the ability to export your files from Draft2Digital, there really is no need.

However you choose to do it is up to you and will depend on the amount of money and time you have.

But don't make the mistake of treating formatting like the ugly stepchild. It is important.

SPECIAL FORMATTING, IMAGES, TABLES ETC.

These are always difficult in ebooks and would be the only reason where I'd recommend a professional formatter.

Things like custom fonts, flourishes, images and other layout features are quite risky as inclusions in an ebook.

An ebook is flowable. You do not get to control the font, the reader does this. Similarly, you also do not control the font size, placing of text or images, the display or otherwise of flourishes like fancy chapter breaks, dropcaps and other formatting.

In attempting to display this on a simpler or older device, the result can range from anything like weird to a mess to completely unreadable.

With every special feature you add manually, you increase the number of people who will not have an "ideal" experience when reading your book.

Therefore, I recommend to either stick within your formatting software's (Vellum or Atticus) capabilities or hire someone. Of course you can also become a formatting expert yourself, but at this point I'm assuming you'd prefer to spend your time writing books.

A hack: if you want to include a small table, simply screenshot the correct formatting and add it as an image.

AN EMERGENCY FORMATTING HACK

If ever you have a formatting emergency, or you need to format a file for Advanced Reader Copies or similar reason, go to Draft2Digital and open an account if you don't already have one (and you should. They're really cool for reasons I'll tell you about later). It's free. Upload your file as new book, then follow the publishing process until you get to the screen where you can download sample EPUB and MOBI files. Do this. Use those files to upload to retailers or send to your readers. It costs nothing, and D2D absolutely allows you to do this. They also do print files.

The service provider site Reedsy also has a similar capability.

CHAPTER 12
DON'T FORGET THE BACK MATTER

ONE OF THE MOST IMPORTANT ELEMENTS IN SETTING UP YOUR BOOK FOR SALE IS quite simple. It's the book's back matter.

These are the About the Author and Also By sections in the back of your book, where you list your contacts, your website and other books you have written.

In the back matter, you get to tell people what to do next.

Make no mistake, people are lazy and love being told what to do.

Do you want them to review the book? Tell them. Do you want them to sign up for your mailing list? Tell them. Do you want them to buy the next book? Tell them. Make a page for each of these things on your website and put links in the book's back matter.

You may ask: is it not better to link directly to the next book on the retailer site? It can be, depending on your aim and you may like to try this.

My aim in the three-year plan is to take control of as much of my audience as I can get. I want as many people as possible on my mailing list, and I want them away from the retailer sites. Of course I will send them back to those sites so that they can buy the book, but I prefer to know who they are first. At the very least I want to know where they came from and how many of them clicked the link.

Also, if you include links to retailer sites, you will have to compile a different ebook file for each retailer, because they will not let you upload a file with a competitor's links in the back. Fancy that.

So, where do you put these links?

The most important piece of real estate in your back matter is immediately following the end of the book, and before the page header for the About The Author section. So you'll finish the text, and there will be a scene break character, usually asterisks, and your closing message will come after that. In my case, it reads something like:

Thank you for reading [book]. In the next book of the series [add a brief tidbit about the next book]. Get [title of the next book] here.

The last sentence would be a live link to a page on my website.

One of the very important things I can do on this page on my website is let the reader know when the next book will be out, if it isn't out yet, and add a signup page to be notified.

But what if you like to link to a retailer page, and you don't have it yet because the book hasn't been published? In that case, use an editable link redirect service like the WordPress plug-in prettylinks. Point the link at a page on your website where you tell people that the book isn't out yet, and insert the redirect link in your book. Then swap over the link to point to the retailer site later. Now you don't need to edit your ebook in order to change the link.

Here is another important thing: When you have a mailing list signup link in your books, make sure you put it in the front as well as the back.

I know it sounds silly. Why ask people to sign up before they've even read the book?

Consider someone who is as anal as I am: when I finish reading a book, I go back to the first page and close the book, so that it won't continue to show as "reading now" on my e-reader.

Say I read a book, and two days later I was still thinking about it and wanted to sign up for when the next book comes out. If I closed the book, I would have to wade through the entire book to get to the signup link at the end.

Even if you're not as anal as I am, and don't get why, put the link in the front of the book anyway. We'll come back to this issue a few times in this book.

CHAPTER 13
YOU ARE NOW READY TO SELL YOUR BOOK

There you go!

You are now ready to start selling your books. They're packaged nicely, look great, you have done your best to make sure your catalogue is of the best quality you can put out.

You have added the appropriate links where they need to be.

Now we can deal with the things you need to do to set up your sales strategies.

Let's start selling this puppy.

CHAPTER 14
THE SERIOUSLY BORING CRAP THAT'S REALLY IMPORTANT

First I'm going to talk to you about accounting. I know, I know, I can hardly think of a more yawn-inducing subject on the planet. Sadly, it's also really important. A wrong decision can cost you a lot of money and involve a lot of work to put right.

Before you start selling, you need the following:

A bank account dedicated to your sales income.

A tax ID for the same.

If you're envisaging setting up as a commercial writer, you're a business—and if you weren't, you probably wouldn't be reading this book—and you should set up a business for your books. How you do this depends on where you live. Consult a local accountant. In general these options probably exist: you can set up as a sole trader or as publishing business. A publishing business is likely to be the more expensive of the two options, but does offer you the opportunity to publish other people's work, and in most countries has the most rigorous protection of your personal assets in case of a claim.

You might be able to set up as a sole trader or equivalent and this would cover just you, with fewer administrative hoops.

Why you should do this: setting up as a business allows you to claim expenses as tax deductions. These expenses can be quite considerable, especially in the beginning: editing, cover design, formatting, ads, the cost of setting up a website. If you're going to start spending this sort of money, it's silly not to set up a business and claim those costs as deductions, because they are costs incurred in producing your income.

Retailers are by law required to withhold tax.

All retailers—listed in the next chapter—will ask you for a tax ID. Give them your business bank account and your business tax ID. At the end of the year, the retailer will send you a statement with how much tax they withheld on your behalf, and you can use this in your annual tax return to claim deductions.

An important point to consider if you have a paying day job: many jobs, especially in higher management, higher education, manufacturing, technology or research, include non-compete clauses in their contracts.

While it is true that a full-time employer can't dictate what you do in your spare time, they have a lot more leverage if you make money from your spare time activity, or if they perceive this activity as competing with your contract of employment. There are also issues surrounding confidentiality, ownership of work or knowledge and income derived from your employment with them.

If you work in a medical research lab and write historical romance, your employer is unlikely to have an issue with it. However, if you wrote medical thrillers, they just might. Especially if your book suddenly took off.

Therefore, dust off that contract and see what it says about other income. You may, as I was, be unpleasantly surprised.

TO DO LIST: ACCOUNTING:

- Set up as company or sole trader.
- Get a tax ID for this entity.
- Get a bank account for this entity.
- Check the contract of employment for your day job for nasty clauses about income or proprietary knowledge.

CHAPTER 15
WHERE TO SELL

CURRENTLY, THERE ARE FIVE MAJOR RETAILERS AND THREE MAJOR aggregators—sites that distribute your book to retailers on your behalf. Most will pay you 60-70% of your book's retail price. I will go through the options here, and list major features of each, but there is much I don't cover. I strongly suggest that you visit the sites mentioned here and read the terms and conditions yourself.

Also, things change very quickly, and it's likely that this page will be out-of-date the day after I finished typing it.

AMAZON KINDLE DIRECT PUBLISHING

You simply have to be here. This is the largest ebook retailer. Features separate retail sites in the US, the UK, Canada, Mexico, Brazil, Germany, France, Spain, Italy, Japan and Australia. You get 70% of royalties for most books priced between $2.99 and $9.99 and 35% outside that range.

Amazon runs the very popular subscription program called Kindle Unlimited for which the reader pays a fixed fee per month and can read up to ten books concurrently. The author gets paid per "page" (ebooks don't have pages, but they make up some figure that you can see on your dashboard). Of course the major drawback of it is that your book has to be exclusive to Amazon to be in the program.

Payment is through cheque or bank account in some countries, or EFT in the US. Outside the US they use "wire transfer" rather than EFT, which can mean a substantial extra banking cost for you if you're not in the US or UK. Get a worldwide account with Wise, which will give you bank accounts in numerous countries. Not only is this much cheaper than transfers directly to your bank, they use far more favourable exchange rates, too.

In 2018, KDP absorbed the print-on-demand company CreateSpace, which then became KDP Print. You can access them through your regular dashboard.

If you're not in the US, they will accept your local tax ID if you're in a country that has a tax treaty with the US.

Amazon's help function is outsourced to some cheap country and gives you copy-and-pasted replies, which is unhelpful when you have a real problem. They're also not always correct.

They can also be draconian, and they ban before they warn.

The only non-personal reason you may not want to list an ebook on Amazon is contained within the first paragraph: if your ebook is a collected bundle that you want to sell for more than $9.99.

Personal reasons for not to want to sell on Amazon can range from having an exclusive release on your website or Kickstarter, basically anything relating to your way of organising your business.

Don't however, buy into the Amazon hate that circulates in certain author groups. Yes, it's a big company, yes, they look after themselves. No, it's not a conspiracy and neither are they out to get you. Nor are they the smartest company. They're just big and lumbering and most of the time their left hand has no idea what their right hand is doing. Like is the case for literally all large companies.

Just list on Amazon at a time it suits you for a price that suits you.

KOBO WRITING LIFE

The Kobo Writing Life portal is one of the prettiest and easiest to use. Who can resist that awesome map that tells you where in the world you have sold?

Payment: 70% of royalties for prices over $2.99. Note: no upper price cap.

Kobo's main office resides in Canada, and this alone makes it a much more international seller than Amazon. They also sell only books, and only ebooks at that. They have recently added audiobooks. You can add them direct on the platform or through Findaway Voices. They sell their own devices and have a free app that everyone can use.

They have a subscription program called Kobo Plus that's very fast becoming very popular. It covers both ebooks and audiobooks and, for the author, doesn't require exclusivity like Kindle Unlimited does.

Your dashboard features a promotions tab which allows you to apply to take part in store-run promotions, most of which won't involve any upfront costs.

Their help function is run by real humans and you can strike a good one, or wait days for a reply. One of the known issues of the accounts is that it's sometimes hard to set up payment. Payment is through Western Union into your bank account, but sometimes it takes a bit of help from their side to set up the bank account correctly.

Is there a reason you shouldn't be on Kobo? No, there is no reason.

BARNES AND NOBLE

Accessed through B&N Press. You can set up accounts in a limited number of countries. In 2018, Australia became one of those, so I boldly ventured into the weeds.

The site is pretty, responsive and easy to deal with. Books are easy to upload. Why, oh why don't other retailers have the "clone book" option that copies categories and other setup features for a new book so you don't have to re-type them?

Sales are reported in real time and payout is into your bank account.

Non-US author warning: expect some difficulty filling in your tax forms. They're very finicky.

B&N Press has a print option which sells print books in their own stores. They use Ingram Spark as their back end.

They also sell audio books, but don't as yet have a function for you to upload them, so you must do so through a secondary party, like Findaway Voices.

If you have an issue, getting help can be hard, because their team appears to be small. They do respond to messages on their Facebook page.

A reason not to be on Barnes & Noble direct? If you're in a country where you can't list direct, and also if you run into too many issues verifying your tax info. It's not that common, but I have seen that happen.

APPLE

You now no longer have to own a Mac to be on Apple, because you can upload online. You do still have to own a Mac in order to run the upload software iTunes Producer. I personally prefer to use the Producer, because there are more options and it's less buggy.

Think clearly how you're going to set up your account structure before you apply. DON'T use your personal AppleID to create your account, because it will take all your details from there. You cannot change this. Create an AppleID specifically for your business and attach all the appropriate business-related accounts, credit cards and tax IDs to it.

Apple also sells audio books, but they have to be accessed through a third party. ACX (Audible) and Findaway Voices distribute to them. I strongly recommend Findaway, because ACX doesn't allow you to set your price.

Reason not to be direct on Apple? Man, they can be such a pain to deal with. Also if you have a closely-guarded pseudonym, they insist on listing your legal name unless you set up a company.

GOOGLE PLAY

The Google Play store is now open for everyone.

The Google Play store is accessible through some aggregators, most importantly StreetLib and Publish Drive, but Google Play requires that you have an account with them before your books are distributed to them even if you use an aggregator.

They now also allow you to upload your audiobooks directly.

On Google Play itself, you get 70% of the recommended retail price. If you've heard rumours that they discount without your approval, they're now no longer doing this.

Google Play takes your local tax ID, and pays into your bank account without silly hoops or fees. They pay 15 days after the close of the month and are as such the fastest paying venue.

The site is a bit onerous, but believe me, it used to be a lot worse, and these days it's reasonably easy to understand, and changes to your books and pricing are lightning fast.

Reason not to be direct on Google? None, really. They do manually check your books when you apply, and when your catalogue triggers warnings (such as you republish a lot of public domain stuff) you may have trouble getting approved.

DRAFT 2 DIGITAL (AND SMASHWORDS)

If all the above sounds too hard, you can use a third party platform, also known as aggregator to list your books on your behalf. This comes at a price of 10% of your list price.

The biggest of these is Draft2Digital. They started as an aggregator only, although they are starting to do some really interesting things, like offering audio books through Findaway Voices, print and a variety of author services, all for free. They've also recently introduced formatting templates for ebooks and they have D2D Print, which operates through Ingram Spark.

In 2022 Draft2Digital acquired Smashwords, which was the first retailer ever that let people upload books to their store (some people still maintain it was Amazon. It was not).

The merger between the two is still playing out in 2024. I can only assume that the Smashwords store was a major attraction for D2D.

Draft2Digital distributes to major retailers including Amazon, except Google Play. The distribute to libraries worldwide. Their reach outside the US is quite limited.

The website is nice and easy to use. They host nifty universal links, where you can generate just one link for your book to use in advertising, taking the reader to their retailer of choice in their country. They pay through bank transfer or PayPal.

A great feature of their site is income splitting, allowing you to co-author books without the admin headache.

Why should you not list on D2D?

Again, no real reason, but since you can set your distribution per book per retailer, I keep the 10% for the major venues like Kobo, Apple and B&N,

but let them distribute to places where you can't set up an account, like Overdrive for libraries and overseas retailers like Germany's Tolino.

There may be a slight issue for Erotica writers. D2D is know to be very—uhm—puritanical and will refuse books based on "objectionable content" that individual retailers will accept. In this light, the merger with Smashwords is interesting, because on Smashwords you can publish stuff that a lot of retailers refuse.

PUBLISH DRIVE

Originating from Hungary, Publish Drive's international focus is clear from the moment you enter their site. Their focus is Asia.

They're a bit different in that their service is subscription based. Their payout percentage is different for each retailer and the plan you're on. Visit the site for more details.

Other services they offer are: getting you into promotions at retailer sites and running your Amazon ads via their site.

Smaller retail sites

Drivethrufiction, good especially for science fiction and fantasy, but the website is hideously clunky.

Smaller aggregator sites

Streetlib (recommended, can get you into Google Play, strong international focus, especially into Africa), XinXii (not recommended, impossible to update and remove books).

SHOULD YOU USE AN AGGREGATOR OR GO DIRECT?

I believe that you should always go direct to sites that give you special promotional opportunities that would not be available otherwise, most notably Amazon and Kobo. Otherwise, it's up to you.

Pros of using an aggregator:

- Less work

- One account to manage

- One payment

Cons of using an aggregator:

- 10% may not sound like much, and it isn't when you earn $60 per month. But it becomes a lot more when you earn $600 per month. When you earn $6000 per month, you can pay an accountant with the money you save.

- You may not be eligible for promotions on retailer websites, notably Kobo

- You lose control over your book's metadata, because the information you fill out will be massaged into a lowest common denominator that suits all automated upload processes with all retailers. This means that you miss out on the funky quirks offered by some platforms, such as drilling down into specialised categories at B&N.

Think carefully, because when you go with an aggregator and then go direct, you may lose all your reviews for that book. Since people are more likely to review on other sites than they are on Amazon, losing 900 reviews on Kobo just because you got sick of paying an aggregator $100 of your earnings per month is a difficult decision. If you intend to move your books across, it pays to email the retailers, because they may be able to migrate your reviews over for you.

FREE BOOK DELIVERY SERVICES

If you want to give your books away and collect email addresses, you may want to get an account at Bookfunnel or Story Origin. There will be much more about these in *Mailing Lists Unboxed*, because these services integrate really well with your mailing list.

Despite the fact that these services both distribute free books when people sign up for your mailing list, they are not the same.

Bookfunnel concentrates on getting the book onto people's devices with the most ease possible. You will realise that this is an important function once you give your book for free to list subscribers and start getting "How do I get this on my Kindle?" emails. Bookfunnel has in-house promotion opportunities, and integrates with platforms that offer direct sales, such as Payhip, Shopify and Woocommerce.

Story Origin is the new kid on the block. Their focus is on author cross-promotion. They also offer opportunities to give your book out to people in return for a review. They've just recently added a direct sales option with a company called Lemon Squeezy, which looks very interesting even if I think it's super-daft name.

KICKSTARTER

This is a new addition to this version of this book.

Ever since Brendan Sanderson's famous 40+ million Kickstarter, interest in the platform has been running hot.

At the time of writing, I've completed five Kickstarters, all successful.

The platform has its own distinct best successful practices, most of which are beyond the scope of this book. If you want to know more, there are books available on Kickstarter. I especially recommend Anthea Sharpe's book, because it covers all you need to know without upsells for courses and the like. Also join Anthea's Kickstarter for Authors Facebook group.

Here is a very brief summary of the basic principles:

- Kickstarter is not a bargain basement platform. You can (and should) ask full price for your books and ask top price for special editions.
- Kickstarter may be known as fundraising platform, but the basis of it is emphatically not "I am poor, gimme some money so I can pay for editing or an audio book", but it is "Here is a really cool book I am going to make [insert beautiful pictures] and here is how you can get a copy".
- You don't need a big audience for a Kickstarter, but the more products you can sell, the more chance of success.
- Kickstarter is a great way to sell print books, especially special editions printed by Book Vault.
- Kickstarter is also great for multimedia projects, art books, comics and other oddball projects.
- Especially for your first project, you POD (Print On Demand) everything.

DIRECT SALES

When I first wrote this book in 2017, direct sales were possible, but still very much a novelty.

These days, an increasing number of authors sell directly from their website. The excellent Bookfunnel app and the out-of-the-box online shop sites have made this possible and profitable.

However, selling direct is an advanced strategy, because it requires that you have a ready-made audience to sell to. When you're new, you don't have this. It's easy enough to add your books to Payhip and use their facility to build a store.

However, this book is geared towards beginning writers and they may already be struggling with setting up accounts on regular retailers.

If you're interested, check out Payhip and Woocommerce if you're familiar with wordpress. Check out Shopify and Etsy and Ko-fi. These are all places where you can sell your books direct. More are springing up all the time.

However, I consider the subject of direct sales to be outside the scope of this book.

Just know that it's an option growing in importance, and worthwhile doing. Later. When you have all the other stuff set up. But if you're at all interested in doing this, don't leave it too long. Payhip is super-easy, free and they handle taxes for you.

TO DO LIST: ACCOUNTS

- Get a KDP account
- Decide how much effort you want to invest into putting your books up at retailers, and decide if you want to go with an aggregator or list direct.
- Get accounts on other retailers
- Start uploading your books!

CHAPTER 16
PRESENTATION

Most sites will give you a few—not many but a few—tools to enhance the presentation of your book on their site.

You will upload your standard blurb and cover to each site, but there are some aspects where the sites differ, notably in the categories and searchability of books.

AMAZON

The most important thing you need to do is make sure you claim your Author Central page. You can do this from your KDP dashboard, or by googling Author Central. If you are registered with Author Central, you can make an author profile page that includes a bio, has an RSS link to your blog, contains images or a video and includes all your books. Not all international stores use Author Central profiles.

Next you have to make sure that Amazon produces a series page for your series. You do this by entering the exact same series name in the appropriate box when you upload your book. Amazon now has a series manager, where you can add books to series if this doesn't happen automatically. You can also enter books as "related material", like bundled editions (they don't always like the word box set, because it implies print books), unnumbered prequels and non-integer volume numbers.

KOBO

Kobo has a nice series feature that allows you to add all kinds of books to your series, because they don't require books to be numbered.

Kobo allows three categories for each book.

You can schedule sales and price changes.

You can choose to be in the Overdrive (library) catalogue.

You can choose to be in Kobo Plus, Kobo's ever-expanding subscription-based program.

The most important part about the Kobo dashboard is that you should make sure that you get the "Promotions" tab. You will find this right underneath the page header. If you can't see it, email and ask. The feature is in beta and they will evaluate each request on merit. If you have only one book or your covers look very homemade, they are unlikely to accept. But you got this far into the book—you know you need nice covers, right?

BARNES & NOBLE

The B&N Press dashboard has a decent array of non-standard (non-BISAC) categories. You need to list direct with them to access these. The benefit could be that there are fewer books in these categories, so people browsing in the store theoretically find fewer books there, and yours will have greater discoverability.

You can schedule sales and price changes. You can apply to take part in promotions exclusive to the platform.

APPLE BOOKS

If you list on Apple Books directly, you will be faced with a staggering number of possible categories in many different library classification systems in the world. I'm not sure how much it adds to fill out all of them, but I'd fill out those for the countries where you hope to sell. Apple also has a unique system of pricing where you can easily gauge whether your price is high or low for books in that country.

You can schedule sales through iTunes Connect, which is the website where you access your sales data, but if you have a Mac, I suggest that you use the iTunes Producer app, since it's less buggy more user-friendly.

GOOGLE PLAY

Like Apple Books, Google Play also has a great number of categories in quite a few different international category systems.

You can schedule sales and price changes.

It's well worth to enter series discounts under the Promotions tab.

You can link your audio and print (on any website) editions.

The most important thing you need to know about Google Play is that their book descriptions are searchable.

TO DO LIST: PRESENTATION

- Visit book pages in your genre on all retailers.
- Look for features that allow your books to stand out that are specific to the retailer.
- Use them.

CHAPTER 17
EXCLUSIVE OR WIDE?

As evidence to the divisive power wielded by Amazon, there is a subscription program called Kindle Unlimited (KU) or KDP Select that will place your book in a library where it can be "borrowed" by readers for a flat fee per month.

On the side of the writers and publishers, it requires your book to be exclusive to Amazon. It also cannot be part of a collection that is available anywhere else—whether on Amazon, and even in KU or not.

Should you enter this program?

Before I'll say anything else, I'll say that this is 100% typically Amazon to instate something as ridiculously divisive as this. They *want* self-published authors to list on this service. The traditional publishers are mostly running a mile from it, probably because of the relatively low compensation, about 0.4 of a cent per page read. Since traditionally published books usually have much higher prices, it makes zero sense for them to list in the program. If they *are* in the program, they are there because Amazon wants them, and often have the exclusivity requirement waived.

Much as I personally detest the program, or rather its exclusivity requirement, I advise you to think about it and consider it carefully.

It might be advantageous if:

- You are a very new writer and feel overwhelmed with the thought of creating accounts and uploading files at several retailers.
- You expect your biggest audience to be in the US.
- You like a set-and-forget approach for the time being
- You are trying out different audiences.

Participation in the program is only for three months at a time, and during this period your book cannot be available anywhere on the Internet other than Amazon, including your own website. I would advocate that if you are considering it, you only enter the program with "virgin" books, ones that haven't been uploaded anywhere yet. Some of the retailers upload your books to resellers or partner sites, and it's often near-impossible to have them taken down.

Here are some of my objections against the program.

- Yes, it is true that books in Kindle Unlimited are often ranked higher in the Amazon US store than those that are not, but how much of that is artificial? Ranking jumps when someone borrows a book, but you only get paid once someone reads the book, and that may not happen at all, leaving you with the false impression that ranking equates money, while foregoing real money you could have made elsewhere.
- While you are in the program, you're not building your audience elsewhere. This affects your long-term sustainability of sales. Note that this book is about building long-term sustainability.
- If you're interested in international sales, don't enter the program. When I have a stand at local cons in Australia, and I tell people that my books are also available as ebooks, the only thing I'm ever asked is if they're on Apple Books.
- Certain genres are dominated by Kindle Unlimited books, does that mean you should be in it, too? Well, how about readers of that genre who browse on non-Amazon stores? They're presented with a diminished choice and are more likely to buy your book if it's well-presented. A crowded genre in KU means a less competitive genre on other stores.
- Amazon can—and does—occasionally pull out the rug from under everyone by making changes to the program or the payment structure. I've seen this happened a few times, and sometimes authors saw their incomes slashed by 90%. Better play it safe and don't have all your books in the program so that you can get by

with income from outside, if necessary. There is no worse time to start building an audience on non-Amazon stores than when everybody else is scrambling to do the same. Start building your audience and put your books wide before the next KU-pocalypse sends in the droves of desperate.
- Not only that, but Amazon cannot actually reliably record the number of pages read. You'll often get reports of people reading one page. Do you know what happens? A reader finishes a book and flips back to the front cover before reconnecting the Kindle to the wifi. And you get paid for only one page instead of 400.
- Amazon also plays around with what constitutes a page. As you know, a page in a digital book is an extremely arbitrary concept. Amazon can decide—and has done things like this—that instead of 250 words, a page is now 260 words, and screw everyone over in the process. Amazon excels at screwing people over like this. Of course, they never, ever communicate with their content providers either, so if you try to fiddle with page length through certain methods you've learned about at forums, next thing you know you'll get an email that your account is suspended. Don't shake your head, I've seen this happen often enough.
- The structure of the program—one that divorces reader payments from payment to authors—lends itself perfectly to scamming. The following still happens frequently: A scammer produces a book full of rubbish, such as a copied book hauled twice through Google Translate so that it no longer trips the plagiarism filters, and then sticks a number of these "books" together so that they make up 3000 "pages", the maximum number of pages allowable for a book in Kindle Unlimited. They then engage clickfarms with Kindle Unlimited subscriptions to borrow and flip through these books so that they get paid for the page reads. It's an entirely closed system that does not rely on readers, but it propels junk books to the top of the charts where they take up spaces, and the "authors" get paid money and bonuses that should be paid to legitimate authors. Amazon does little to stop it. Do you really want to mix with that nonsense?

Well, make your decision, and run with the consequences. Some people do really well in the program, and I only suggest that you consider it.

The only thing you should absolutely avoid is to flip-flop between being exclusive and wide. There is no better way to annoy your readers. People in Kindle Unlimited are a different audience. You should see it as a separate store, but one that requires you to exclude all others. People with a subscription are likely to be in the US, read a lot, and are concentrated in Romance. They do buy books, but many prefer to read them as part of their subscription.

People who are on the other stores are generally happy to pay a bit more than people on Amazon, they are more likely to be outside the US, and they don't read quite as much.

Before you say that it's obviously better to go where voracious readers are, it may be that those voracious readers don't happen to be in your genre. And that your work may not appeal as much to US audiences as international audiences.

My point is, the audiences who read in KU and those who don't are not the same people.

Each time you pull your books from other stores and go into KU, or vice versa, you start over with another audience and annoy the readers you already had. Make up your mind and stay there.

TO DO LIST: EXCLUSIVE OR WIDE

- Consider who your audience is likely to be, where they are likely to be, and decide if you want to be exclusive or not.

CHAPTER 18
FIRST FREE OR 99¢?

As you will have noticed in the brief outline of the three-year plan, I told you to make book 1 of each series free.

Lately, there has been a bit of backlash against free books from within the writing community, because "There are too many free books," and "The permafree is dead."

What they mean to say is that, after a fairly brief honeymoon period when people were going on free book binges, getting readers to download the free book has become *work*. You have to lead the readers to the free book. They won't discover it by themselves.

Yes, there are a lot of free books, and yes, having a free book still works, if you use it correctly.

NOT using it correctly means making the book free and sitting back waiting for the hordes to come.

Using it correctly means telling people, "Here is book 1 in my series free," and leading them to where they can download the book.

Many, many companies use the tactic of the free sample. They have done this since the beginning of commerce and I suspect they will continue to do this until the end of the world, possibly even after.

Giving away free content in order to entice people to buy the rest works:

- If your content is good.

- If you make sure that people see that content.

Say I ran a butchery that had just won an award for sausages, and I created an offer that said "Get 10 sausages free with a kilo of steak!"

I printed the offer on flyers showing nice juicy sausages and I wanted as many people as possible to see it.

Would I:

- Put the leaflets in a stack on a table in front of the post office in the shopping centre?
- Pay the next-door neighbour's teenage daughter to put 500 flyers in letterboxes around the suburb?
- Pay the teenage daughter and her friend to come to the shopping centre on a busy Saturday morning, give them sausage-themed shirts and put them inside the entrance of the shopping centre with a barbecue with sizzling sausage pieces people could try and vouchers for free sausages with your steak right there at your shop which happens to be just inside the entrance as well?

Each of these options would cost increasingly more, but I bet the more people can try, the more they will buy.

(Excuse me, now I feel like eating sausages.)

Free works if you put in the effort to make it work. You make your book free, and then you run ads. These could be ad sites, or Facebook or Amazon ads (accessible via your KDP dashboard) or cross-promotions. Point is: you need to advertise your free book.

But the above example is also exactly why I no longer have my free books on retailer sites. Most of these sites don't like the top spots in their genre rankings to be cluttered with free books. They want the George R.R. Martins and J.K. Rowlings to occupy those spots. They have reduced the visibility of free books and sometimes even cheap books, and made it much harder for people to find them. Therefore you, the author, drive the traffic to these books. Therefore, also, you can drive the traffic to where *you* want these people to download the free book. In my case, I want people to go to a place where they need to leave their email address in order to get the free book.

So what, then, if you no longer have the books free on the retailer sites, should you price the books? Some people say 99¢, but I've put all mine up to $3.99. Why?

Because, similar to free, 99¢ only gets attention if you run a sale. Therefore if you're *not* running a sale, put the price up so that you have somewhere to move down to if you do want to have a sale.

But won't those people get annoyed if they buy the book and then find out they could have gotten it for free?

You remember how I said to put your signup link in the front of the book? It will probably say something like "Get this book for free if you sign up for my mailing list." It will show up in Amazon's "Look Inside" and the link will be live. You thought you couldn't enter live links in your author profile or your book pages on Amazon? Yes, you can.

People who are sensitive to the "Could have gotten this for free" issue will see it and will sign up. Problem solved.

The most important thing to take away from the free vs. paid debate is that free is a tool. Amazon, Kobo, Apple Books etc. are mere delivery methods. When considering whether your book should be free or not, this should go hand in hand with your consideration of *how* you're going to use the tool and what methods you will use to get the free books into the hands of potential readers. Just "make it free" by itself is not a method.

My books are still free. Readers can get them by signing up for my mailing list. I use platforms other than the retailers (I use Bookfunnel but StoryOrigin and MyBookCave are also options) to deliver the free books. At this point in time, those are my methods, but they will likely change in the future.

THE BLINDINGLY NON-OBVIOUS ISSUE FOR THE NEW WRITER

How do you make a book permanently free on Amazon? Because the upload menu won't allow you to do it, yet you can see the free books on the site. How on Earth did the writers do that?

First, you upload your book to other retailers, and make it free there. If your book sells reasonably well, Amazon is likely to make the book free on its own. It's quite sensitive to prices on Apple Books and Google Play in particular.

If your book doesn't sell so well, an email may be called for. Grab the links to your free book on the other retailers (don't forget the links in other countries), and email KDP support with those links, using the link in your dashboard. Ask them to make it free, because the book is free on Apple and Kobo and Nook, and look, here are the links if you guys want to check it.

Once you've sent the email with the links to the free book in the US, UK, Canada, Australia and wherever else Amazon has stores and you want it free, they will send you back a snarky canned reply that "free is at their discretion" or some rubbish like that. But they will make it free anyway*. In the few very limited cases where it doesn't happen, email again. You're highly unlikely to hit the same grumpy customer rep. If you want to make it free because, say, you snagged a free Bookbub, send this email not too long before the ad. I advocate two weeks. Amazon will make your book free in all nominated territories, but mainland Europe has funny laws about free and low pricing and won't *keep* the books free in Germany. Germany is a fairly sizeable proportion of my market, so that's something to consider.

---

* Funny anecdote: I originally published the Unboxed books in 2017. The third book, *Going Wide Unboxed*, is free. It's only short and describes the philosophy of not tying yourself to one publisher. I've never had Amazon refuse to make any of my books free. Except this one. Since 2017, it has been free on all the retailers, and my website, but Amazon has never pricematched it.

TO DO LIST: STRATEGY

- Decide what your sales strategy is going to look like. Will you use retailers as the delivery mechanism for your free books, or will you collect the email addresses of people who download your free books?
- Decide how you are going to advertise your free books.

CHAPTER 19
WHAT ABOUT PRINT?

MANY WRITERS DREAM OF SEEING THEIR BOOKS ON THE SHELVES IN THEIR favourite bookstore. There is something romantic about paper books that can't be replaced by ebooks.

Sadly, this part of the book industry is stitched up by the traditional publishers. They have the investment-heavy channels that supply the books, the reps that travel around to the bookshops that sell the books to the owners, and the back-end system setup that bookshops use, with a scan of the ISBN, to order or re-order their stock.

There is a huge industry that lies behind the books that you see for sale on the shelves.

The Recommended Retail Price (RRP) is the benchmark price that everyone agrees to sell the book for, and compensations for the various parties are calculated backwards from that price.

Bookstores want a discount of at least 35% but preferably 40% off the recommended retail price (from which they need to pay their staff and their rent), the distributor gets 15% (which they use to pay their reps and transport and warehouses), the publisher gets the rest, from which they pay the author usually 7% (from which the author needs to pay their agent), and the publisher needs to pay for printing, transport, editing and advertising. If a book is $10, the store gets $4, the distributor $1.50, the author 70c and the publisher $3.80.

Well, but you self-publish and you don't have those costs, right?

No, wrong.

The store wants their 40% regardless of how the book is published. The distributor is Ingram Spark. They take the 15% and don't really advertise that fact. But they do (this is why you need to set your discount at 55%, not 40% on their dashboard).

But now you have an issue, because it's pretty much impossible to have a book POD printed for $3.80. And you need to pay yourself. And pay for postage. So this model doesn't work for us unless we raise our prices. So please do that from the start. Make sure that you earn whatever you want to get from each sale. I suggest the same as you want from your ebooks, but at least $2 is generally considered to be a good margin. In that case, you have a little bit of a cushion when there is a price increase that you failed to notice or forgot to do something about.

In the traditional industry, stores takes books on consignment, a sale-or-return model. If the store doesn't sell the book within three months, they can return it to the distributor, who then reverse-bills the publisher and either sends the book back or destroys it.

We can't accept those conditions. Please always make your books non-returnable because you don't want to be reverse-billed by Ingram Spark. Really, you do NOT.

Yes, the fact that you need to jack up the price in order to make a profit and the fact that you cannot offer stores returns makes the print book channels less likely to want to sell our books. MUCH less likely.

I know, it's not fair. But it is what it is. And, as they say, life is not fair. It never was. Rather than rail at the injustice, find the corners where you can go and large companies cannot.

So should you even bother with bookshops?

I'm not entirely saying don't do it, because there are some cases where you might want to give it a go, but it's very hard to make decent money selling print books via bookstores.

If you write non-fiction, especially non-fiction that is tied to your locality, if you're a local author and are well-known locally or if you write picture-heavy non-fiction, you will find that your sales will naturally skew towards print anyway and you may try.

But it's hard and a lot of work.

In 2000, I published a full colour non-fiction book. I had it printed in Hong Kong, shipped to Australia, and I paid the customs duties. I sent flyers to about 800 bookshops and visited whichever ones I could reach while also having young children. It was a lot of work, but because I knew the—very specialised—market, I sold a lot of books. Would I do it again today? Nup. I'd probably make a pay-for-content website. For one, do you realise how *heavy* books are?

For many self-published fiction authors, especially of general fiction, print is far less than 5% of our sales. One would say this is an opportunity for expansion, but many find it really hard to branch out into print bookstore sales.

If you rocked up to a bookshop, managed to be there at the time the book buyer was in, held the book under her nose, why would you think she would even consider you?

Just imagine being in her shoes.

She probably gets asked the same question by at least 2-3 suckers published by vanity presses per week. She's probably been burned a few times. Some authors are really rude about it, too. They don't understand the traditional book industry and expect the world to move for them. Their refusal to deal with self-published authors is a form of self-defense.

SO, SHOULD YOU DO PRINT BOOKS?

But now I'll say something that completely contradicts the previous.

You should offer your books in print. Absolutely, you should.

But unless you like self-flagellation, don't beat yourself up about getting them into stores. Just offer them as print-on-demand option on the retailers that take them. Which means you upload your file and a copy gets printed and sent to the buyer when someone orders one.

Amazon will sell them to readers, so will B&N. A huge selection of bookstsores and library suppliers will sell them to their customers. The latter get their inventory through Ingram Spark.

It's a very good idea to add print to your available formats, but do so only if you can do it easily or cheaply. Format them yourself through Vellum, Atticus or Draft2Digital.

However, only ever consider offering your book through print-on-demand. NEVER do print runs unless you have an extremely good reason for doing so, for example if you have pre-sold the books already or you are 100% certain that you will sell the books, for example, they are part of a pre-arranged course or publicity package where the fee included the book.

PRINT OPTIONS

If you want to go the print route, there are a few companies to consider.

KDP Print (formerly CreateSpace) is the easiest to deal with for most people. They're owned by Amazon, accessible via your KDP dashboard, will automatically upload your books to Amazon and link them with your ebooks. Uploading books there is free. They can also supply you with an ISBN for free, and distribute your book to a few other online sellers. They do limited sizes and limited formats and paper types. They are not good for full colour books like children's books, because you need to print on coated paper.

IngramSpark are the behemoth in the print-on-demand market, used by many publishers. They have printing plants worldwide.

They require an ISBN; they can do hardcovers and distribute your book to retailers and allow you to set the appropriate discount. As said previously, you will need to select the 55% discount option for the bookstore to get 40%. Bookshops and libraries will order through them and will refuse to order from Amazon, because Amazon won't give them the discount they need.

They offer standard printing, standard binding and few paper options. They don't offer coated paper.

Book Vault is a fairly recent addition to the selection. While their parent company has been around for a long time, servicing the traditional presses, they have recently started to make inroads in the self-publishing sphere. They have tapped into a new market: that of making beautiful print editions for special projects like Kickstarter.

They've been a blessing to authors selling beautiful books direct. Now you can print a book with colour pages, reversible dust jackets, with foiling, photo-quality coated paper, with ribbons and printed end papers on a Print-On-Demand basis (in other words: no print runs).

They also distribute to a few retailers like Amazon, but their network is not by far as extensive as Ingram Spark's.

At the time of writing, the absolute explosion of authors wanting to use their services has left the site a bit buggy. They have integrations with Shopify and Woocommerce and are working on Payhip, but there are some teething issues for some people. I assume these are a victim of their success and will be ironed out in the future.

In summary, if you want to sell pretty books direct to your readers either via your online store or Kickstarter, you can't go past Book Vault.

Lulu has been active many years, but it has been getting a bit of attention recently. They allow you to distribute to major retailers, like Ingram Spark does. They're a bit more expensive, but they have their own printing providers, unlike some of the other services which use Ingram Spark's. People speak highly of the quality of their products.

The website is an absolute breeze. There is no cost for uploading or changing files.

They offer a service called Lulu Direct that will integrate with your Shopify or Woocommerce store and will dropship books to your customers without your involvement.

Lulu also print full colour books on coated paper, as well as coil-bound books, calendars and other products.

Smaller venues

Barnes & Noble also offers the option to upload print books, but they use the Ingram Spark print facilities.

The same applies to **Draft2Digital**, which can be an option if dealing with the rather ossified Ingram Spark gives you the heebie-jeebies.

It's marginally useful to upload on these venues. I use B&N but not Draft2Digital, since I deal with Ingram Spark direct, but $%$# why do these gigs all use different-sized templates for their covers? Seriously.

Which print venues do I use? How about: all of them. Once my book is done, I upload it to KDP for Amazon sales, Ingram Spark for library sales, B&N for sales in their stores and Book Vault for direct sales. I'll even use Lulu for special projects.

Each of these venues has their own reach and there is nothing that says you can only be on one.

WHAT ABOUT FORMATTING FOR PRINT?

You'll need a print-ready PDF to upload to all the places mentioned in this chapter.

Professionals make print-ready PDFs with InDesign, which is not easy to learn and not cheap. Done super-properly, the print PDF is not an easy document to create. If you really want to do this in a nice way, and especially if you have in-text illustrations and tables, you should probably hire someone who knows about placement, about rivers and valleys, about kerning and headers and footers, master templates and whatnot.

But.

You can also make a very nice file with Vellum or Atticus. Draft2Digital also produces PDFs.

Both the Vellum and D2D options are of the "this'll do" quality. Print book formatting to professional standards absolutely requires a real human. It's also a dubious investment if you have to pay for it, because print sales are unlikely to be a major source of income. Will readers care or even be able to tell? I suggest not. But professionals will, absolutely. Does it matter? Meh, not really, especially for fiction.

Full disclosure: this book is formatted with Vellum. I looked into other options like InDesign (too expensive) and Affinity Publisher (Eh. I was used to InDesign, and this is a whole 'nother level of stuff I need to learn and life's too short). So it does the job. Quite a nice job, actually.

Vellum has had a couple of very nice additions recently. Full-page illustrations and chapter headers and backgrounds have made formatting for special edition Kickstarters a lot easier than it would otherwise have been.

TO DO LIST: PRINT BOOKS

- Decide if and when you want print books, and why.
- Decide on a formatting process or service.
- Open an account at IngramSpark.
- Upload your book.

- Make sure it gets linked with your ebook on Amazon (you may need to email KDP if this doesn't happen within a few days).

CHAPTER 20
DOES YOUR BOOK NEED AN ISBN?

The question of ISBNs in self-publishing comes up a bit. Does your book need one?

If you live in the wonderful countries of New Zealand or Canada, you can skip this section. ISBNs are free, so go be merry, ask for a bunch of them and stick them on all your books.

For the rest of us poor sods who have to pay and then register the damn things with some daft agency…

Traditionalists are adamant that an ISBN is "essential" and that it makes you look "professional".

I have to admit to being a bit allergic to that latter word: "professional". It's a word that's making a beeline for my list of hated words, because in the writer space, it's so often used to put down "people who disagree with me".

In the 1990's in the heydays of my non-fiction bookselling, I dealt with a publishing company in Germany. They had about 40-odd books out and made a living from this. None of their books had ISBNs. To me, it was a small pain in the butt, because I listed their books on websites that liked to get ISBNs and not having them put their books in the dungeon of the pre-1960s books that did not have ISBNs.

So here is the most important thing about ISBNs: Bookshops need ISBNs to enter books in their system, and so do libraries. The ISBN is a stock identification number that gives the person at the checkout something to scan so that the person who does the ordering for the store knows what to order. That's it.

Despite failing the traditional publishing industry, the German publisher's books sold quite well. They were books on diving and sea life and I suspect many were sold through specialist retailers, like dive shops. This was in the publisher-controlled, pre-ebook time.

Back then, I published some books and bought ISBNs for them, because bookshops needed them. I even bought a block of ISBNs for my first lot of ebooks. But after I did that, I found it impossible to register them through the Thorpe-Bowker website. They gave me no help and didn't reply to my emails, so I gave up and had a rethink: what do you actually pay for when you buy ISBNs?

For ebooks or audio: nothing.

Amazon doesn't require one.

None of the other ebook retailers require ISBNs. In fact, one of the Author Earnings (website now sadly defunct) reports looked at the ISBN situation for the top 120,000 books at Amazon. A whopping thirty percent did not have ISBNs. Earnings and sales do not suffer. In fact, the report shows higher sales and income for books without ISBNs. Now before we all draw conclusions from that, let's just say that sales do not suffer.

Think about it: self-publishers say (and this has been proven right) that the vast majority of buyers do not care who published a book. Certainly buyers can rarely name the publisher of books they buy. Why then should they care about whether or not it has an ISBN?

"Oh, but it looks PROFESSIONAL!"

Seriously, bollocks. All an ISBN does is line the pockets of an industry that, by self-publishing, we have already chosen to step away from.

In the words of Author Earnings:

"What we can say for sure is that the clear lack of any material benefit in the marketplace makes the cost of purchasing an ISBN for an ebook very difficult to justify—the same money would be far better invested instead in better professional editing, proofreading, formatting, cover art, and the like."

If you want to publish in print, however, things may be a little bit different.

The primary function of the ISBN is to act as a unique stock management identifier, and bookshops and libraries will use it as such. The vast majority of print books have an ISBN. If you want to sell through bookshops or print wholesalers, you need an ISBN.

However, does that mean you need to buy them?

If you're using KDP Print, they can provide you with free ISBNs. The owner of the ISBN will be KDP Print and the author will be you. Will bookshops order these books?

The fact that many bookshops refuse to order from their rival Amazon (and that even if they did want it, their margins for bookshops are poor, as discussed in the previous chapter) is probably a greater impediment to sales than the ownership of the ISBN.

If you're going with Ingram Spark, you may have to provide your own ISBNs.

You can choose to use their free ISBNs. This won't harm your sales but may limit what you can do on their site and where you can distribute.

You can also upload a book without an ISBN if you do so for a Kickstarter or for sale on your own store, but you don't plan to distribute your book through retailers.

However, I consider the ISBN question for print books an advanced problem.

You still don't need to buy an ISBN even to put a print version up on KDP Print.

You don't need your own ISBN to upload to Barnes & Noble. They can provide you with one. If you do want to provide your own, they won't take the same ISBN that you also used for KDP print or Ingram Spark, even if you own the ISBN. Keep that in mind. Better use the free one.

The hairy thing about ISBNs is that every time you decide to make an update to your book, as soon as that update touches the main body of the text, you need a new ISBN. When you're new to publishing, you're likely to take some time before you find your feet, and you may want to go through several versions of your book before you settle on the right branding. This would cost you a new ISBN for every iteration. This gets

80 ENJOY SELF-PUBLISHING

expensive quickly, and is very uneconomical to boot, unless you can buy a block of 100.

Getting your own ISBNs for your print books is something you can do later, and I advocate that you wait.

TO DO LIST: ISBNS

- If you want ISBNs, get them now. Buy them in a block owned by your company, don't go into one of those share-buy schemes.

CHAPTER 21
OTHER FORMATS

WHERE ELSE DOES IT MAKE SENSE TO MAKE YOUR BOOK AVAILABLE?

AUDIO

Audio books are becoming very popular. People listen to them on public transport, in cars, while walking. They are good for sick people, older people, little people, active people, blind people, and people who are just sick of looking at a screen.

Some audio books do exceedingly well.

It is also, however, exceedingly expensive.

Why?

Because you have to pay the narrator. Audio books fall or stand with the quality of their production and the voice of the narrator. Therefore it can hurt you to go with the wrong narrator. People won't like the production, they will give bad reviews, and you won't recoup your investment.

Audio files are generally paid for per finished hour. This is the length of the file once it's for sale. The good narrators generally ask $300 per hour for their work. Each hour of the finished product typically takes them 4–5 hours to produce. An average book is 9–10 hours long.

This is to illustrate that it's not cheap.

There are not half the number of promotional tools available for promoting audio books as there are for ebooks. But if you promote the ebook, the audio book will get sales, too.

Still, I don't advocate doing audio books until you can afford to lose the money. Not that you will, but it might take you quite a while to recoup.

WHAT ABOUT AI NARRATION?

A number of venues, including Google Play and Amazon if you're in the US, now offer AI-narrated audio, currently free to authors, but this will probably cost in the future.

Setting up AI narration involves a fair bit of setup and a lot of proofing and fiddling, at least if you want to do it to the highest possible standard offered by the software.

For the listener, even if the quality is improving all the time, you can clearly pick an AI-narrated book. Not everyone minds.

A lot of authors are rushing out to put their books in audio through this service.

I see AI-narrated audio as accessibility service. Audio buffs will not touch it, but you aren't marketing to audio buffs. You're marketing to people who don't want to—or can't—access the written version. Opening the market to new readers.

I've even seen it suggested that AI-narrated audio is a temporary state, because soon the built-in AI voices in our devices will be good enough to take over completely. So you can already tell Siri to read a book, but she (or whatever voice you choose) will read it to an increasingly high standard that no longer justifies that the author should prepare these files.

Maybe if you want to do a multi-character production, but that is a serious amount of work and I wouldn't recommend doing it when you are starting out.

If you're going to sell AI-narrated books, I'd advocate making them the same price as the ebook. They're the same, just in another format.

OPTIONS FOR AUDIO

Price for audio consumers is less of an issue than with other formats. By far the majority of listeners have subscriptions. To them, audiobooks are "free".

If you want to do audio, you have a few options.

- Narrating the book yourself can be fun if you're familiar with the technical requirements and have had at least some voice training.
- Paying a narrator is expensive but saves you a lot of time. Although you still have to proof the book unless you also want to hire someone for that.
- You can access the ACX platform if you're in the US, UK or Canada. You can find narrators there, even ones who are willing to take a no-upfront payment royalty share deal.
- In other countries, you can use Findaway Voices. Note that they no longer offer the narrator marketplace.
- You can also try to find a third party to do it for you. Companies like Tantor pay you a one-time advance.
- AI-narration. I'd only do this in parallel with the ebook as accessibility feature.

For more information about audiobooks, see the interlude about this subject.

TRANSLATIONS

Some writers have ventured into having their books translated into other languages. This may be a viable option, especially if you know there is a market for your genre in that language. It's a huge benefit if you're familiar with that market or you can hire the help of someone who is. For this reason, I suggest that translations are something to consider once you're out of the beginner stage.

Knowing the market is hugely important. A well-known writer in the self-publishing community paid to have his books translated. The books sold well in English, so why not? The translated books sold very little. The problem? He wrote "prepper" fiction and no one who is not in the US even knows what that is.

So: do your research.

If you decide to go ahead with it, there are a few options:

- Going with a translation site, like Babelcube. They're like an aggregator for translated books. They have price structures to pay the translators. Cons: how do you check the quality of the translation?
- Paying a translator outright. In some European countries, there are laws that force you to do a royalty share with them. You can't just pay and be done with it, unless you find a translator of a European language who does not live in Europe. Cons: this is an obvious minefield. Also, how to advertise in a language you don't speak?
- AI translation: there is a lot of talk about this, but I cannot, with all the will in the world, as someone who speaks more than just English, see how machine translation on its own can be near good enough to replace a human. AI is a tool in this space. A tool you can use or one a translator uses. But checking by a real human who is a native speaker of that language is essential. Idioms, metaphors, figures of speech, there are just so many places where AI will, guaranteed, get it wrong. Don't upload your AI-translated book directly on retailers, please. It's an insult to speakers of the target language.
- Find a publisher to do it for you. A publisher in the country where they sell should be familiar with how to advertise and where to sell. They will eat the translation costs and hopefully recoup them from sales. Cons: you may be required to sign a contract handing them the rights for a number of years. The publisher "should" know how to market, but it doesn't necessarily mean that they will.

LARGE PRINT

Most people who are vision impaired have gone to e-readers. You can enlarge the font without having to purchase an expensive and heavy book. As added incentive, few books are available in large print.

But it may be worthwhile doing a large print edition of your book when your book appeals specifically to those who typically read large print and you know how to reach them.

PDF FILES

Once you start accumulating a mailing list, you will occasionally get requests from people for PDF files.

Should you make your book available in PDF?

On the one hand, it doesn't need to cost you much, if you know how to convert it.

On the other… if pirates are going to offer your book, it's always in PDF. I don't worry too much about piracy, but don't want to hand them my book on a platter either.

Whether you do it or not, think about it: Amazon and the major retailers don't offer PDFs. So: the people who ask for PDFs are unlikely to buy your books anyway.

TO DO LIST: OTHER FORMATS

- Consider what other formats are available and whether you are or may become interested in them.
- Sign up to some service providers to get their emails on the latest news.

CHAPTER 22
AAAARGHHH! HERE COME THE PIRATES!

Many new writers are dismayed to find their books pirated only a few days after they have published them.

They come to forums, upset, wondering what to do about it.

Some people advocate sending DMCA takedown notices, but I usually tell them don't worry about it.

Why not? And why do I recommend ignoring Google Alert messages about your books being available on sites where you haven't authorised them to be? I even say: don't click that link!

Well, in the first place these sites are rarely legit. If you have virus software installed, it will often go berserk when going to these sites.

That's because they try to infect your computer. This is the main aim of the site: to install a Trojan on your computer. So: Rule 1: don't even click that link.

If you did click the link, you'll find, in at least 90% of the cases, that they don't actually have your book. They've downloaded the sample from a retailer and have put that up. In order to get the rest of the book, you have to either join the site or hand over your credit card details, at which point —surprise, surprise!—your computer will freeze up and you'll have to wipe the viruses off.

These are phishing sites. They don't sell books. They plant malware or collect credit cards.

In the small percentage of cases where the site does have your book and people can download it freely, think about who would visit such a site:

- People who like to read but have no money.
- People who possess the level of geekery necessary to sideload a file and not import embedded viruses on their computer. In other words: smart people with no money.
- People who believe everything on the Internet should be free.

The first two groups have a habit of getting good jobs later in life, and with a good job comes the willingness to pay for ease of access. One click, and it's on your phone, tablet, e-reader and laptop. They'll pay $5 for that no problem, once they've finished their degree.

The last group: you'll never sell anything to them, but they may become fans and recommend your books to their friends.

In fact, I try to lure those people into my ARC team, where they get my books for free if they write reviews. They can turn into very loyal and thankful readers.

TO DO LIST: PIRACY

- If you want to go down this route, find a standard text for a DMCA takedown notice and paste it in a template in your email service.
- Or simply disable Google Alerts and ignore pirates (I highly recommend this option).

CHAPTER 23
DO THESE THINGS

ADVICE. AS ANY WOMAN WHO HAS EVER BEEN PREGNANT WILL KNOW, THE world is full of unsolicited advice. Once you put a book out there, you will attract no end of it.

Many people are going to want to give you advice, and many will even try to charge you money for it. You will get advice such as "Self-publishing ruins your career prospects" (yes, people like that still exist), or "You need an editor," oddly accompanied by the notification that the giver of advice is, in fact, an editor, and probably a pretty poor one at that.

People will tell you to write this or that genre, or not to write this or that genre. They will tell you to get more reviews, as if that alone will make your books sell better, or to enter competitions which, surprise, surprise, charge an entrance fee.

In the endless morass of advice you will get, only a few things are important:

- If you asked for the advice, it's 1000 times more valuable than if it was given unasked.
- If the giver of the advice benefits personally from the advice, discard it immediately.
- If it sounds like something that you, with your skill set, are willing or able to do and it doesn't cost a huge mount of time or money, then try it.
- If you find something that works, then do more of that.

- If something doesn't work, stop doing it.

HOW DO YOU DETERMINE WHAT WORKS?

All this requires that you have a pretty solid idea of how well your books sell as a result of actions taken by you. Keeping records of what you sell and when is necessary to please your accountant, but it is also useful for checking the effectiveness of ads or other promotional activities.

Some people make a study of data and do amazing and pretty things with it, but for someone who would rather write, some fairly basic book-keeping will do.

Things I like to record:

- A rolling total of sales over 30 days, to check if overall sales are trending up or down.
- Total sales per book over the current financial year and over the lifetime of the book.

There is no number wizardry necessary to obtain these records. All retailers allow you to define the time period over which they give data. I simply keep an eye on the 30-day moving total.

HOW DO YOU KEEP TRACK OF IT ALL?

There are not that many options for recordkeeping.

The standout new kid on the block is an online service called ScribeCount that will collate all sales data in one place. It covers a lot of retailers (but not absolutely all). It does not read your passwords and produces really cool graphics. On the downside, since it deals daily with about 6-8 different APIs (how sites talk to each other), it's likely to be less stable than something that you download onto your computer and upload spreadsheets into. And it's a subscription.

There is also the schnazzy app called Book Report that's used by a number of authors. It's free if you sell less than $1000 per month on Amazon, and $20 per month if you sell more. To be honest, it's pretty, but utterly useless to me, because I need something that handles all retailers, not just Amazon. They have very recently launched a version with a couple of additional retailers.

(Ah, the fun of a constantly changing landscape)

But, whatever way you spin it, all these services are going to wax and wane, since all of them depend on just one person and thus depend on the level of enthusiasm that person has, or is able to display, for the service. Competition, health issues, marriage breakups and deaths (yeah, people die—fact of life) are all going to be disruptive to your ability to track your sales.

Hence, I favour the humble spreadsheet. At least make sure that at any of these services you subscribe to, you can export your data when the service goes south.

I use Google Sheets and developed my own master workbook. One sheet per retailer/sales venue (I have about 20 of these sheets) and a few to put the data together in the way I like to see it.

At the very basic level you can add up titles and monthly sales in a simple spreadsheet.

In any case, do this, track your monthly sales per retailer and per title, because it is your most important vehicle for checking if your money and time spent on promotions is spent wisely.

No one can tell you with certainty that a promotion is going to work. You can only check this for yourself. Check it, because if it doesn't work, stop doing it. Stop wasting your time and money on stuff that doesn't work.

TO DO LIST: SALES TRACKING

- Set up a system that tracks sales and allows you to see how much you're selling on a daily, monthly or yearly basis. Mostly this will involve some type of accounting software or spreadsheet.

CHAPTER 24
FOUR STEPS TO STARDOM

It was a little while ago that bestselling romance writer Courtney Milan wrote her famous "Regions of Discoverability" post on the Kindleboards.

In a nutshell, it defines four stages in a writer's career:

Stage 1, where no one knows you, you have perhaps one or a couple of books out, and everything seems an uphill battle: not just selling books, but getting reviews and getting people to sign up for your mailing list. Literally everything. Promotions are hard. You get a little spike but the sales go back to the same level the day after, and that level is pretty much nothing. You struggle to sell a book a day, or earn more than $100 per month from your writing. You feel there must be something you're doing wrong: maybe I'm not spending enough on ads, maybe my covers suck, maybe my books suck.

At stage 2, a writer becomes more well-known, and sales grow, as well as effectiveness of advertising. People comment that there is often not that much time between reliably selling $100 per month and selling $1000 per month. When you're doing this, obviously something is going right. You will have more books, people will be familiar with your series, and you are likely to have more than one. Because readers see that you have complete series, they know that you're not going to abandon them. Maybe they've seen your name somewhere before. Promotions become more effective.

At stage 3, quite a few people know who you are. You don't need to push advertising so much anymore, because a new release will sell itself. Your audience will be your most important sales vehicle.

At stage 4, the retailers will know who you are and will give you special promotions. You will have reps at the retailers.

The hardest part, of course, is getting out of stage 1. You're advertising your socks off, nothing works, everything seems an uphill struggle. You're publishing new books to a very small audience. You may get a small bump in sales, but it's not lasting.

Don't fear, most of us have been there. And yes, it's not easy, but this is where you put your head down and keep writing your series. Stop the series that sell the worst, expand on the series that people like best. Give the readers more of what they like. And make sure that new readers can find your books in places where they like looking for books, such as the free and discounted lists on the retailers.

It is also my strongest belief that once you are out of stage 1, you should forget about the other stages and just get on with it and enjoy yourself. Don't worry about having bestsellers or being famous. What goes into your bank account is far more important than your ranking on the retailers. It's all the little bits coming together that form the basis of your career. Sales from all the series, all the formats, all the retailers put *together*.

… and this is essentially what this book is about. More books, consistent effort and output, more readers. Rinse and repeat.

We're now going to talk about how to advertise your book. But first I want to kill another myth…

CHAPTER 25
THE BIGGEST MYTH IN THE HISTORY OF PUBLISHING

A VERY PERSISTENT MYTH OUT THERE SAYS THAT REVIEWS SELL BOOKS. THERE IS a pretty graphic that goes with it, exhorting people to review books for their favourite authors, because once the book has fifty reviews, Amazon will start promoting it for the author. You will see it rehashed every so often, especially by traditionally published authors, on social media.

It's bunk.

Of course it is true that authors very much appreciate reviews, and that reviewing their books is a nice service you can extend to the authors whose books you read. Of course it is also true that a book that has a ton of reviews will look more attractive than one that has none.

But the statement that Amazon will promote a book that has fifty reviews?

It's bunk.

It's utter, complete bunk.

The fact that people believe this rubbish is one of the reasons that services exist where you can buy reviews.

So what is the relationship between reviews and sales? Do reviews sell books?

What really sells a book is social proof. If people see that so many people have commented on a book, more people will buy it. But you must understand that this is a function of the book having sold a lot in the first place.

HOW DO YOU GET REVIEWS?

Reviews are a function of sales. The more books you sell, the more reviews you get. The more reviews you have, the more books you will have sold. A good ballpark figure for likely reviews is: one review for every 100 sales, one review for every 1000 free downloads. Want more reviews? Get selling! Lower your price, run some promotions, give your books to anyone who wants them. Don't badger them for reviews, but simply mention that you would love a review.

HOW ELSE DO YOU GET REVIEWS?

The best trick to get reviews was pointed out to me by a friend of mine, Carolynn Gockel. She said: every time you get a review, put a thank you message on whatever channels of social media you use. No need to mention the reviewer in person—they might be embarrassed—just say thank you for another review. That's it! No begging, just saying thank you.

USING ARCS

Advanced Reader Copies are a powerful way to get reviews, but you first need a mailing list and some readers. Ask people on your list if they would like to get the book free if they write a review. Keep them in a separate mailing list. Bookfunnel has a paid option where you can make sure that only the people on this list can download the book. It's called "Midlist with Integrations". Give these people the download link to the book a couple of weeks before the book goes live.

It's also possible to organise an ARC team over social media. Especially Instagram (Bookstagram) and TikTok (Booktok) are good for this. You can also approach book reviewers in your genre to ask if they would like to review your book. Make sure that before you contact them, you read their requirements about what kind of books they take.

Personally, I don't make too much fuss over whether ARC reviewers post a review or not, although the integration with Bookfunnel allows me to see who has downloaded the books and I should be able to tell who has reviewed from my Amazon page. I may choose to do something with that information later. At this point in time, I don't.

REVIEW SERVICES

There are a plethora of review services where you pay for a service to send your book out to reviewers who then post reviews on various sites. While Amazon will object to "paying for reviews", these services don't fall under that banner. You pay for access to their database, but not for the reviews themselves, and definitely not for the content or star rating of the review.

So if you want, you can use these services. Just don't expect a certain number of reviews of a certain rating. They don't (and are not allowed to) promise that.

In the end, it all depends on how quickly you want the reviews and how big your existing audience is. If you're new, maybe use a service like this, because you don't have the audience to post a number of reviews quickly.

Never go with services that promise you anything, like the number of reviews or the star rating.

A warning: don't ask friends or family or other authors to review your books. On Amazon, reviews by people who are deemed friends or relatives will be disallowed and removed.

TO DO LIST: REVIEWS

- Start gathering your mailing list and ARC review groups as soon as you can.
- Decide if you want to use a paid service and if so, check out their requirements and booking schedule.
- If you want to find reviewers on social media, take notes of possible accounts to contact and start creating a package including blurb, cover and other information about the book that you can send out to people who request it.

CHAPTER 26
YOUR LIFE'S WORK IS IN YOUR HANDS

When writing four novels a year, you are constantly adding to your inventory of intellectual property. After three years of work, you will have twelve books that you can sell in many different forms, on many different platforms, for as long as you like. This body of work is your capital that makes you your income.

This is the very important concept that goes hand in hand with the rest of the Three-Year Plan. You keep working on your overall intellectual property, and you keep doing things that keep those books selling.

A body of work is your stock in your virtual shop. You need to nurture it, look after it, give it a new lick of paint every now and then, and you need to make sure that it presents a unified picture.

People need to be able to see, at a single glance, which books go together. The collection of books on your bookshelf needs to look *pretty*.

Covers can't look too dated, the formatting has to be adapted if new formatting options arise, and your links in front and back matter should be kept updated.

A catalogue of books requires *maintenance*.

It requires a clean brand.

The word brand is, of course, very much a marketing word, and it's on the receiving end of a fair bit of ridicule from the "I write for my art" crowd. But a brand is no more than graphic elements that allow a casual observer to tell that the book in question is yours and that it belongs to a certain series.

Think about it by imagining that you were walking into a fashion store. If half of the clothes on the racks were for teens and the other half were geared towards women over 60, then you'd feel weirded out.

You wouldn't buy at a shop that sold widely different items for no good reason, so why should authors present their output as vastly varied? This applies especially when you write across very different genres and have books of varying length that are not in series.

It's a fine balance to find between lumping too much together and fragmenting your catalogue too much. If genres are very different then it may be worth going with a pen name. However for each pen name you will have to do double the work in maintaining a website, mailing list and advertising. Is it going to be worth the effort? That is something you will have to decide for yourself.

I have always resisted splitting up my work for this reason. If you have trouble sending regular updates to your mailing list when you have one list, just think about what your work is going to be like for two pen names.

TO DO LIST: BRAND & UPDATES

- Decide on your brand and communicate this clearly to your cover designer.
- Put evaluation, and upgrades if necessary, on your calendar.

CHAPTER 27
PLATFORM AND SOCIAL MEDIA

You will often hear marketers talk about the term platform. What they mean is how many followers you have on the various social media sites, like Facebook, TikTok, Instagram and the like. Also how many people read your blog or are on your mailing list.

But I hear you say—gulp—I don't have a mailing list, and I use Facebook for my friends and I don't understand the rest. Is that a bad thing? Do I have to become one of those horrible writers shouting Buy My Book on social media?

No. In fact I recommend that you *don't* become one of those writers. There are quite enough of them already. Also, most of those writers don't really understand how social media works.

Much as it might sadden you, your social media engagement can be quite important. It is not how people buy your book, but it is certainly how people find out about you. If you entertain them on those platforms, it's more likely that they will eventually buy your books.

But you have to be engaging and post stuff that they are interested in reading.

You don't have to do all of it. In fact, you don't have to do it at all.

But if you can at all abide it, do set up accounts on each of the social media platforms. Make those accounts different from your personal account if you already have a personal account talking about other topics that have nothing to do with books. On Facebook, make an author page and don't use your personal profile.

Decide which social media site you're most comfortable with. Don't try to do all of them, because you'll end up tiring yourself out and being effective on none of them.

Say you like Facebook.

(For those who say Facebook is old fashioned, yeah, it kind-of is, but a lot of people hang out in groups, because Facebook is forum software, and the creation of groups is made infinitely easier by the fact that half the planet is on the platform)

Post something on your page every day or at least a few times a week. It could be something about the book you're currently writing, something about a movie you saw, a book you read, or it could be about your rabbits. People love animals, so the rabbit post will probably win in engagement hands down. If you don't want to go to Instagram to post the same thing there, there are ways to set up that posts are shared on a number of social media sites. Tools like Hootsuite can help with this. Wordpress blogs have the option to post updates about new posts on a range of social media sites. Use them.

If a platform allows you to have a sticky post that people will always see when they visit your profile, use it to give a link to your website or mailing list signup page.

Tiktok, and most notably, BookTok, has been making some waves recently, with people crediting their success to the platform.

A few thoughts about this:

- If the thought of TikTok, or, better put, "yet another social media site" fills you with despair, then never mind, it will pass. As with any viral app, or anything viral, *it will pass*. If it's not your thing, don't worry about it.
- TikTok is a hoot. I love watching the 30-second videos of people making art.
- Did you notice the absence of the word "books" from the previous point? If you can manage to engage with the BookTok crowd, then absolutely, go for it.
- If, however, BookTok is not your thing, then don't worry about it.

You will find something else. Put away your FOMO and keep truckin'. It's a fad. Fads will pass. They always do.

Whatever you choose to do social media wise, reply to comments you get. Social media is about engagement. It has to be fun and relaxing. No point doing something if you hate it.

Now if you regularly engage with people on social media, those people will be much more likely to buy your books or even recommend them to others. This is how social media works.

Don't want to do it? There are other ways of becoming known to readers.

TO DO LIST: SOCIAL MEDIA

- Make accounts on social media separate from your personal accounts.
- Set up a Facebook author page.
- Set up an author Twitter account, and on any other platforms you like.
- Choose which platform you're going to use most.
- Set up cross-posting from that platform to the ones you don't plan on using.

CHAPTER 28
A WORD ABOUT GOODREADS

GOODREADS IS A SOCIAL MEDIA PLATFORM BASED AROUND READING. ON IT, you can place books on virtual bookshelves and post reviews, comment on reviews made by other people, create or vote in book lists, join reading groups and friend people.

The question whether there is any point in a writer investing time into Goodreads is one that often comes up on forums.

The Goodreads reader community can come down like a tonne of bricks on any writer who self-promotes too much, or who infiltrates groups for the sole reason of promoting.

Goodreads gets the rap for being nasty, but it merely reflects the general feel in the community: nobody likes people who constantly self-promote. Nobody likes the author who goes ballistic online about a bad review. Goodreads is just extraordinarily good at ridiculing those writers.

For one, Goodreads is a community for *readers* to talk about books. Many of those readers feel uncomfortable when the author of said book is looking over their shoulder. So tread with care. Don't be one of those people.

Join Goodreads as a reader, not a writer. Join groups to talk about books you've read. There are corners where you can announce your freebies or new books. Stick to these places if you want to promote at all.

The minimum things you should do on Goodreads is to claim your author profile and make sure your books are linked. Goodreads is owned by

Amazon, so if you put a book up on Amazon it will automatically find its way to your Goodreads page.

Another very useful and low-maintenance thing you can do on Goodreads is to syndicate your blog, so that blog posts show up on the site.

CHAPTER 29
YOU MUST ADVERTISE

Once you have a decent set of products, for example you have completed a series of three books and have started another, about a year or so into the plan, you should start to think more seriously about advertising.

Note that I don't think it is necessarily wrong to start advertising earlier, but I would also caution against not spending too much effort or money, unless something works really well, and then of course, do more of it as I said earlier (but not to the exclusion of writing).

Sometimes new writers get sucked into the notion that they need to "launch" their first books with a lot fanfare, without having an audience to fanfare to, and without having a clear idea where to spend their money. They buy expensive ads and try to mimic traditionally published book launches, forgetting that the publishing industry sells to bookshops, not to customers, and that the purpose of a traditional book launch is to impress first and sell second.

It is also very easy to spend a lot of money on ads that don't work, like newspaper or magazine ads and pay per click advertising.

Even if you have a very large budget, it's often hard to find where to spend money effectively. Sure, it's easy enough to blow huge amounts of money on Facebook ads and Google Adwords, but they're unlikely to be very effective if you've never done this before.

Things that traditional publishers rely on—print ads, radio slots, interviews and print reviews—don't actually have much effect at all. People don't read about a book in a print newspaper and then go to the effort of searching for where they can buy it online.

Effective advertising opportunities are extremely rare. As an independent writer, you are usually presented with the following broad advertising options:

LISTING SERVICES

These are websites that, for a fee, will post your book for a discounted price to their list of subscribers. Some of these are reasonably effective, especially, at the time of writing, Bookbub, Ereader News Today, Freebooksy, Book Barbarian, Robin Reads and Booksends. New sites come up and drop off all the time, so find out which are the best sites from the friends in your writer groups.

Note that most of those sites are unlikely to give you an immediate return on investment, unless your book is the first in a longer series. Most charge anywhere from $5 to $70, which, in terms of bang for buck, makes them reasonably expensive compared to the hallowed and pricey Bookbub, which almost never fails to make your money back, sometimes significantly more than the (quite steep) fees. Bookbub is by far the best bang for your buck, even if to start with you have to shell out a lot of bucks.

If you hear of a new site that you've never heard of before, check them out. Look to see how easily people can sign up as readers. Look at the sales rankings of some of the most recently advertised books. Check the site's Alexa rankings for an independent verification for how many people come to the site. If the price is reasonable and they look otherwise fine (in other words, readers can sign up and they send out regular newsletters), try them.

PAY PER CLICK/DISPLAY ADS

These are Facebook ads, Amazon ads, Bookbub pay per click ads, Google Adwords and a whole raft of similar services, where you pay (and often bid) for the display of your ad or clicks on the ad.

This option is not for wimps and it's not for people who fear losing money on experiments. Often it takes quite a lot of experimenting to get ads working, and then they might still be too expensive. You often end up bidding against people with more expensive product to sell than a $3 book, and they can afford to pay much more per click.

If you're interested in this option, I advise doing some research on how to best set up your ads. You can find a lot of information on the Internet, or you can take a course. Learn Self-publishing, formerly known as Self-publishing Formula by crime writer Mark Dawson, offers a set of three introductory videos that are an excellent primer to Facebook ads for self-published writers. He also offers some courses. While they are not cheap, I can state that I utterly respect the team behind them and that they act with the utmost integrity. They teach you the ins and outs of the platforms and don't claim that you will find guaranteed success.

How much you will get out of his courses depends on your level of knowledge and the level of commitment you're willing to make.

From my perspective the problem is that making pay-per-click advertising work for you takes time, often a lot of it. Then there is the maintaining of ads and constant creation of new ones, as well as the regular scramble whenever an advertiser suddenly pulls the rug on ads that worked well.

Would you be better off spending that time writing? That's something you'll have to answer for yourself before going down this route. I suspect, for many writers, the answer will be yes. I would not recommend it as something essential for beginners. Decent results will be much easier to get once you have more books out.

CROSS-PROMOTION WITH OTHER AUTHORS

These are activities where you pool resources, in this case your social media reach, to pull in more people interested in books. This works very well if promotions are genre-targeted, and where all participants write fairly similar books.

The best promotions are those you do with friends and that are not run by a promotional site. The downside is that it usually requires some work from your side, and for it to work you need to have some level of social media footprint already. If you can find no cross-promotions to join, you can make your own. All you need are a couple of friends whose work you respect who have a decent social media presence that's different from yours. You can make the promotion a group sale, where you all reduce one of your books to 99c and put them on a page where people can see the promotion and click through to the buy links. Or you could bundle the books into a set and sell it cheaply or give it away for free. You will need a cover and someone will need to format the file.

These days, we also have Bookfunnel and StoryOrigin where we can host these promotions.

But the last method of advertising is the most powerful of all, and I'll devote an entire section to it: your mailing list.

But first let me remind you...

TO DO LIST: PROMOTIONS

- Investigate the best bang-for-your-buck promotion sites for your genre.
- Look at their requirements.
- Look at promo results and Alexa rankings of all smaller sites before booking.
- Inform yourself about Facebook ads before trying to run any
- Join author cross-promotion groups.

CHAPTER 30
WORK IS A FOUR-LETTER WORD

THERE ARE AS MANY PATHS TO ACHIEVING YOUR PUBLISHING AIMS AS THERE are writers, even if that aim is making a living from your writing. Without fail, all of those paths involve work. A lot of hard, consistent work.

People who do work regularly and who try consistently and stubbornly always prevail over the ones who don't. Even if, at the beginning, the work mostly leads to failure; and make no mistake—it usually does.

If things don't go the way you want and your sales are poor, get some advice from a few people you trust, readjust whatever needs readjusting and keep working.

A big discussion is perpetually going on in the self-publishing world as to whether publishing success is determined by luck. On the one hand there are those who say that all their success is due to their own hard work; on the other there are those who complain that at the time that others found success, things were easier or they got lucky.

It's a bit of both.

But without a good product, you will never get lucky. Without your constant involvement in activities where readers can find you, it's unlikely they ever will.

Writers who have tried to get a traditional publishing deal will be familiar with the concept of rejection. Self-published writers know rejection, too, except they don't realise this. Not selling a book is a form of rejection. If you have high hopes for a book and they don't come to fruition, that is rejection. In self-publishing you always get a chance to sell it later, to repackage the book or advertise it in a different way, but it's a rejection nevertheless.

The path to success is paved with rejection.

In my livejournal days when I was still trying to sell to a traditional press, an online friend and I made a bargain: we were going to get 100 rejections in a year. Nothing about acceptances, just 100 rejections.

Of course, in order to get these rejections, you need to have something to submit, so we wrote stories like crazy. I didn't make the 100 that year, because I sold a few stories (oops), but the year after that I got 132 rejections, as well as five acceptances from pro-level magazines.

That's the type of work you need to put into your career: not to take rejection (or failure to sell) personally, but dusting yourself and your book off and trying again in a different way. Forget about lofty hopes and fairness, just do the work.

There is a saying that lucky breaks most often happen to people who don't need them, and this is indicative of what you need to do. You have to make sure that you don't need the lucky break in order to survive. You also need to put yourself out in places where luck can find you. You never know where that may be, so try as many things as possible at least once.

CHAPTER 31
MAILING LISTS

The author mailing list!

I would personally consider it the most undervalued and underused tool in the author's promotional toolkit.

I started using email mailing lists in 2000, when you could still simply collect email addresses of your business contacts and email them regularly without having to ask for permission, without having them sign up and without mandatory unsubscribe options.

In fact, none of the services offering all these things existed. I ran an online non-fiction bookstore, and I would buy batches of specialist books from people who were selling collections, then send the inventory to the 150-odd people on my list. They were rare and often very expensive books. I'd sell hundreds of dollars worth of books within an hour. It was magic!

Of course then Amazon came along and flooded the market with of some of these books, while the ones that were truly rare became completely unobtainable, and the gold rush ended.

I went into other things like fiction writing and forgot about how well the mailing list used to work until the issue of mailing lists became a hot topic in the author sphere. At that point, a lot of authors were using their mailing list as a back-end service only. The idea that one could use a list to actively advertise and sell, and invest in a mailing list in lieu of advertising, is still quite new to some people.

The mailing list is your most powerful sales strategy. The people on the list are yours, they have either read your books or have given you permission to try and sell them your books. So, sell them books!

How?

In the next section, I will list the basic things you need to set up a mailing list.

CHAPTER 32
HOW TO SET IT UP

How do you set up a mailing list?

There are several things you will need:

- In the first place, you should sign up with a mailing list provider, a third party website that hosts your list and deals with subscriber vetting and unsubscribes.
- Then you need somewhere to set up your information about your list that you will use in your emails. This will most likely be your website.
- You will need a way for subscribers to sign up. Most likely, this will be a form, preferably on your website. It is important that you won't need to change this form frequently. Preferably, you will never change this link.
- You will need to know how and where you will get your subscribers. If you want them to have read at least one of your books, get them from links in the back of a book (but notice how I told you to also put the link in the front of the book?)
- You will need a plan; what are you going to do with this list and what are you going to send these people? Is it a chatty newsletter? What will you talk about? Any particular subjects? Will you talk about your books, about writing, about the background information relating to your books, or research you did for the books? Will you review books in your genre and talk about those?

The list is endless. But it's best to define a brand and a style, and stick to it.
- You will also need some graphics that you want to use as a header. This could be as simple as a photo of yourself, or a graphic that includes your books. It's worth spending some money on this, because this header will be your brand.

In all, setting up a list is quick and easy. Sign up for an account with a list provider, make a signup form and you're done! But setting up a list for maximum benefit will take a bit of thought and planning.

The next section will cover the basics of mailing list operation. There is a lot more to be said about how to run your list, how to get people to subscribe and how to engage them. This is covered in book 2 of this series, *Mailing Lists Unboxed*.

CHAPTER 33
WHERE TO HOST YOUR LIST

If you want to have a mailing list, by far the easiest way is to sign up with a company that provides mailing list hosting. Many of them have free plans for small lists or for a limited time.

At the time of writing, the options used by many writers are:

- Mailerlite. Free plan for up to 1000 subscribers. Mailerlite is based in Lithuania and their help team is from all over the world. They offer a decent array of service on the free plans and are very much across Europe's GDPR laws. I use them and they're awesome.
- Mailchimp. Free plan for up to 2000 subscribers. Cost climbs very quickly after that. Pretty lousy help service, even if on a paid plan.
- Convertkit. Expensive, but offers extensive tagging options that some people really like.
- ActiveCampaign. Quite popular with writers, even though it's not the cheapest. Has consistently good delivery rates.
- Email Octopus. A decent low-priced service that looks good if you just want to send newsletters and don't need advanced features like ecommerce.
- Sendfox. A service that has a unique billing system where you pay a one-off fee for your chosen number of subscribers and no monthly subscription. Many writers use it.

Whatever you do, unless you really know what you're doing, please ignore the voice of your little tech-savvy cousin: you are highly unlikely to be able to run your mailing list from your self-hosted WordPress site. It's not that it's impossible—larger marketing companies run their lists with custom software from their own servers and it's not technically difficult—but doing so carries a huge number of risks that you will be unaware of as beginner, let alone know how to avoid, such as:

Risk #1: Having your account and website cancelled

Spam is huge. In today's situation where your Internet service provider catches most of it, nobody even realises how huge. It used to be that domain owners were subjected to the full brunt of it. I could tell you about the day I received over 1000 spam emails, most of them in Arabic, but the expletives would send this book to the "adult" dungeon. Take it from me: the vast, vast majority of spam is caught before it ever reaches your inbox. The Internet is hypersensitive to anything that looks like spam.

So how does this risk affect a private author with a small list? After all, all you want to do is email some people about your new release?

Well, how does sending 2000 emails from a private email address sound? There are cheery plug-ins you can get, for free even, that will manage your newsletter. They will do as advertised, but please use this option for very small newsletters only, not the type I'm talking about.

Every Internet service provider has guidelines for banning spam or what looks like spam, or anything that could get *them* into hot water. That's why they don't want you sending thousands of emails from their servers, and why your account may get cancelled if you do.

Risk #2: Having your emails end up in people's spam folders or never be delivered

Now I have to say one thing: there will *always* be some of this happening. It's pretty much unavoidable. If it happens to someone who complains about it, ask them to use a different email address. This will almost always solve the problem.

Of course having your account cancelled is much more serious than your emails getting stuck in spam folders, but the effect is pretty much the same: people don't get your emails. Fortunately, there are some things you can do to avoid landing in the spam folder. Avoid using trigger words in the subject line (like FREE). Be specific with the email subject line so that people know what they're going to get. Don't try to be clever, because if people don't understand the message, they won't open. If they don't open, the email software will assume they're not interested and will automatically move the next email messages to spam.

Another thing you can do is to avoid using your free email provider address (like Gmail or Yahoo) as your "From:" address. Because many real spammers use free email addresses, this is often automatically a red flag.

Manage your list at a reputable email list service, which does its best to maintain the highest possible relevance rating for its customers. These companies have servers that are especially geared up to send huge quantities of email in a short period *and* not get flagged for sending spam.

In evaluating what company to choose, consider your current and future needs. Consider whether you are going to use your list as a service to existing readers or aggressively recruit email addresses and look at the company's price structure. Consider whether they have a free trial number of subscribers, and what level of automation they offer if they have a free subscriber level.

Consider how integrated they are with services you use to gather subscribers, like Facebook, your website or Bookfunnel. Do they transport email addresses straight from Facebook or Bookfunnel to your list or are you going to have to import CSV files?

Consider whether you want your email service to integrate with your store if you decide to sell books direct to readers. Having this integration is a huge boon, but if you're never going to sell on a direct store, then there is not much point in paying for a service you're not using.

Choose wisely according to your future budget, because moving a list is a major pain in the behind.

There are basically two types of email services: those that offer the full gamut of services, with an accordingly high price tag, like MailChimp, ActiveCampaign, ConvertKit and the new Mailerlite, and those that are more basic like Sendfox and Email Octopus.

Basic functionality you need:

- The capability of producing all types of signup forms, including the ability to embed the form on your website.
- The ability to segment or group subscribers.
- Basic automation that triggers when a subscriber signs up.

Functionalities I strongly recommend considering:

- Automation based on parameters other than when they signed up, like when a subscriber clicks a link.
- Automation that puts subscribers on different lists and unsubscribes them based on actions in a chain of events.
- Ecommerce integration! The Woocommerce-Mailerlite integration is awesome!

Don't listen to people trying to push their own (expensive) favourites on you. Look at what functionalities you are likely to use and decide based on that.

TO DO LIST: MAILING LISTS

- Consider your needs for a mailing list now and in the future.
- Look at companies' options. Ask other writers what they use and why.
- Get an account at the provider of your choice.

CHAPTER 34
SIGNUP FORMS

Once you've set up your account on the provider of your choice, you will need a signup form. You may also need some landing pages.

Now, you understand what a signup form is, but what's a landing page?

In short, a landing page is a page that focuses on one issue or item. It's a page where you send people to see an ad. The single function of a landing page can be for people to sign up, or it can be about ONE single book. At the bottom of the page, there is a link to buy the book. There are no other links on the page. No distracting menus, no links to other posts. This page is about this one single issue only, and if a visitor doesn't click the buy button, the only other way to get out is to close the tab.

The reason you send people to a landing page rather than a regular page on your website is that you don't want them to become distracted, and you don't want the design of your page to distract from the reason they clicked on the link. A landing page is specifically designed to display that single item in a way that a web page is not. On a web page, you might have sidebars, a header and footer all cluttering up the page.

How do you make forms and landing pages?

Most providers will make pretty forms for you. Many will even offer the option of making landing pages. I strongly recommend AGAINST using these. Why? Because you will advertise these forms and pages wide. The links will be in your books. If you ever decide to change provider (a massive pain in the behind already), those forms are owned by them. You cancel the account, you lose the form. OK, OK, you can just make a new form at the new provider.

Yup, but what about all those 20,000 books you gave away in your last free Bookbub promotion, which all still have the old link in them?

Oops.

At the very least, use a link redirect for example through the plug-in prettylinks for WordPress. Services like those will provide you with a dummy URL that points to another URL *that you can edit later*.

Better still, of course, is to self-host the form.

By self-hosting the form I mean put the code somewhere on a page you own. This means that if you wanted to change your list or your provider, you only need to change the stuff on the page, not the page's URL.

How does this work?

Make a form for the list on your email provider's site, then copy the form's code (mostly through the "embed" option) and paste the code into your website.

You often have various design options, from a full form with added text and pictures to a "slim" design, which consists only of the form fields and a "subscribe" button.

Hint: this and the WordPress plug-in prettylinks won't work if you're on a free blog platform.

This is why you really need a website.

Guess what the next chapter is about?

TO DO LIST: SIGNUP FORMS

- Make one or more forms so that people can sign up to your list.
- Embed this form in a page on your website—don't use the URL given by your mailing list provider.

CHAPTER 35
ABOUT WEBSITES

ONE OF THE FIRST THINGS YOU ARE GOING TO NEED TO SET UP IN ORDER TO have a successful mailing list is a website.

I mean a proper website, not one of these free blog jobs (oo-er that's uncomfortably close to some other kind of "job") from WordPress or BlogSpot. Why? Because some things you need to do you can't do on free websites. If you're really cash-strapped, do get a free WordPress site, but make upgrading it to a self-hosted site a priority.

What is the main function of your website?

If you said *To display your books* you'd be only halfway right.

In the three-year plan method, the most important function of your website is that it forms a place where you can send people. It's a place where you can host your landing pages independent of retailers or other places that control who visits.

If you don't think this is important, consider Facebook.

Not so long ago, when you posted on Facebook, every one of your friends would see it. If you had an author page, all the people who had liked your page would see it.

These days, you can be lucky if a mere 10% of the people who have liked your page will see the update. If you want all of them to see it, you have to pay.

If you have invested a lot of time and money into getting likes on Facebook, you have a good reason to feel duped by Facebook. They can, with a few lines of code on their website, ruin the audience reach you've spent years to build up. Or they can go out of fashion. Remember Myspace?

So the three-year plan avoids the Facebooks of the world. It doesn't allow companies that have control over who sees your material to serve as an important link in the chain of contact between you and your reader.

This is the function of your website. It's a home to put things you want people to see, where you, and no one else, controls who sees it.

Of course, your website should contain pages for each of your books, but it should also contain sections where you can send people in your mailing list automation sequence. This can be landing pages for your books, but also interesting blog posts, cross-promotion sales, additional information about books, and even registration-only member sites. The possibilities are endless.

At the very least, your website should host your forms and your landing pages.

So, landing pages.

There are all sorts of programs you can buy to generate your landing pages. Most of them are subscription services (URGH!) and they do far more than you will ever need as author. So here is a hack for reasonably computer-literate people:

Go into your website's directory using your ISP's file menu. Create a new directory. Mine is called "pages".

Go to your ISP's app directory, and find WordPress. Install WordPress, but tell it to install the software in the directory you have just created, not in the root directory. This won't affect your normal website at all.

Then when it's completed, log into your new sub-site, go to the WordPress free theme directory and find a theme that allows you to turn off everything: the header, the footer, the menu, sidebars, post titles, post dates, commenting, social icons, EVERYTHING.

There is also a plugin called Full Width Page.

You want to be left with a blank page, maybe with a border. Make sure the theme is mobile-friendly. I use the theme Tempera for both my website (where I have all the stuff turned on) and my pages (where I have everything turned off). It's free. Then simply start creating pages. They can be pretty basic, or Tempera has a very easy box where you can add your custom CSS to make it look a little bit more fancy. But landing pages are simple by definition, so simple will do. Title, cover, blurb, buy buttons. That's all you need.

While some options for creating and maintaining landing pages will charge you $10 per month—including fancy stuff you'll never use—this costs NOTHING.

TO DO LIST: WEBSITES

- Get a self-hosted website.
- Create signup pages and landing pages for your books on your website.

CHAPTER 36
AUTOMATION

So now I have a list and a website, what about this thing called automation?

Automation is an action that happens according to a trigger you set in your mailing list provider's menu.

For example, when a subscriber joins a list, they automatically receive a welcome email in which you introduce yourself. If you give subscribers something for free, you would do it in this email.

Then, two weeks later, another email goes out automatically in which you ask them if they got the book and maybe ask them another question. Then two weeks later you might give them something else or send them another question.

I use this standard automation sequence on most of my lists. It requires none of my involvement and always runs in the background.

But there is much more you can do with automation. Because, in the third email, people get the option to click on a link that tells them that they'll be sent an introduction to my series, a different series every second week. It tells them that if they don't want to get it because they already know about my series, click here and Hey! They won't get those emails.

Meanwhile, another four automation sequences keep track of which people downloaded which of my free books. For each of those links, it makes a list of people and a set number of days later, sends them an email asking if they enjoyed the book, if they have any questions, if they'd like to review and introducing the second book in the series.

Meanwhile, in another list, I give people an option to click a link and they'll be automatically moved to another group. When they click, it automatically removes their name from the group and presents them with a form to enter an email address. It's called "change your address".

But, if people have been on my list for six months and have opened none of their emails, they'll get an email that says, "Here is a free book." If they don't open it, a month later they get another email that says, "Here is another book for you." And if they don't open that one either, they get an email that says, "Do you still want to be on this list?" At this point, the automation automatically unsubscribes the people. But if they click on the link "yes" they will see a form where they can enter their email address and resubscribe.

These are just a few examples to show that there are no limits to what you can do with automation.

A word of warning: designing complex automation will hurt your brain.

At the very least, I recommend that you have a short welcome sequence that introduces people to you and your work and that gives them a few free things.

I go into much more detail about automation in part 2 in this series, *Mailing Lists Unboxed*.

To do list: automation

- Set up a basic automation email that welcomes new subscribers to your list.

CHAPTER 37
ABOUT MANDATES

IT IS IMPORTANT TO UNDERSTAND THE ETHICS OF OPERATING MAILING LISTS.

In this case, ethics means: people must understand what they're signing up for.

When signing up, you make them a promise, and you should stick to that promise. You shouldn't suddenly change the name and subject matter of your list.

You should never port lists from one author name to the next, or import mailing lists from other businesses, even businesses that you own.

If people haven't signed up for it, they have every right to be upset about being sent emails.

Every one of your emails should have an unsubscribe link that leads to a simple unsubscribe page, or, even easier, unsubscribes them with one click. People don't want to go through a hassle to get off a list. They will report you for spam instead.

Even if you do all this, you will get plenty of people who don't remember signing up, or who didn't read the part that said that by signing up for a competition, they would end up on the authors' mailing lists.

When you operate a mailing list, you will soon find out that there are a lot of crazy people out there. Don't give them any more reason to go nuts than necessary. Define what you're going to do, stick to it and never import anyone who hasn't given their email address with the understanding that you will be emailing them.

TO DO LIST: EMAIL PURPOSE

- Decide what your list is for and write out what you'll promise people in their first email.

CHAPTER 38
YOU ARE NOT YOUR OWN TARGET AUDIENCE

But, you will say, I hate mailing lists.

I hear you. Personally, I rarely sign up for them either. My inbox is full enough as it is.

But there are obviously people who like to sign up. They like getting deals, or they like conversations. They may have more time than I do, or they just like to get email.

One of the most important things you have to realise: selling books successfully is not about you, the author, nor is it about your personal preferences. It's about doing things that are proven to work.

Therefore, you must test a lot of things, even things that you as a person would never respond to.

Get this: you are not your own target audience. That's OK.

Plenty of people love being on mailing lists and love hearing from authors. Some people will be there because they're your fans. Some people will be there because you give out the occasional free book, and some will be there because they're lonely and like getting email. You can never know who is who.

Do what you said you would do when they joined your list, give them reasons to open the email and click links.

Remember to judge people primarily by their actions, not their words. Mailing list providers give you stats on who opens, who clicks what. A few loud people will email you all the time and complain, but your mailing list not about appeasing the few loud complainers. Watch online what the majority of them *do*.

Which links do they click most? Which emails with which titles do they open?

If something unexpected happens, try to find out why. Send them a survey. People love answering surveys and giving their opinions. Don't ask "What would you do?" but "What did you do?"

Questions like:

- Which authors do you like?
- Which genres do you read besides mine?
- Where do you buy your books?
- Which of my books have you read?

Especially the last question will surprise you. Authors frequently assume that people on their list have already read all their books. Most of them won't. So, make use of that fact. They're interested in you. Remind them that you have all these books that they can read, and hey, here are some buy links. Use automation to do this.

Once you free yourself from the assumption that all these people's likes and dislikes are just like your own, there are no limits to how you can engage with these people who have told you, by signing up: "Entertain me."

CHAPTER 39
HELP, I'M F(L)AILING

Hang on a moment, I hear people say. I did everything you told me to do. I wrote books in series. I set up a website, started a mailing list and automation, did some cross-promotions and I now have 4000 people on my list. There is only one problem: they don't buy my books! They're just costing me money.

This happens from time to time, and it's never easy to treat or even diagnose when you can't see the whole process. Therefore you must continuously evaluate your results. But here are some common reasons that people continue to struggle:

They're impatient

I would give the whole process at least a year to start giving consistent results. If you give away free books, you need to give people the time to read them. Many people who download free books will have massive collections on their devices. They must be reminded a few times that your books are worth a try. Your automated email sequence should do that.

But still, virtually no one reads a free book immediately. Give them time.

The ad copy does not draw them in

Because people have so many free books on their devices, they need to make a decision about what to read first. Only the truly anal people will read on a first-received, first-read basis. Most people will browse their libraries and will pick the book that they've heard most about or that sounds the most interesting. So it's not enough to give people a free book. You have to make them want to read that book.

Your blurb needs to be interesting. Whenever you mention your book in your emails, it needs to draw people in.

To be able to do this well is an art, and it's called copywriting. Grab a book or two about how to write ads, and about how to push people's buttons with words. You'll be glad that you did.

The book fails to deliver

This is the hardest thing for a writer to hear: the book just doesn't draw enough people into the series. How do you know that this might be the issue?

People buy book 1 but after a year, few have bought book 2, even when you've advertised a fair bit.

You're having a lot of trouble getting reviews, and a good proportion of the ones you do get are of the "meh" variety, or they mention specific issues, like characters being unlikeable or shallow, the ending being unbelievable or unsatisfactory or the plot being stodgy, slow or confusing.

The book has failed the basic rules of writing: don't bore the reader, don't confuse the reader, don't annoy the reader.

Ask advice from a developmental editor and make changes if you can. But mostly, your best investment is to use what you've learned in another series. Start something new. Make it slightly related to the rest of your work so that you maximise potential sell-through.

A note about cliffhangers

A cliffhanger is a book that ends on a major new reveal or a point of tension where the reader has to buy the next book to find out what happens. TV series are masters at cliffhangers.

At any one time, you can find any number of heated discussions about cliffhangers. That readers hate them and how much they hate them, and that they feel duped into buying the next book; that there are such things as "good" cliffhangers and "bad" cliffhangers, where the good ones supposedly resolve certain plot points, but the bad ones are only to dupe the reader into buying the next book.

Yadda yadda yadda yadda.

The only thing that counts is this: are people buying the next book? Have you made them *feel* enough that they click "Buy"? No matter how much they complain? No matter how angry they seem to be?

If the answer is yes, cliffhang away. If the answer is no, they probably never complain about your cliffhangers anyway, because they give up reading long before they get to the end.

Remember: at any one point in your career, if you strike a rough patch and try to figure out what to do about it, don't listen to what people *say*, other than, if you've judged that they're qualified to give you advice, watch what they *do*. Test, analyse, decide.

Don't be a circlejerk

When you're down on your luck and feel depressed about your sales and wonder what to do about it, you'll likely stumble across groups of like-minded authors who have devised various schemes to hold up the illusion of selling. They review and even buy each other's books.

Don't waste your time doing this stuff.

You only need to have made an ill-chosen return-review arrangement once to know that it's a bad, bad idea (that's aside from the fact that Amazon doesn't like it when authors review other authors). How so? Well, imagine you exchange reviews with someone and they read your book quickly and give it a glowing review. You, however, are busy and don't get to their book for a while. Then you open it and oh my, is it awful! What do you write in that review? Seriously, you do *not* want to be in a situation like this.

I'm not even going to talk about buying each other's books. That's just dumb, because, circlejerks aside, it's treating the symptoms, not the cause.

You're not selling as much as you like. A poor ranking and a lack of reviews are *symptoms* of poor sales, not the cause. Readers are not stupid. They can pick a book with a high rank that's unlikely to have gained that rank fairly. They can pick canned reviews.

Propping up rank artificially and fishing for circlejerk reviews at best makes your book look odd to prospective buyers. At worst, Amazon will cancel your account.

If you're not selling and your next release is a while off, you can do these things, in increasing order of investment in time and money:

- Change the categories.
- Do some marketing.
- Change the cover.
- Change your book's description.
- Rewrite the beginning.

Better still: write another book using all the stuff you've learned.

CHAPTER 40
YOU ARE THE SECRET SAUCE

Here is a word of advice if you're new and feeling overwhelmed. You came into this writing gig because you loved telling stories, and now you're told that you need to do all this STUFF?

There is good news for you: writing a good story is still what sells you the most books. All the things I've discussed in this book are to augment the reader's experience of the books you write. They are designed to get the most out of the books you write and to set you up so that you don't have to spend 80% of your time running around yelling, "Buy my book!"

This is a note to make sure you understand that there is no secret sauce. No magic thing you can apply to your book that will make it start selling, other than to write an engaging book. In fact, *you*, dear author, are the secret sauce. But it's not a fast-working sauce, and it does not come with a ready-made recipe.

You often see that newer writers are very keen to get their books going as quickly as possible. They buy expensive ads, watch their rankings of their single book like a hawk, and panic when they don't sell as much as they want.

What are they doing wrong? Why aren't they having the success that is owed to them?

Well, they weren't writing their next book, for starters. They got suckered down the rabbit hole by some big name author uttering that launch is important.

It is, sort of.

It's actually a lot more important if you're a traditionally published author, because your book gets a six-week window in which it has to prove itself, in which ads, if any, will be used to prop up the book, in which the book launch will be scheduled, and any book tours. And then if the book doesn't sell huge amounts of copies, it's left to fend for itself.

There are definitely benefits to starting off a book launch with a bang, even if you're self-published. But this bang gets bigger when your number of backlist titles grows. The bang is bigger when you're a bigger name, so don't sweat it too much when you've just started.

Write the next book already.

Rather than rabbit on Facebook, or even run Facebook ads, write the next book.

Rather than fiddle with your current book, write the next book. Make it the second book in your series. Don't start another series; don't start another genre. Write the next book. There will be time for diversification later.

Don't worry about reviews so much. OK, send your book out to everyone who is a reviewer and wants a copy. Don't be precious about this. Give them the free book. Don't hound them for writing the reviews; just give them the book.

Also ask for reviews from the people on your mailing list. Don't beg; just ask. If someone says they can't afford to buy the book, give it to them if they'll review it. Don't go nuts if they don't end up reviewing. You'll want one less review a lot more than a protracted argument online, or a vengeful bad review because you pissed someone off. Send the book and then let it be, whatever it is that will end up happening.

Write the next book.

If you happen to run a few small promotions and they go well, try to capitalise on it as much as you can, but don't let yourself be distracted that you lose sight of what will drive the sales once the buzz dies down: your next book. (You knew I was going to say that, right?)

There is a saying doing the rounds amongst authors: you're only as good as your last book. If your last book was a year ago, this is going to suppress sales a good deal, because almost all the retailer sites thrive on churn. They want the newest, the best-selling books by the bestselling authors. What's on the front page gets rotated out very quickly. At some sites more quickly than others, but this is the general principle of it. If you haven't released a book in over a year, you can't expect any kind of support from recommendations through retailer sites.

Write the next book. That's what's going to give you the most bang for your buck.

I know it's hard work, but if you want a secret sauce, there it is: write books in a series, place them in a reasonably popular genre, make sure the covers are genre-appropriate, automate your mailing list and then concentrate on the next book. Keep doing this for a few years.

It's called the Three-Year Plan.

INTERLUDE: AUDIOBOOKS

CHAPTER 41
SHOULD I SELL AUDIOBOOKS?

Should I sell audiobooks? This is the first part in a four-part interlude on shoestring audio for self-published authors.

There is a lot of talk about the rise in audiobooks. Some articles show that the sales of audiobooks are surging. So if you don't have audiobooks, better get in there while you can, right?

Well, maybe.

There is a lot going on in the audio book sphere and a lot to consider, and not all of it is good.

Many of the reports in the media need to be taken with a grain of salt, because several of the much-hyped sales figures are based on trade published books only, and for years, the traditional publishing industry has been pushing buyers away from ebooks.

Still, there is no denying that audiobooks are both becoming more prevalent and cheaper, with various subscription services, including Spotify and Kobo Plus, offering them. Many authors are getting into audiobooks. Should you do the same?

The answer isn't clear-cut, and will depend on what you write and where you are in your author career, and frankly, how much money you want to invest in it.

Commonly advice given about the feasibility of audiobooks is that if your e-book isn't selling well, your audiobook won't either. It's not easy to market audiobooks on their own, so their sales will always be related to the e-book sales. I feel that this is an artificial issue, since Amazon demands that an audiobook must be tied to an ebook, but there is literally no logical reason why you can't have audio-first or audio only. In fact, the text of this interlude has been audio-only for years.

The issue is that many retailers have treated audio as add-on and poor cousin of the ebook and print. The discoverability of audiobooks on retailers is, to excuse my French, piss poor, and your ebook sales will have to do the heavy lifting.

But it's not the entire story and also, things are changing.

Audio is an entirely different market. People who listen to audiobooks don't always read e-books and vice versa.

Not all genres do well in audio. Audio is more expensive to purchase, so genres that are populated by readers who don't have much money, such as young adults, or people who read at such volumes that getting books cheaply is important, such as romance, tend not to do as well.

On the other hand, the Science Fiction and Fantasy categories are populated by books that are long and part of series that make satisfying listening for audio consumers. And of course non-fiction is big in audio.

Of course, there are exceptions to these general observations. If your ebook sells well, the audio will sell, too, regardless of genre.

It's also important to understand the audio landscape. How do listeners consume books?

Most listeners use an app, and many listen on their phones while commuting or doing something else.

The biggest player in the audio book market is Audible, but the ground is shifting under the feet of the audio world. Kobo, Nook, Google and of course Apple have their own audio apps, and so have a whole slew of other places, including Everand (formerly Scribd), Bookmate, Storytel, Nextory, and library apps like Libby and Hoopla. Spotify now offers audiobooks. Library listening to audio is becoming huge.

There is a lot of subscription-based listening in audiobooks.

How do you get your audiobooks in these places?

The elephant in the room, that I will deal with first, is ACX, which feeds books into Audible and Apple. ACX is owned by Amazon, and is the biggest audio distributor. But it's very important to realise that it's not the only place to upload your books, that it's not the best market and it has a number of very important and limiting restrictions.

You can't distribute direct to ACX unless you're in the US, Canada or the UK.

Audible is a subscription platform. They also sell audio on a non-subscription basis, but the subscription option is pushed hard to customers. Audible subscriptions are available in the US, UK, Canada, Germany and Australia.

Hang on! Authors in some of those countries can't upload to the platform direct.

Yup. Welcome to the quagmire that is ACX. This is one of the benign idiosyncrasies of the platform.

So, let's get into the not-so-great things.

ACX advertises that they pay you 40% for an outright sale if you're exclusive and 25% if you're not (meaning if you want to sell elsewhere). But because most of the "sales" are through subscription credits, they use an infuriatingly opaque royalty calculation that will end up paying you less than $1 per sale. Keep that in mind.

You can't set the price for an outright purchase on the site, so you can't run promotions. Of course you can run promotions on the ebook and hope audio listeners see it. They do, in modest numbers.

On top of that, the site is full of scammers and shenanigans.

For example:

- People "claim" your book on ACX/Audible and produce an illegal version (possibly using AI)
- People produce scam audio to defraud creators and narrators giving the industry a bad name.
- ACX/Audible encouraging listeners to "return" books so they can reuse the monthly credit. Of course when a book is "returned", the sale vanishes off an author's dashboard.
- ACX banning author accounts based on automated detection of some sort of transgression that's never explained, with the author having no avenue for recourse.

At this point in time, ACX is literally the worst company self-published authors have to deal with. Long audio approval times, repeated weird rejections of books that shouldn't be rejected. Returns, garbage reporting, garbage website that's keeps crapping out, garbage back end service. It's high on the "tread with extreme care" list. They keep promising big things, and when they change something, it's just a cosmetic touch-up of the dashboard.

OK then, what else?

Findaway Voices is an audio aggregator that will distribute to ACX/Audible on your behalf. They will also distribute your book to a whole host of other venues including Google Play and Apple and all the other venues mentioned above, over 40 in total, including to libraries. They were bought by Spotify and distribute to the platform. They take a cut of your sales on top of the retailer cuts.

You can upload your audiobooks direct to Kobo. The site is fast and efficient, and the book gets approved quickly.

If you're lucky, you can now also upload your audio files direct to Google Play. They're in the process of rolling out this capability to everyone, but, typical Google Play, they're doing this slowly and without fanfare.

Bookfunnel can also deliver audio direct to your readers, but you have to set up the sales platform. You can use Payhip or Shopify or Woocommerce, but you need your own website.

There are other audio distributors, like Authors Republic.

Finally, you can upload your audio to Youtube. You can't sell your books there, but it might be good for loss leaders. If you can monetise your channel, you might be able to make some money, but it will always be much less than you'd get from virtually all other channels.

The audio landscape is one of subscriptions and while you may hate subscriptions, they're not going away any time soon.

Audible pushes their subscription model pretty hard. There are many other subscription services. I highly recommend Kobo Plus.

Findaway Voices will get your book into library subscriptions and other services, such as Hoopla and Everand (formerly Scribd). Like Audible's credit system, these don't pay much per read, but they can add up.

So should you get into audio? If your e-book has been selling very well, you might already have received an offer from a production company. Companies like Tantor or Podium are well regarded.

But even if they make you an offer, there are a few things you have to be wary of.

Audio is expensive and time-consuming, so it's tempting to let someone take it off your hands.

Reputable as they are, these companies are still likely to orphan a series if the first book doesn't sell well by their benchmarks. It means they will take and produce the first book in a series, and maybe another book or two, but won't complete the series.

If that happens, are you then going to produce the other books by yourself? They are going to be even harder to market than audio already is, because you have no control over the first book.

If you receive an offer, it means they think they can make money, which means you could probably make more doing it yourself. And keep control of the series.

How frustrating would it be not to have control over the first book in your series and be unable to enter it in promotions.

In general, there are two rather depressing aspects to selling audiobooks. One, the cost of production is much higher than e-books and two, sales are likely to be lower. On top of that, you get a much smaller percentage of the cover price.

So yeah, tread with care. This is not for beginners.

On the other hand, even if your book is not a bestseller, it can be worth producing an audiobook if you can keep production costs low and fully funded by sales you have already made. You can keep costs low by either recording it yourself, or by hiring it out to someone cheaper, including using AI if that's your jam.

Look for part two on how to find a narrator. I'll say a few things about AI in part three.

Or you can do it yourself. More about that in the last part of this miniseries.

One fact holds for both ebooks and audiobooks: the more books you have in your catalogue, the easier they become to sell.

And related to that, the more control you retain over your books, the greater your ability to take advantage of opportunities, or create your own.

More promotion opportunities are coming up all the time. You want to retain the ability to take part. Exclusivity or farming your production out to others does not do that.

Also, don't gamble any money on audio production that you can't afford to lose.

In short, I wouldn't recommend audio to first-time authors with a first book, unless the book takes off like clappers and continues to sell well.

I would recommend paying for audio out of sales of existing books, rather than putting your own money into it.

I would also make sure to retain control over both the book and the pricing, which means not to be exclusive to ACX/Audible. Direct sales from my website are both much cheaper to listeners and more profitable for me.

CHAPTER 42
FINDING A NARRATOR

AFTER ALL THE DISCOURAGING FACTS IN THE PREVIOUS PART OF THIS SERIES, you have decided that you want to bring out your books in audio. Good on you, and I think you should. Audio is just a field you should get into when you've heard the facts and still want to do it, because you love audio, or you just want to do it.

How do you find a narrator and what do you need to watch out for?

This is going to be infinitely easier if you are one in of the few countries with access to ACX: the US, UK, and Canada.

(Note, I am not in any of these countries, but I do have an ACX account through an option that existed a few years ago, but that is no longer open)

If you have access to ACX, you can submit your book in two ways: you can upload files you already own, or you can go through an audition process where you solicit auditions from potential narrators interested in narrating your work.

When initially setting your book up through ACX, you have a further option to make your book exclusive with ACX (don't) and if you didn't heed my suggestion in brackets, you can use Royalty Share (DON'T!!!!). I suggest you make your book non-exclusive and set your price per finished hour to what you want to pay, not what "people" say you "should" pay to get "professional" auditions. A lot of air quotes in that. If you don't get enough of the type of auditions you want, you can try again with a higher rate.

So first of all, why don't I recommend Royalty Share? It's a great way of getting the books into audio if you don't have the money to spend on production.

While this can be true, the Royalty Share contract is particularly onerous and ties you to the platform for seven years. After that, you have the option to extend or negotiate something else with your narrator, but in that case, you have to take the book down and re-upload it.

OK. You could do that.

You can now take your book out earlier than seven years but only with approval of the narrator, presumably because you paid them out.

But what if you want to do this, your narrator goes MIA or otherwise won't cooperate? They decide narrating is not for them and they no longer respond to your messages or they refuse to cooperate or ask unreasonably high payouts? Then you're stuck for seven years, at the mercy of the notoriously opaque and inflexible customer support people at ACX.

I strenuously advise people to avoid the Royalty Share option, and if you can't afford audio otherwise to save up or do the first books yourself. You can take those down later if you wish, because you are the narrator and control everything.

But we were talking about finding a narrator.

Narrators come in all kinds for many types of books and budgets.

Some people in the community make a bit of fanfare that you should hire "only the best" and that "narrators have their own followers". Yes, and yes. But like cover design, this is a typical case where cost and effectiveness are not always in step. Because if you're on the fence about audio and the cost worries you, the narrators who have lots of followers are not the ones you can afford, so forget about that.

So. You want someone who can 1. Read the book, 2. In a pleasant voice that suits the book, 3. Without mistakes, 4. With enough knowledge about the tech to produce audio that passes quality control. That's it.

You can snatch someone who's doing this as a part-time gig, or someone who is just beginning as narrator. In the latter case, you may have to consider that you may have to pay a higher price to have later volumes recorded.

Cost reduction of the production is absolutely crucial unless you're breaking the bank with sales. But if you're reading this, I assume you're not. Don't go with a super-expensive narrator just because people say you should. Find the cheapest possible suitable narrator who delivers a decent product.

The narrator who was the cheapest is also my best one. He makes the fewest mistakes. I've also given him the most work. It's a trade-off for both parties. The narrator wants to work, you want a certain voice type and production quality.

The ACX audition process is a decent way of finding a narrator. You can use it regardless of how you want to distribute your book.

But what if you don't have access to ACX?

Findaway Voices used to have a process to find a narrator. Sadly, they closed this down. But even before this happened, I found their narrators too expensive.

Honestly, you're better off doing your own legwork. Uploading your own audio (rather than letting narrators upload to ACX) has huge benefits. You simply pay the narrator, then take the files because they're now yours, and upload them yourself. You control every part of the process.

How do you find a narrator if you're not going to do auditions at ACX?

Ask your author friends for recommendations of people they've worked with. Contact these people and ask about their preferred way of working. Discuss a rate and time frame.

Listen to some samples.

Remember that you're looking for someone who can 1. Read the book, 2. In a pleasant voice that suits the book, 3. Without mistakes, 4. With enough knowledge about the tech to produce audio that passes quality control.

It may be that you will need to loosen your preconceptions about what the book should sound like, and about the voices of the characters. The narrator brings their own artistic interpretation to the mix. It's not your job to micro-manage them. Don't be a pain in the arse, for both parties' sake.

The narrated book is about the listener, not the author. Authenticity of the accent, or nationality of the narrator is much less important than this: does the audience find the voice pleasant to listen to?

If authenticity of the accent is super-important, hire someone from that area. Yes, narrators can do voices, but they're not depositories of sound files. Their sound will be 95% their own voice and 5% variation to indicate who speaks.

A discussion I heard recently went like this: how come British actors can do American accents, but when Americans do British accents, it sounds horrible? There is one answer to this question: the asker was British. That's all you need to know.

Listeners will care far less about this than you do. Guaranteed.

But as author, what is important to your relationship with the narrator?

Ask for a sample narration of a few pages of your work.

Do you like the voice and does it suit the book? Are they reading with emotion? Do they distinguish the tone of dialogue spoken by different characters so you can hear the difference?

Do they make mistakes, no matter how small? I've found the issue of dropped syllables a very common problem, even for highly-paid narrators. Sure, this can be fixed, but do you know how much of a pain in the butt audio proofing is? The less of it you have to do, the better.

If they drop a syllable in the audition, they're out.

Hire someone who makes no mistakes in the sample.

As author, it's your responsibility to deliver a manuscript without errors and to give them a pronunciation sheet if your book contains unusual names.

Make no mistake, you will find some errors, because that's what happens when someone reads a book word for word. Accept that if there are a lot of errors that they need to re-record, and those errors were in your manuscript, you'll have to pay them extra. Really, don't give them garbage to read. Wait until not only an editor and a proofreader, but a bunch of readers have gone through the manuscript and a number of the most egregious typos have been fixed (never ALL, it's impossible to find *all* typos in a manuscript).

Then it's also your responsibility to pay the narrator in a timely fashion and to credit them as narrator in whatever boxes the retailers provide for this purpose. And you should mention their name on the cover if possible.

So this is finding a narrator in a nutshell. Use the audition processes at ACX, or ask your friends. You may need some patience until you find the right person for the right price, but the only reason to hurry into audio is if your book takes off and then you can afford a more expensive narrator anyway. Watch and learn, and jump when an opportunity comes your way.

CHAPTER 43
AI NARRATION

I'm going to attempt to say something about AI narration, even if this subject will be out of date very quickly, probably even before this book is in readers' hands.

By AI narration I mean the process where you get a program with an artificial voice to read your audiobook for you and you then upload the files in a similar way to human-narrated books. I don't mean the built-in AI capability of apps and devices.

There are a few different options available if this is what you want.

The upside is that it's cheaper than regular narration.

Google Play has this option, KDP has introduced the option for some writers. Most people I know use a company called ElevenLabs.

In most cases, you get the option of different types of voices. The people whose voices are used are properly compensated for the use of their voice. Some people even have created doubles of their own voice, for practical reasons. These are usually narrators or podcasters, and having the voice double helps them with edits.

As author, you can also hire out the production of AI narration. This is just to illustrate a wide range of options when it comes to AI narration.

Many authors choose AI because they baulk at the cost of human narration. Books that don't sell well would otherwise never be made into audio. Not all readers mind.

The pros include the reduced cost.

But a note on this: it's not quite as cheap as you might think. If you use the best option (ElevenLabs), you will need a subscription. If you use the capabilities by Amazon or Google Play, you're going to have to extensively fiddle with the text to get pronunciations, intonation and spacing right. This will cost a lot of time. It should cost a lot of time. You want to deliver as good a product as you can.

Is it good enough?

I've tried it with some of my books or blog posts. It's better for non-fiction. I'm currently listening to a non-fiction audiobook written by someone else.

When you use human narration, you get a human to sit in a recording booth and record them reading the book. They will probably go through an edit, taking out the parts where they flubbed up, maybe re-recording a few sections or taking out the sections that are already re-recorded. The file then goes into mastering. This is an electronic editing process that takes out some of the impurities and makes the file comply with the standards of the audio platforms. They look at things like extraneous noises, but also the loudness and variability in loudness to make sure that all their audiobooks meet a particular standard. For those who think that mastering is something mysterious, it is not. Once you have decided on your parameters, it's more or less a set and forget thing. You run the file through a couple of plug-ins and that's it.

If you're careful about recording, your file won't need a huge amount of external mastering, at least not to meet the platforms' guidelines.

When you use AI narration for your book, you have to choose a voice, and then you have to manually mark up your manuscript for made up or unusual words and for intonation. When a human reads a text, he or she uses that amazing human organ that makes us unique, the brain. And because the brain is such a beautiful thing, the brain comprehends meaning when we are reading. It comprehends changes in pace and changes in tone. It can comprehend the difference between two different words that are nevertheless spelt the same and pronounced differently in different context. Things like desert and desert for example. Before you give your file to have an AI narration produced of a good quality, you have to manually mark all this. You have to mark for loudness for softness for speeding up, for emotion if the software allows that. And so you have to go through your manuscript with a fine tooth comb and look at each and every word.

At least, if you want to do a decent job.

This was not done for the book I'm listening to. It's a non-fiction and there are some really bad bloopers that, in my opinion, should have been fixed. Things that I would not have wanted to include in any book I offered up for sale. There are not a huge number of them, but enough for my brain to go NOPE. I would never want this in my own books.

So this is the most important: spend the effort getting it right. Listen to all of it and fix the weird pronunciations and the wrong emphasis and the strange pauses in the middle of a sentence.

You mark up you manuscript, then you haul it through the generator and you probably find that you have forgotten a few things or things that didn't work, or places where the software just mangled words for no obvious reason. There is extensive proofing involved. Much more than for human narration.

I presume that you can already see where I'm going with this, namely that producing AI narration is not a simple press of a button. It requires an extraordinary amount of preparation, of proofing and reading back. And this, sadly, is work that only a human can do.

After all, as humans, we use our brains, and we can make subtle distinctions that are far beyond a computer's ability.

When you give a manuscript to a narrator, they will get a few things wrong, and they will even pronounce a few words in a way that is unexpected to you. But sometimes this has more to do with their dialect then that they are wrong. A human mispronounces a word for a reason. It's either a cultural reason or one that feels natural because everyone is doing it, for example mispronouncing commonly used French words in the English language. You can then decide whether you're going to be a stickler for the correct pronunciation, if there is such a thing, or if you're going to let it slide, because the way they pronounce it is an accepted pronunciation just not the way you would have chosen it.

But when an AI mispronounces a word, it will just be a random word, and there will be nothing natural about it. It is simply something that has to be fixed for the sake of the quality of the manuscript.

I guess by now you realise that this is an extraordinary amount of work and that you either have to do this yourself or pay someone to do it. All of this makes it that producing an AI narrated audiobook to a decent quality is not as cheap as people would expect. It can be marginally cheaper, but still very similar to costs I've paid for a human narrator.

So, what are we really competing on if we want to use AI narration? We are trying to reduce costs to us, but in the market, the market doesn't care about what something costs us, as long as the quality is acceptable. But we cannot compete on quality with human narration especially in fiction. Some of the AI generated narration is quite good, but it comes nowhere near a human in the area of expressing emotion and subtle varieties in speed and tone. People who love their audiobooks do this because of the performance. And the performance includes the narrator's interpretation of the work. The only way AI narration can get close to this is if someone puts a lot of work into generating similar emotions. I have no doubt that it's possible, but I'm not sure how much money you would save and whether it would really come close enough to human narration.

The book I'm listening to now very much suggests that it would not.

So seeing as we're not competing on quality, are we competing on price?

Most of the major audio platforms don't allow AI narration. ACX and Findaway Voices distribute audiobooks to the vast majority of the outlets so your scope to sell AI narration at the moment would be quite limited. ACX also already sets the price that you can charge for your audio, and while it is quite expensive, the proportion of sales vs subscription credits you will get through direct sales on the Audible platform is very small and shrinking by the minute.

Most people get their audio through subscriptions. On Findaway Voices, you can set the price for your audio, and this means that a lot of people already do. Some people like to stick to the high price that ACX charges for an audiobook, but many other people already make their audiobooks quite cheap or even free for the first in series. Also, when people get audiobooks on subscription models, they don't physically need to pay for them. They just pay the monthly fee and a book itself is then free. So, price is not a very good thing to try to compete on in audio, because that model is already smashed with the vast amount of subscription services.

Since we can't compete on quality with AI narration, and competing on price also doesn't look viable, what else can we think of that would be attractive to the readers? Because a reduced cost of producing audio maybe attractive to us, but ultimately if there is no market for it then it won't be successful. You can produce an AI narrated audiobook, and sell it on your website for 99c, because it only cost you $600 to produce in total, but I can tell you that there are already plenty of authors who have human narrated audiobooks that they produced for much more, or that they narrated themselves and they're giving those books away on their website or on Youtube.

There's got to be something in it for the reader.

The only place where I can see AI narration make inroads in audio is to make available books of a large back catalogue that otherwise would never be available in audio. But a read-aloud option will be a built-in feature of many reading apps. They are going to get better and better, and hey, you can choose the particular voice that's reading to you! All for free with the app.

It maybe an option for the many books and different languages that would otherwise never be available in audio, but I always find it a bit funny when people talk about other languages as if the readers of those languages have a diminished mental capacity. Of course someone who wants their audiobooks to be in Afrikaans is not going to want to listen to an AI read it to them and make even worse bloopers than it does in English. They will just wait until a narrator does it for them, or they're really desperate, they will get their software to read it out for them.

Where does this leave the author?

You can go into AI narration, but it's not an easy button to do it well. Try it if you want and see what happens as long as you keep control over the files and can take them down if you want. What I would not do, however, is spend a lot of time and money on this technology that is very fluid right now.

CHAPTER 44
NARRATING YOUR OWN AUDIOBOOK

Narrating your own audiobook? Yeah or nay?

As I have said previously, producing audiobooks is expensive. You may economise on it by finding a cheaper narrator or using AI narration, but audio production still costs a fair chunk of money. If you have a large back list, especially one that is not breaking the bank in sales, even a cheap narrator maybe too expensive if you add up the amount required to do all your books.

Having these books in audio can still be very good, because the more books you have in audio the more they will sell, the more fans you will have, and the easier it is to advertise. At this point in time, we have more options to advertise our audiobooks than we have had in the past, so it would be worth putting out your entire back list in audio. The problem is, if you have fifty books, even if you could find the cheapest possible narrator (and honestly, you don't want to underpay them too much, because they do their work fairly), it still would cost you tens of thousands of dollars.

You don't like, and don't want to do, AI narration.

So what gives?

The solution is fairly simple: you could narrate them yourself.

I started on this adventure during the pandemic, and it has both increased my income, and completely transformed my attitude towards audio and my writing process.

I started with my non-fiction books, because I figured that readers' tolerance to having an author read their own books is the highest for non-fiction. After all, it's fun being given the author's advice in the author's voice, isn't it?

Unless you're already a podcaster, to take the step into recording audio is quite a big one, but most of it is mental. Yes, you have to learn some technical stuff, but not half as much as you think or what you needed to learn in the past.

This chapter will set out the basics.

I also want to dispel some notions about why you shouldn't record your own audio, so let's do that first.

I HATE MY VOICE

I did this as well, but it was a choice between me paying $60,000 to have my books put in audio or doing it much more cheaply, and I chose the money. Once I started recording, I found that I got over this hatred of hearing my own voice in about three seconds flat.

You may feel that you don't have a voice for audio. I think this is tied in with the first objection. While some people do have annoying voices, the funny thing is that what I find an annoying voice is not the same as what the next person finds an annoying voice. There are very well-known, well-paid professional narrators whose voices I simply cannot stand. They sound too American, too fake, too squeaky or whatever for my liking. The operative in this sentence are the last three words: for my liking.

If you can read a piece of text in a clear voice, enunciate all the syllables properly, and do this for a limited period without mistakes, then congratulations, you can at least read a short story or a piece of non-fiction.

There are roughly two types of audiences in audio. There are the listeners who go for the celebrity big name narrators. These are people who have a following of their own, and listeners buy the audiobooks because of the performance. Most of these people are either professional performers or they're well-known identities. These people are also very expensive to hire, and the fact that you don't have that kind of money (because otherwise why would you be reading or listening to this) means that you can't afford them.

But a very large section of audio listeners are people who just like someone to read the book to them so that they can look at the traffic while driving (always a good idea!) or listen on the train or while they're walking the dog or doing anything else that does not allow them to sit down and look at a screen or paper.

As long as you don't make too many mistakes, your voice is not too much of a monotone or annoys too many people, you will be just fine.

So get over the stage fright.

You're expanding your catalogue into different formats for material you have already written. That will increase the audience for your existing books. If you so desire, you can at a later date hire a professional narrator to re-record the material. However, don't be surprised if a sizeable portion of the audience prefers your voice.

REQUIREMENTS

With that out of the way, let's get started on the details.

In order to record in audio, you will need several things.

You will need recording software. You will need a decent microphone and you will need a set of over-ear noise-cancelling headphones. Most importantly, you will need a space to record. I will now go through these things.

Software to record in audio can be free or paid. The paid versions are better than the free ones because they have more options. The recording quality is the same for each and does not depend on the software. If you have a Mac you can use free software already installed on your machine. It's called GarageBand. The options are fairly limited, but I put out several full-length audiobooks before I upgraded to paid software. ACX has a program called Audacity which is free to use. The advantage of this software is that it will work with some important editing plug-ins. ACX also has its own user library of how-to articles and videos, and Audacity is dedicated to recording audio books (unlike Logic, which is what I use, which is much more multi-faceted). Other options are Reaper and Studio One. It doesn't really matter what you use. As they say: pick one and join the Facebook group to help you get the best out of it.

This software's function is to record the audio files and do some basic editing. The level of editing necessary to pass audiobook quality standards is not huge, and if you have the time and are still experimenting, a lot of the necessity for editing can be eliminated by simply re-recording the offending paragraph.

You will find in the audiobook narrator community a lot of dogma about which type of software you should use, usually based on the preference of the group's moderator. It doesn't really matter.

You are going to need a good microphone. If you get a USB microphone, this may not be terribly expensive. I got a Blue Yeti Nano podcasting microphone that I plug into the computer, simple as that. If you google "recording audiobooks", you will often see people recommending that you get extra hardware, but at the level that you're at, presuming that you're not turning into an audio engineer, you don't need this.

You do need a decent set of over-ear headphones. Noise-cancelling headphones are the best, because you will often find that there is a very short lag between your speaking and hearing your voice recorded through the microphone in your ears. You can also pick up slight background noises or rustles of your clothing or tummy rumbles, and when you hear it in your headphones, you know it's on the file, so it's best to re-record while you're still in the booth.

By far the most important thing you're going to need is a decent recording space. Fortunately, most houses come with one of these pre-installed. It's called a closet. A good recording space is a room that sounds muffled, where there is no echoing of sound. Large cavernous rooms with hard floors as are popular in modern houses are terrible for recording audio. You need to be in a space that's covered with soft material. Closets are ideal.

Famous podcasters have made a recording cubby by putting up a beach umbrella in the middle of the room with a doona over the top. It really is as simple as that. Of course, your recording space also needs to be quiet. Things like traffic, planes, dogs, a busy road, a washing machine or renovations next door will interfere with your recording. You can choose to do it at a time when it's quiet, or you can insulate your room. Sound recording booths are extremely expensive, but again, the good old closet with the door shut dampens a lot of sound. Some sounds, like the rumbling of air-conditioners, can be edited out if they're not too loud. But it's preferable by far not to record the background sound in the first place.

YOUR PERFORMANCE

The final component is your performance. You have to put energy into your voice that reflects the material you're reading. You may need some practice. Record a small piece and listen back to it to see if you like the sound. If you do, ask a couple of friends. They have to be audio book listeners, because those are used to listening to someone reading a book rather than talking in a conversation. An audiobook is like a lecture, it's not a conversation. Make sure that you enunciate clearly and that you do not miss any words or syllables. This may take some practice. Also, if you've been reading for a minute without making any mistakes, you're doing well. Don't expect to read a 4000 word chapter without mistakes. You will need to edit them out.

When I make a mistake, I leave a silence of a couple of seconds, and then repeat the sentence that contained the mistake. I find it easier to do this as I go, because if I stop the recording and listen back to it, often the sound of my voice changes. Experiment with this and see what you like best.

Should you do "voices" in fiction?

Most books were not written for audio, and you will find this out for yourself if you start recording. Editors encourage us not to use too many dialogue tags. But when you have more than two characters speaking, this very quickly becomes confusing. Audio can become confusing even if there are only two characters. You will find you may need to add some dialogue tags to your text.

Of course you can do this by changing the sound of your voice, and this is why listeners like it when people do "voices". This is not as much about acting ability as it is about clarity. If you're determined you're not going to do voices, you definitely need the extra tags. But you may be like me.

I was all like I'm not going to do voices because I'm not an actor, I was never trained, and I have no illusions about my ability in acting. But when I came to read some fiction after I did my non-fiction books, I found that I enjoyed it a lot more than reading non-fiction. Fiction allows you to put a lot more emotion in your voice and perform the book rather than simply read it. Non-fiction read with an extremely emotional voice becomes ridiculous, so non-fiction narration is usually much more like a lecture read from notes. Which of course is exactly what it is.

With fiction there is so much emotion that happens off the page between the words, that you can express this in your voice. You may find that you really enjoy that process. At this point, you may also decide that you want to take some acting classes or voice coaching. But at that point you will transition into a different world.

THE TECH

The last issue is meeting the retailer sites' quality parameters.

They all spell these out clearly on their websites, and ACX has detailed instructions on how to edit your recording. If you have recorded correctly in your audio cubby, without too much extraneous noise, with a decent microphone, you should be able to meet these specifications. If you have trouble, there are online communities where you can get help, but do make sure you read the instructions for your chosen software first, because editing recorded speech for an audiobook is really quite simple. I can't include instructions, because I can only do it for the software I use, which is not the most common, and each software package is going to be different. If you can google and read, you should be able to master this. There are some Facebook groups like Authors Who Narrate Their Own Audiobooks where are you can ask questions, and someone will point you in the right direction.

As it turned out, my jump into audio has been very good. I got the equipment in December 2019, and then started recording my non-fiction in December and January. In January I went on a trip, and when I came back, COVID hit and closed the airport for months. We are under the flight path and planes interfere with my recording. I've had a great time in my audio booth. Find your own journey and have fun.

INTERLUDE: HOW TO BOOTSTRAP PUBLISHING

CHAPTER 45
WHY YOU SHOULD BOOTSTRAP PUBLISHING

As I promised, here is a short interlude on how to bootstrap your publishing.

There are several reasons why you would want to do this.

In the beginning of your career, you are highly likely to make mistakes, for example about the best genre for your book, about going with a cover you find pretty vs one that sells, or hiring an editor who doesn't do a good job. You are, guaranteed, going to make mistakes. Please make sure they're not hugely expensive ones.

It is possible to publish both cheaply and to an acceptable standard.

Many of the things I'll mention here are going to be viable for you in all stages of your career, while some of them are probably a little bit more advanced.

But I want everyone to understand that the lack of money, or the lack of willingness to spend money on a particular project, does not need to mean that you can't publish it.

There is no advantage, least of all to yourself or your surrounding community, to loudly proclaim the notion that because you can't spend xyz, you can't publish. It's elitist, it's snobby, and it's not even true.

I want you to understand this: self-publishing is free.

Get out your calligraphy set, write it in huge letters on a sheet of art paper and hang it on the wall above your desk.

Self-publishing is free.

While there are very valid and extremely useful reasons to spend money, don't ever let anyone tell you how much to spend, especially when they're elevating the bar so high that few people can clear it.

There is NO restriction on what you can publish and when.

There are only actions (yours) and consequences (as evidenced in reader reactions). And those consequences are not set in stone.

Spending more money does NOT automatically lead to better sales.

WHY YOU SHOULDN'T GO ALL OUT ON PUBLISHING YOUR FIRST BOOK AT GREAT COST

It could be that you're mentally not in a place to spend a lot of money on putting out your first book. You're just testing the waters, and you don't have the financial security to trust yourself to make that money back.

Because it's your first book, you're likely to make mistakes. If you knew what they were going to be, you wouldn't make them, so this concept is part of publishing. There will be mistakes. You don't know which ones yet, but since books are such interconnected projects, a failure in one area is likely to affect another.

You could, for example, spend a lot of money on a beautiful cover that doesn't sell the book or gives readers the wrong impression of what's in it.

It could also be that you have already published quite a lot of books, and you're growing tired of the cost of publishing each of them. While you have a small following, and small is the operative word in that sentence, you have little interest in spending a lot of time marketing. You want to keep your costs low so that you can at least not lose money while publishing.

It could also be that you're publishing something temporarily, like a box set that is not going to stay up for very long, or a bundle of short stories or articles that you want to later take down.

IT'S THE ECONOMY, STUPID!

Honestly, there are many reasons why you might want to publish cheaply. But the most important one is this:

Don't spend more than you earn.

This is basis of every business and every household budget.

But! You must invest money to make money.

Yes. Up to a point. However, when you start out you have absolutely no idea, not even the faintest clue, where that point is, or how to reach it.

So the following chapters contain my hacks.

CHAPTER 46
EDITING

EDITING IS GOING TO BE YOUR BIGGEST BUGBEAR, BECAUSE I AGREE WITH people who say that it is very hard to spot the mistakes in your own writing. There are several things you can do about it, but first I want to talk about what society at large (in other words, the main body of readers) actually means by an edited book.

THE ABSOLUTE BASICS

In the previous section about editing, I said that when a reader will notice something amiss in the quality of your editing, and comments that a book needs editing show up in your reviews regularly, it usually means that either there are typos or continuity errors.

These are fairly easy to fix. So as the bottom level, cheapest, number one hack for editing just make sure that there are no typos and no continuity errors. This is not a magic process, and there are ways in which you can do this.

You could ask a group of friends or beta readers to help you. You're probably going to have to read their manuscript in return, or you're going to have to pay them in some other form.

To be honest, this is probably my least favourite method, because you don't really know how good those people are. Not everybody comes with a ready made supply of friends whose knowledge of language is impeccable. "My cousin is an English teacher" is no guarantee, sadly.

A very good hack for finding those nasty typos is to get your computer to read your manuscript back at you while you're looking at it on the screen.

This is a task that requires quite a lot of concentration, and you will probably only be able to do it for short periods at a time.

You could help matters by reading the chapters backwards, so you're not thinking about story structures or about the characters while you're trying to follow the text on the screen.

Yes, it takes a long time and it's also very, exceedingly, mindnumbingly boring, but it costs nothing.

I used to keep a jar on my desk with all the chapter numbers, and I would randomly draw one out for a chapter that I was going to look at that day.

One thing I have also found very useful is to read the book aloud. This was an additional benefit from reading my own audio. You're guaranteed to find all the typos that two editors have missed and even find some of the continuity errors.

But some extra tools would be useful at the very least.

If you have any money at all and you have to choose where to spend it, this is probably the place.

For a really modest sum, you could buy a subscription to editing software, since using most packages will cost you at least some money. In this space, I prefer ProWritingAid, which also gives suggestions for style improvements.

As I have said before, this software is not always right, so you have to be vigilant, but it does give you reasons for the suggestions. You can google them to judge for yourself.

Of course this means you have to acquire knowledge yourself. After all, this is what a good editor does: learn about language rules. You can learn these, too. Google is pretty good for checking.

The more trouble you have with your ability to spell and use grammar correctly, the longer it's going to take to unlearn the bad habits. You might not be able to get all of them.

Really, editing is one of the first things you should pass off to someone else, even if simply for the time saved.

DEVELOPMENTAL EDITING

For comments and advice on the story structure, you can go to a writing workshop. This usually involves a group of people who each read each others' manuscripts and comment on them.

I've always used online versions, such as the Online Writing Workshop for Science Fiction, Fantasy and Horror. I still have writing friends from the time I spent there.

In these groups you will get suggestions about whether the things your characters are doing make sense, whether your story makes sense overall and all those kind of big plot structure things, as well as an infuriating amount of talk about the writing rules.

Again, you can read up on those rules and ignore the comments suggesting religious adherence to these "rules".

But unless you've been a stickler for those rules for even a short time, chances are you don't feel in your bones why those rules exist.

(Hint: It's about not confusing, not boring and not annoying the reader).

Getting "over" those rules, putting them aside as a thing you know but don't always abide by (nor should you) is all part of the learning process.

Some people will say there are times rules can be broken and the trick is knowing when you can do so.

But I don't believe that.

There were never any rules so they cannot be broken. However, your prose should do only one thing: engage the readers without boring, confusing or annoying the pants off them.

"The rules" are merely crutches, and pretty imperfect ones at that.

Opponents of writing groups will say that suggestions you get from other wannabe hopefuls are rubbish. And yes, they often are. But, plot suggestions you get from editors can be rubbish, too. Again, it depends on how good the editor is. Like humans, they're a mixed bag. It also depends on how well you understand and can handle their suggestions.

Good story craft is a very rubbery science. There are story structures that you can learn about. There are character types and genre expectation. Those are things you can learn that are guidelines. But no one can give you a paint-by-numbers instruction on how to best construct your story.

Whether you're in a workshop or you hire a developmental editor, both have the same function: they make you think about the hows and whys of your character's journey and, if done properly, the process should leave you with important questions:

Does it make sense?

Do people act like this?

Why does the character not do this other thing?

How are we meant to ever like this character if they're such a jerk in this scene?

A developmental editor is very useful because they know and remember to ask these questions. Working with them means you'll remember to ask these questions yourself with your next story. But if you don't have the money for one, workshops are a good second option, providing that you take the time.

CHAPTER 47
COVER DESIGN

There are also very good reasons to spend a bit of money on cover design. However, it does not need to be a huge amount. I'll discuss some of the options here and also give a few warnings.

CHEAP AND EASY SOLUTIONS

There are quite a number of places where you can get fairly cheap premade covers. These are covers where the design is set and the only thing you get to change is the title and the author name.

Some people want to be very precious about what's going to be on the cover of their book, but this matters far less than that it communicates the genre. If you choose a premade cover that indicates your genre well, by the time readers have gone into the first chapter of the book, they have already forgotten what is on the front cover and it doesn't matter. By that time the cover has already done its job.

In 2024, we also have the wonderful Ukrainian website GetCovers, where the covers are ridiculous cheap.

WARNINGS

I highly recommend that you use one of the above options before you try to cobble something together or get an acquaintance to do it.

I do not recommend getting someone in your circle of friends or acquaintances who is a graphic designer to make the cover for you for free.

Book cover design is a very distinctive art, and even if you have a design background, but know nothing about book covers, then the cover is not going to be terribly good.

What is worse about services you bartered with friends or family is that you feel compelled to keep using them, even though you know that the cover is less than ideal. I honestly advise against doing that.

A lot of authors use Canva to make simple covers. Beware that if you're using their free images, you cannot use these commercially. It's better to bring your own images.

Your Canva cover will probably not be super pretty, but it will be serviceable, and honestly these types of apps are getting better all the time.

I would caution you against using an image and slapping some text over the top, because it unfailingly looks amateurish if you know nothing about typography. Use Canva to do that for you.

If you have a particular image that you want to use, you can get someone on fiverr to put some text on it in a pleasing way, in fonts that are not one of the 12 fonts you got for free with your computer, because honestly readers can tell if you have used one of these.

If you want to use an image you've sourced yourself, make sure you have the rights to use this image. You cannot use images from Pinterest, Instagram or other online sources. At the time of writing, you cannot use AI images unless you have paid for their creation (subscription or otherwise). You cannot use someone else's photos, and you need to be super-careful with downloading images from free photo sites, even if the site itself says images are OK for commercial use. Most of those sites don't check the images that get uploaded.

LEARNING TO MAKE YOUR OWN COVERS

If you're that way inclined, go for it! You can be as creative as you want, republish with new covers as many times as you want.

But it's neither easy nor as cheap as you think. Good work will require good resources, including the images you will need to purchase, licensed fonts, tools like Photoshop or similar, and of course, learning materials including books and courses on how to make awesome covers, or to make them even more awesome.

And that single resource that no one counts but that is very important: time.

I like art and make my own covers. The main reason is that the cover has become part of my process. I like having it early so I can write towards the right "feel" of the book. I also like not having to wait for it, or having to fit in with someone's schedule.

Note the absence of the phrase "saving money" in that paragraph. I would probably be better off writing in the time I spend making covers. Except I can't write every hour of the day.

But yes, in summary, you can make your own covers. But you need to spend time learning how to do it.

CHAPTER 48
MARKETING

The umbrella of all the activities that fall under "marketing" is very wide. When talking about marketing, people's thoughts go foremost to paid ads, but much of marketing is free.

In fact, the best marketing—word of mouth—is completely free. Of course it's also hard to generate. But there are other marketing actions you can take that will cost you nothing or very little.

WHAT IS MARKETING FOR?

This may be a stupid question, but what is marketing actually for?

Many authors would answer this with: to sell my books. While that is not entirely wrong, it's a very author-centric way of thinking.

The best book marketing is about the reader. What do you have to offer the reader to make the book attractive? A reduced price? A large bundle? A new title? You have to make it attractive for the reader. A free book? There is nothing that attracts people like getting something for free. How about a free collection of books or a whole page full of free books?

Marketing is not spraying your information as wide as you can, but it's presenting something attractive to the right people.

Following that angle, you can see that good marketing does not need to cost a lot of money and that a good proportion of it can be free.

Paid ads are a multiplier. They work best on offers that have *already* shown themselves as appealing to readers.

THE POWER OF FREE OR CHEAP

There is a reason that the three year plan tells you to make your first book free. In my experience, and observing many other writers, by far the easiest way of selling at least some books is to make a book free. It has to be done with a decent amount of strategy behind it, such as it being the first book in series, but if your book does the job of engaging readers, you will, guaranteed, sell copies of the second volume.

Of course, having a free book by itself is not a sales strategy. Free is a tool. You have to use it well. There is also no reason why the tactics you use with free books can't also work on heavily discounted books, such as the first book in the series that is 99c.

Having a book free or cheap is about the reader. It is about reducing the amount of friction for the reader to decide that they want to give you a try.

So, since free is a tool and not tactic, how can you employ free books to make more sales?

As I already said, it works best if the free book is part of a series or otherwise well branded collection.

Since a certain percentage of people are going to buy the rest, it is your task to get as many copies of the free book into the hands of readers.

There are several way of doing this that don't cost you anything.

Of course you could just put it for free on the retailers, and their algorithms will show the book to those who are looking for free books.

But as so many people like to point out, this also attracts a fair number of people who are just looking for free books, and are not interested in buying any books.

As aside, I strongly dislike it when authors label these people "freebie-seekers" and talk about them in derogatory fashion. People who have downloaded a free book but have not bought are "unrealised potential". They are inseparable from people who have downloaded your free book and who are going to buy but haven't bought yet. It's your book's job to make them want to buy it.

What is more, even if you were to ask your list "Do you buy books?" and one of the options is "I only get free books", I can guarantee that there will be lots of people in that category who *want* to get only free books, but do actually buy when they want it badly enough.

People are weird that way.

But ultimately, your free book won't appeal to everyone.

It's your job to direct the right kind of people to your book.

You can do this with promotion swaps with other authors.

If you have a friend who writes in the same genre, promote their free book to your audience so that they can promote your book to theirs.

Of course this requires you to have an audience in the first place, so better get started on that mailing list.

Of course you can also do this on the social media channel of your choice.

In this space, the mailing list, Facebook pages or TikTok accounts are just a tool. The idea is that you promote somebody else's book to your audience and they do the same for you.

Alternatively, you could get together with a couple of authors who all have free books, put these books on a page and advertise that page to your audiences.

These are cross promotions that you can do even on a simple free blog page if you don't have the money for a paid account at BookFunnel and you don't yet have a website.

The important part is that you will select authors who write in the same genre and are in the same stage of their career as you are.

You can even grab all these books, format them together into a box set and offer that for free. Downloads of set of free books are much higher than those of single free books, and they generally do not require much advertising, if any at all.

HOW ABOUT A MAILING LIST?

There are a number of services that involve a free tier for subscribers. Most of the major email list services have at least some form of free tier. Your account may be restricted in what kind of extensions you can use, such as e-commerce and things like that, but any mailing list is better than none, and when you have only a few subscribers, it doesn't really matter whether your mailing list is automated. Just start collecting the addresses and then do something with them later, when there are more of them and you have a better idea of what you want to do.

Substack, Medium, Patreon and Ko-fi are free and while they're subscription services, you can create a free tier where your updates get posted to subscribers for free.

MAILING LISTS UNBOXED

CHAPTER 49
THIS IS A BOOK ABOUT EMAIL MARKETING FOR AUTHORS

I hear it on podcasts, on forums, everywhere I turn. Self-published writers ask the same old question: how can I keep my books selling?

Invariably, they are advised to run a few ads, to lower their price, to run Facebook ads, or to do a cross-promotion—all valid techniques.

But none, absolutely *none* of them mention the most powerful way to keep your backlist selling: your author mailing list.

Oh, many authors *have* a mailing list, and talk about gaining subscribers, but once people are on that list, the authors are not quite sure what to do with them.

Is it because authors are shy?

Because they're afraid to bother people?

Because they're afraid to sound like a salesperson?

Or they're just afraid they'll happen to annoy someone?

I don't know, but many authors are sitting on this bunch of potential in the form of a few thousand email addresses—and they're doing next to nothing with it.

They complain that their books aren't selling in between releases, and that they need to fight for sales, *while doing nothing with the people who have already shown themselves to be interested in their books*, or at least have shown themselves willing to receive emails from those authors.

I know, it's nuts.

So in this book I'll be doing something about that.

This is not a book for beginners without a list. If you want to know the principles of a mailing list and how to set one up, I have described the basic processes in *Self-publishing Unboxed*. In that book, a 101 guide to self-publishing, I described what you need in order to run an author mailing list, I've discussed websites, landing pages, companies to use and things to look out for. If you don't have a list yet and want to know what you need, go and read that book first. That's what it's for.

In this book we go into much more detail about what you can actually *do* with your mailing list once you have all these things set up.

This particular book, and the entire concept of the Three Year Plan, was born from my belief that authors are not using their mailing lists to their full potential. A mailing list is not just a service of the author to their reader, it is also an extremely powerful marketing tool.

This book will show you the basic principles of different types of mailing lists, how to use your list to engage your readers, how to set up your list to perform basic automated tasks that help you sell your books, and how to set it up so that you will never have to buy an ad on another listing service again.

Who am I to write this book? As I said in *Self-publishing Unboxed*, I used mailing lists back in the early 2000's when I didn't understand anything about mailing lists or know why they were working so well. Back then, there were no services to handle mass email ("mass" meaning more than 20 emails, LOL), and there were no services to deal with any of the things that we now consider standard, including spam blocking. There was a lot of spam, and it all went into your inbox, especially if you owned a domain.

Anyway, back in those days, I sold non-fiction print books. They were specialist books that were often rare and never cheap. I would sometimes buy libraries from estates of the deceased, make a list and email it out to the 150-odd people on my mailing list. Yes, the only way you could do this was by copying their addresses in the Bcc field! And by doing this, I noticed the efficiency of marketing through lists. No ads to buy, no stuff to photocopy and staple, no folders to mail. It was a huge saving especially in terms of time. And it was much easier to reach people.

Fast forward to the present, and I'm writing fiction. I self-published my first book after selling some stories and books with traditional publishers. But unlike selling physical books—where you always get the buyer's address, because otherwise how can you send the book?—with ebooks you have no idea who your buyers are. Amazon does. Apple does. Kobo does. So when your book is delivered to the buyer, you can't slip in a flyer for something else that you think might interest the buyer. This had been a major source of sales for me. I would colour code the paper of the flyers so I knew where it came from if someone mailed me an order (you remember mail and postage stamps?). You can't do that with ebooks delivered by a third party.

I was not used to that, and didn't like that situation at all, so when people started talking about mailing lists, I jumped on the bandwagon. Over the past few years, I have made a liveable income doing this.

CHAPTER 50
WHY YOU MIGHT NOT LIKE TO READ THIS BOOK

THIS BOOK IS NOT GOING TO BE FOR EVERYONE.

This book is about mindset and strategy. It's not about paint-the-dots examples. This book is designed to make you think, not to tell you what to do. This book also assumes that, armed with the ideas you will get and your wits, you'll be able to read the help files of your mailing list provider (or, for that matter, Google) to check on how exactly to set things up in your particular mailing list provider. Each of them (MailerLite, Mail-Chimp, ActiveCampaign, ConvertKit, Sendfox) treats lists and subscribers in such a different manner that it would be impossible for me to give a single step-by-step how-to in this book. Besides, I don't want to. It's boring stuff, and seriously, you can read, so check the help files. That's what they're for, and they're always the most recent and up-to-date source of information.

Also, I would say that you need an open mind to dive into the possibilities of what you can do with your list.

But it could be that you have already decided that you only want to use your list to talk to your existing fans about snippets of new books and your cats.

That's OK. It's a valid use of a newsletter and I like cats. But in this case, if you have made such a clear decision about how to use your list already, then you may not get a lot out of this book, because this book is for people who want to use the full potential of mailing lists. A chatty newsletter to your readers is just one very small part of how you can use it. Not that you *shouldn't* use it like that, not at all. I do. Except I don't have cats.

But you can do so much more with your list. So even if you're such a writer and you're curious, or you're wondering if you're somehow missing out on something good, then read on.

Especially if you're a writer who fears "bothering people" by sending email to the subscribers on their list.

Because you know those preconceptions you have about who is on that list and why? They're mostly wrong.

CHAPTER 51
LEAVE YOUR PRECONCEPTIONS AT THE DOOR

Come in, come in. The door is open and everyone is welcome here.

There is a little table next to the door, where you can leave your preconceptions, your *assumptions*, your *opinions* about mailing lists. You can deposit your opinions on landing pages there, as well, and automated emails and—gasp—popup forms, too.

It's OK, no one will touch them while you read, and they'll still be there once you finish reading. Warning: I'd hazard a guess that you may not want some of them back. For that purpose, there is also a bin next to the table.

This book operates under only one principle, which I feel you should apply to your whole career:

If it doesn't take a huge amount of money or time, try it. If it works, do more of it.

Don't ask fellow authors if you should do something. If you ask fellow authors, you will find that there is no shortage of assumptions and opinions when it comes to mailing lists, processes to recruit people and what to do when those people are on that list. Most of those opinions are negative. Most of them are self-destructive.

You know the schtick:

- "I hate popups!"
- "I never subscribe to mailing lists!"

- "They just send me spam!"
- "As soon as a site asks me to sign up, I leave and never come back!"
- "People who subscribe are just after freebies!"

And so on, and so forth.

For the most part, those opinions and preconceptions get in your way. Why? Because the preconceptions may only apply to a small percentage of people, vocal though they are. Because you believe that these people do as they say.

For example the people who say that they'll never come back if a site has a popup that asks them to sign up. Do you think they *really* follow through with this? Well, if they did, most of the Internet would be off-limits to them. And just think about all the energy they would need to spend trying to remember which sites ask for sign-ups. They might even need to keep a *list* of these sites.

Of course these people don't follow through with their statement. Not only that, but when they want to get something, they'll sign up. They'll complain to high heaven, but they'll sign up. It is not about these people. At least, it's not about them as individuals.

Your task is to figure out, through testing, which method gives you the best results for the aim you have set. Determine which result you want, try it, and see what happens. Use a pop-up sign-up form on you website for a set period, and don't use one for another period. Check how many sign-ups you get for each 100 unique visits for each period. Make your decision based on this, not on the comments of a few.

So here is lesson one: decisions related to your mailing list should not be about what people *say*, but about what people *do*.

The above just concerns the preconceptions of other people. Never mind the most damaging preconceptions of all: your own.

You don't want to do something because *you* would never be swayed by a certain tactic. You don't want to do something because you don't like this thing.

As an individual, you are but a grain of sand in the avalanche of humanity. Don't get me wrong: so am I, and so is everyone else. But in your mind, you, and your way of thinking, are majority speak. For successful marketing, this mindset gets in your way. You may indeed be part of a majority opinion. Most likely, you are not. At any rate, you can't assume that you are or aren't for your particular audience.

So what can you do?

You test it on your audience. You evaluate the results. Don't let yourself be led by a few loudmouths who don't do as they say, or by your own preconceptions.

Oh, while you're at it and you're still in the hall, put your sense of wanting to be liked by everyone in this little box here. Yes, it's called a *safe* and I'll throw the key into a deep and cold pond. I'll give you a net at the end of the book, but you probably won't need it.

Go forth, step into the inner sanctum, and be preconception-free.

CHAPTER 52
REPEATING THE THREE-YEAR PLAN

NOW THAT WE GOT THAT OUT OF THE WAY, I'D LIKE YOU TO READ THE original text of the Three-Year Plan again. In *Self-publishing Unboxed*, we have visited the areas that need to be set up: the quality of the book, the cover, the description, the branding of the series, your website and how to set up your mailing list. Now read it again, taking note of the points lower down in the plan.

THE THREE-YEAR, NO-BESTSELLER PLAN TO MAKING A SUSTAINABLE INCOME FROM YOUR WRITING

I. The Product

1. Write a series of three books in a genre you like. It's best if the books are full-length of 70-80k words at least. There are people who can get away with novellas, but selling well gets harder the shorter your books are. Unless, maybe, your genre is erotica or romance. Maybe. Just make the books full length, OK? It makes life so much easier (insert whisper that sounds like Bookbub: many advertising sites don't accept short books).
2. Make the first book free.
3. Play around a bit with advertising if you feel so inclined (I mean— why the hell not?), but don't worry about stuff that takes you away from writing too much.
4. Make sure you have the following in all your books: a link to your

mailing list sign-up form, and, at the end, a live link to the next book in the series.
5. When you finish the series, or even while you're writing it, start the next series. Make it a slightly different subgenre, or use a different setting and characters. Make sure that people don't need to have read the other series in order to follow it. Write three books. Make the first book free.
6. Repeat 5. Twice, if you can. Three years @ 4 novels a year = 12 books = 4 trilogies.
7. Advertise your freebies, but don't fall down any rabbit holes that take you away from writing for major chunks of time (insert snort that sounds like Facebook advertising).

II. The Marketing

1. After a while, your mailing list will start to build up a bit (see point 4 above). Get a paid account at MailChimp or wherever you are. If you are not at a list provider that allows automation and segmentation, and most importantly, automation *based on* automatic segmentation, move your list.
2. Set up mailing automation. When people join your list, send them an email with the freebies, even though they're already free. Don't email the freebies to them, but include download links in the email. Then booby-trap those links so that you can track who downloads what. You'll be using this later.
3. Next, send your subscribers to an automated program that sends them something at regular intervals (Amazon genre newsletters arrive every two weeks, that's good enough for me). What do you write about? About you, about your fiction, free short stories, you ask them questions, tell them about tidbits of research you've done, or places you travelled for your writing. Tell them about box sets you're in, and even plug your friends with similar books. Anything. Booby-trap any links to your books so your MailChimp/AWeber/whatever account knows who clicked what.
4. Siphon people who clicked all the links to series 1 (and downloaded the freebie!) off to a side list, and say three months later send them an email saying: hey, this is book 2 in the series. Do this with all books 2 in all your series.
5. Repeat steps 3 and 4. Create new emails, use the links and who clicks them to segment your list and send them further information based on who clicked what.

6. Pronto! You have now created your own marketing machine that crawls like a giant slug over your subscriber list.

III. Your Tasks

It's now really clear what you need to do:

1. Keep writing new books that people want to read, continuing your most popular series, starting new series maybe (make book 1 free again). Add new emails about those books to your mailing sequence.
2. Keep feeding people into your giant mailing slug.

The things we dealt with in *Self-publishing Unboxed* were all extremely important to get right before you do anything else. In fact, they are the foundation of the plan. Everyone knows that without foundations, you have a lousy building. Without at least one series with multiple books, and a decent sell-through, none of this will work. If you don't have this, if your sell-through is not good, if you have trouble getting reviews on your books, even with thousands of people on your mailing list, then go back and work on your foundations.

This book will deal with the points described in parts 2 and 3.2.

CHAPTER 53
THE TRIFECTA OF MAILING LIST RULES

If there are any "rules" that govern the long-term success or otherwise of mailing lists, they are these:

1. Mandate
2. Purpose (that's in line with the mandate)
3. Delivery (in line with the list's purpose)

MANDATE

The people on the list should understand what they signed up for. Be clear when they sign up: is your list an author newsletter, a new-releases-only list, a list that advertises cross-promotions? Say so when people sign up.

It could easily be that later on, you want to change the focus and branding of the list. In this case, you no longer have a mandate and it's best to ask for people to re-confirm their mandate.

PURPOSE

Do you want to sell books, inform people, keep a chatty conversation, talk to ARC readers, or talk about your cat? Tell people what you're doing from the outset. Stick to it. They have given you their permission to talk to them about this stuff (mandate).

DELIVERY

Do as you promised. If you have an author-focused list, and you get bitten by the author cross-promotion bug but now need a place to advertise cross-promotions, start a new list. Don't do this to your existing list. People will get pissed off and report you for spam.

Do the three things above: ask their permission, be clear about what you'll do, and stick to it.

Oh, and if they don't like it, give them a super-easy way out. Put that unsubscribe button at a super-obvious place in flashing neon colours. Yes, people will unsubscribe. This is a good thing.

Pretty simple, right?

A SMALL BUT VERY IMPORTANT NOTE

Because it still seems that people don't get it.

It is ILLEGAL to add people to your mailing list who haven't given you permission to do so. Permission would include filling in a form or downloading a book from Bookfunnel or StoryOrigin or another site where it is clearly stated that people will be signing up to a list.

Anything else is NOT ALLOWED.

To do list:

- If you have a mailing list, examine it in the light of the three principles: mandate, purpose and delivery. I hazard a guess that it's going to look pretty sad. Never mind! We've all been there and done that.

1. You know I'm joking about the neon colours, right?

CHAPTER 54
WHAT TYPE OF LIST DO YOU HAVE?

In a very black-and-white kind of world, there are two types of mailing lists. Of course, it isn't quite as simple as stated here, and you can have both types of lists, and there definitely is crossover; but for the sake of the argument, let's keep them separate, at least for a very short time.

THE BACK-END LIST

This is the type of list that people sign up for when they have read one of your books and get to the end, where they find a link to sign up to be notified when the next book comes out. A back-end list is a *service* to readers. Even more precise: it's a service to existing readers. A back-end list preaches to the choir. You can develop awesome relationships with the people on this list, because they're interested in your books and in you. You can post pictures of your workspace, your holidays, and of your cat. You can post snippets of the book that's about to come out, enlist help from your readers in spreading the word, hold competitions, use your readers' names as characters in books, and so on and so forth. But they're not new and they're already your fans.

THE FRONT-END LIST

The subscribers who join a front-end list often do so because of an incentive. They may part with their email address in order to get a free book or in order to take part in a competition. You may have advertised this book or competition solely because it will get people to sign up for your list.

Subscribers of a front-end list typically have not read many of your books (or indeed any of them). Obviously, this limits the type of things that will be attractive to them. However, they are also excellent subjects for pimping books.

While there are obvious differences in the two list types, there are also similarities. Both types of lists will be heavily populated with people interested in books, and, if you have done your homework and placed a few safeguards, even the people who entered just to win a Kindle will be interested in your genre.

So some things you will need to do differently for the list types and some will be the same. And you know what? No one says that you can only have one type. You can have both types of lists on the same account. In fact, I recommend that you do so.

Let's look at the different types of lists, sign-ups, inherent qualities and possibilities.

TO DO LIST: MAILING LISTS

- What type of list(s) do you have?
- What are the unique characteristics of each?

CHAPTER 55
THE BACK-END LIST

BY BACK-END LIST, WE MEAN A LIST WHERE PEOPLE SIGN UP FROM A LINK IN the back of your book. By definition, this means people have read and presumably liked that book. They want to know when the next book comes out, and are interested in you as a writer.

Most of this book will deal with incentivised, or front-end, sign-ups, so this chapter will contain most of what I'll say about organic, back-end sign-ups.

And I truly don't need to say much about the subject, because people understand back-end sign-ups. These are your fans. They don't need an incentive to sign up. They have read your work and want to know about you.

Most authors, even many of the traditionally published ones, have a list like this. They notify their fans of new releases. Sometimes they also send newsletters with personal details. Some authors have elaborate structures such as street teams and Facebook groups for fans. I'll say a bit more about these later. They have rallied a keen group of readers who review their books and buy the newest book as soon as it is out.

These people are gold and you need to treasure them.

There are also unlikely to be many of them, at least at first, and their numbers grow very slowly.

It's a rough average that you get about one review for every hundred sales. I have not seen any stats on sign-ups, but you are likely to get fewer sign-ups for every hundred sales. It's a slow, slow business.

What can you do to increase back-end sign-ups?

I have seen some authors have great success with giving them an offer of a bonus story that explains some aspect of the book they've just read. The story will typically only appeal to those who read and liked the book, and the offer will only be made at the end of the book.

Another way to get people to sign up is to make people feel special about being on the list. Give the list and its members a name. Ask them special questions and give them special tasks. Often authors know these people quite well.

These are your early reviewers, your last-minute typo hunters, your beta readers. These are people who will come to your book signings, come to your stand at shows, people who will truly delight and maybe even embarrass you with their fandom. I mean—we all suffer impostor syndrome, and I'm not *that* good to deserve this treatment, am I?

Seriously, these people are awesome, wherever in the world they are.

Treat them well.

One of the major drawbacks of back-end sign-ups is that this method won't give you a workable list within a reasonable amount of time if your books are not selling like hotcakes. The premise of this book is that you want to use your mailing list to sell books. Since subscribers to a back-end list accrue slowly *and* are much more likely to have read all your books already, this type of list is a poor candidate for generating sales except for the occasions when you have a new release. I'll have more about this in a chapter on open rates, later.

The reality is that authors who want to use their list to generate sales will *need* to accrue front-end subscribers, or their lists will remain stuck under 100 subscribers, and you can't do much, nor expect much result, from a list that size.

TO DO LIST: BACK END LIST

- Examine your back-end sign-up process and whether you might be able to increase sign-ups by offering something special related to the book people have just read.

CHAPTER 56
THE FRONT-END LIST

MOST OF THIS BOOK WILL DEAL WITH FRONT-END LISTS. THIS IS MAINLY because if you have chosen to use your mailing list as a way of advertising your books, this is where the biggest potential is.

Back-end sign-ups accrue slowly, especially in the beginning when you've only got a few books out, and no one knows your name. Your list has no serious advertising potential if there are only a hundred people on it. For some, even that may sound like a lot.

If you want to use your list to sell books, you need a significant number of people on it, and front-end sign-ups are the way to go. With front-end sign-ups, you can quickly increase your list to a size that you can do something with, which allows you to evaluate the results.

So what are front-end sign-ups?

These are the people you get on your mailing list as a result of an activity that requires them to leave their email address in return for a benefit. This could be as simple as an incentive to sign up so that they can get one or more of your books for free. Or it could be something as elaborate as a joint promotion with other authors, where you pool your money to give away a fairly large prize, like a Kindle, and collect the entrants' email addresses.

There are many varieties of non-organic sign-ups, and in this book we will discuss a number of them, their effectiveness and things you have to look out for.

While it is true that the subscribers you get this way don't know you from a bar of soap, it is also true that they have given you a mandate to email them. These people are your custom audience. They have parted with their email address in order to get something of yours.

You will probably have heard a lot of preconceptions about these types of sign-ups and promotions, and we will discuss them next. However it is absolutely true that with a bit of work, enough of these people can be turned into loyal readers to make recruiting them worthwhile. Note that the operatives in this sentence are "work" and "enough of these people."

Let's hunt a few more preconceptions first.

TO DO LIST:

- Consider the different methods of front-end sign-ups in terms of your own list. What would you be prepared to do now, and what may need to wait?

CHAPTER 57
LET'S KILL SOME DANGEROUS PRECONCEPTIONS

...Right here, before I go any further, let's kill some preconceptions and assumptions that can be quite harmful to your overall mailing list strategy.

If people sign up for your list organically, they have read all your books

Nope. And nope. Not even on your pure, 100% back-end list. Especially if you have more than one series. They may have read the books in that series, with the emphasis on "may". They may have read one book, or all of them. If they haven't read all of your books, then why did they sign up to be notified of the next one? Good question, but people are people and people sign up for mailing lists for all sorts of weird and wonderful reasons.

If you're in doubt about how many books, and which ones, people have read, ask them. People love answering questions, and a survey doesn't do your engagement rate any harm. Use Google Forms or a free account on SurveyMonkey.

People who sign up for a free book only want free books

Nope. Sure, some of them do, but don't worry about those people. In fact, get rid of them as soon as you've worked out who they are. It's about the people who like getting free books as an introduction to a new author. Those are the ones you want to keep.

If you do giveaways, your list open rate will plummet and unsubscribes will soar

They may, for a little while, or they may not. It depends on where you sourced your sign-ups. It also depends on how well you weed your list out, and how engaging your emails are. Furthermore, I will show you later in this book that nervously checking open and click rates, and making decisions solely based on them, is not productive. So it may or may not be true, but it's actually not terribly important.

The subscribers you get from giveaways are yours

Nope. Non-organic sign-ups have given you one thing: their mandate to email them. It's up to you to engage them. Have a good first free book, and enough of them will buy the second one to make it worth your while.

However, they are not your fans and you cannot expect them to buy your books without first making them want those books.

People who sign up organically are going to be yours forever

Nope. No matter how they signed up, you will still have to keep giving them what you promised to keep their interest. Later in the book, I'll write about mailing list decay, but you'll also need to understand about the honeymoon period, so let's tackle that first...

TO DO LIST:

- What are your preconceptions?
- Which barriers are you putting in your own way and what is your rationale for maintaining them?

CHAPTER 58
THE HONEYMOON PERIOD

I ALWAYS FIND IT SURPRISING THAT SO FEW PEOPLE TALK ABOUT AND acknowledge the influence of the honeymoon period on your sales, on a new release or a new list.

Here are some examples of how it applies to your fiction and to mailing lists:

- When your book is new, and if it started selling without much of your involvement, it will keep doing so for a while, but inevitably the newness will wear off and readers will move onto something else.
- When someone joins a new mailing list, they are more likely to open the first emails than they are when they have been on the list for a while.
- When you advertise your new Facebook group, a few people will join and keep conversations going, but unless you get involved, they won't keep doing this. The novelty wears off and they move somewhere else.

The underlying principle is the following: as humans we are programmed to want churn. When something is new, we find it wonderful and use it, talk about it, and get involved all the time; but after a while, it is no longer new and exciting. It becomes more comfortable and a bit more pedestrian, and unless the thing or activity keeps delivering awesome new content, people are going to look for something else new.

This happens with everything and everybody, like it or not.

Even marriages.

How does this apply to mailing lists? Well, when people have just joined, whether they did so organically or not, they are more likely to open your emails. After a while, you'll find that the people who joined a few months ago are not opening your emails as often anymore.

There is a "catch-em-while-they're-hot" quality about this. During those first few months people are most likely to buy your books and become fans.

So let's get into this part of the process.

CHAPTER 59
THE MAIN TOOLS FOR GETTING SIGN-UPS

The number one tool for getting people to sign up is your book

Remember how in *Self-publishing Unboxed*, I spent the first few chapters talking about your book, its quality and attractiveness, and genre appropriateness? This is why. You need to put out the best book possible, so people will *want* to sign up to read more when it's available. You need to put out the best book possible, even if you're going to give it away for free to new mailing list subscribers.

This book is your honey to attract the bees.

Don't give out a short story with a rubbish cover that has nothing to do with the rest of your work. You can give that once people are your fans. To attract fans, give your best work only.

In the next few chapters, we will go into the different methods you can use to deliver this free book, because some of these offer further opportunities.

Furthermore, when you want to give out a free book, you have to make sure that there are books available for people to buy after they've read the free one, that these books are clearly labelled as part of the same series, and that they're full price and available in as many different places as possible.

The number two tool for getting subscribers is your landing page

I talked a bit about landing pages in *Self-publishing Unboxed*, but I talked more about what's *not* on a landing page, namely anything other than your offer. No menus, no links to other parts of your site, no distractions, nothing.

The primary content of the landing page can be really simple.

Typically, a landing page for sign-ups will display the cover of the book people are going to get, it includes a sales pitch for the book and a field where people can enter their email address and a subscribe button.

Keep the design simple. No busy backgrounds, no strange colours. No orange letters on a black background. Remember that many people will look at these on their phones. Anything that reduces readability has to be eliminated.

KISS: Keep It Simple, Stupid.

The field and the button are an embedded form from your mailing list provider as I described in *Self-publishing Unboxed*, so that when people enter their email address, it is taken straight to your list, at which point your automation sequence will kick in and deliver the free book to them.

I usually only ask for an email address, not a name. Ultimately, whether you have people's names or not doesn't matter in the operation of your list, and people tend to be less likely to sign up the more details you ask them to provide. So: email address and subscribe button—that's all your form needs.

This landing page is your giveaway offer.

Armed with these two tools, you go into the wide world…

TO DO LIST:

- Before you go any further, re-examine your sign-up form (hosted on your own website as explained in *Self-publishing Unboxed*) and your landing page.
- Does the offer look attractive?
- Does the page look attractive or is it confusing?
- Is it clear what people will get?
- Ask a few people.
- Make sure you update graphics. If your graphics are homemade, pay someone to make an attractive graphic. Poorly made graphics, poor typography, illegible fonts and garish colours can all turn

people away. Basically, people don't want to associate themselves with something that they think looks ugly.

CHAPTER 60
FRONT-END SIGN-UPS AND THEIR RISK

IN THIS CHAPTER I'LL TALK ABOUT THE DIFFERENT WAYS THAT YOU CAN get incentivised, or front-end, sign-ups. I've divided them into three groups, and will discuss the methods for each. I also talk about the "risk" associated with each of these methods. For this purpose, the term "risk" refers to recruiting the wrong type of people to your list: people who never open your emails or are not the right audience, or people who are likely to report you for spam.

GIVE AWAY ONE OR MORE BOOKS FOR FREE

This is the simplest and some would say the most harmless way of getting people to sign up to your mailing list non-organically.

Grab the URL of the landing page that details your sign-up offer, and put a link to that page in the sidebar on your website, or in the front of your book—and remember how I told you to put the sign-up for your mailing list in front of your book as well as the back? This is why.

Put it in your website's header, in pinned posts in your social media accounts. Put it in a pop-up form that comes up when people visit your website. Yes, I can hear you gasp right now, "Everyone hates those things!"

Do they? Why do so many websites have them? Do you want subscribers or are you afraid to show people the awesome book they can get for free?

Try it, and see if it works.

On my website, I have chosen to put the sign-up graphic in the page header, because I found it more elegant than a popup and couldn't see a major difference in sign-ups, but there may be a difference for you. Try it.

This type of non-organic sign-up can still be quite passive. You can just put a link on your website, on your Facebook author page, on your Twitter profile, and wherever else you are active on social media or elsewhere on the Internet. You can even have it printed on business cards or flyers you give away at cons. The possibilities are endless.

As well as passive, this method of getting non-organic sign-ups is relatively harmless or idiot proof because, although they have not read your books, the people who sign up have already visited your book's page, your profile or your website. They are people who are likely to be at least somewhat interested in what you write.

FREE BOOK INCENTIVES WITH ADVERTISING

It could be that even when you're giving away a free book as I showed you above, your sign-ups are quite slow, because no one knows about you, you have few followers on Twitter and no one visits your website. So you may decide that you want to give your free book offer a bit of a push. You want to advertise your offer. You will pay to advertise the landing page that you have created as described in the previous chapter and *Self-publishing Unboxed*.

There are several ways to do this, which I will address in later chapters. They can be very effective or very ineffective, and very expensive or very inexpensive, and everything in between.

Again, the people you recruit in this way most likely won't have read your books, but in addition, they have probably never heard of you. They saw "free books" and thought "goodie!" They came over and downloaded the book.

They may indeed only be interested in free books, but you don't know that yet. They are at least interested in books and probably in your genre, because you would have targeted genre readers with the placement of your ad. Or your covers, if done properly, would advertise what sort of books they are. People would self-select. If you write romance, people looking for crime books would not download your freebies and you would not get their email addresses.

With this method, there is obviously a little bit more risk involved, namely that you attract readers who only want free books, but this is still a very good method of recruiting people to your mailing list.

GIVEAWAYS AND COMPETITIONS

This is the most high-risk method of recruiting subscribers, even if it can also be one of the most effective. But you have to know what you're doing, and you have to be really careful in selecting the giveaway organisers that you are willing to work with.

The giveaway has to be related to reading, related to your genre, and preferably organised by another author in your genre. It's best if the prize is genre and/or reading related. Giveaways for gift cards and iPads might attract a lot of entrants, but you get a fairly high number of people in these who have never read a book in their lives. You want to avoid those giveaways.

The best giveaways are for books in your genre—because who would want to win books if they never read?

You also have to be quite careful with importing the resulting subscribers lists into your email provider, especially if your list is still quite small. I will say more about importing subscribers later.

I would not recommend you jump into this method straight away because it can get you into hot water. I would also say the method does not make much sense if you have only one or two books out. You need books for them to buy when they have read the freebie, because otherwise you remove the immediacy of recommending something to them that they can buy right now. Remember the honeymoon period? You want the honeymoon period for subscribers to this list to coincide with a period where you have as many books for sale as possible.

I've been doing competitions since 2014 and a large section of my mailing list was built that way. With careful weeding, you can absolutely find new readers who become loyal fans.

TO DO LIST:

- Decide which incentive you'll use for front-end sign-ups.
- Make graphics and sign-up pages.

CHAPTER 61
SUBSCRIBER-ADDING SHORTCUTS

Although I mentioned in the previous chapter that using incentivised sign-ups with advertising is more risky than simply waiting for people to sign up by themselves, it is also a very powerful method of quickly building your list.

It is especially useful if you're starting out, you don't have many readers, you are launching something new or you want to start a new list.

In the next few chapters, I will give some ideas of methods, both free and paid, to increase incentivised sign-ups. Your tools will be your landing page and your free books.

The question remains: how do you get your free books to the subscribers?

Please don't attach the book to an email. They may be reading their email on their phone, where it's cumbersome to deal with attachments. They may not want the book on their computer, where they receive email. They want it where they read it.

For several reasons, it's much better to upload the book somewhere and include a link in your email. This way, you can track who clicks which links.

But where? Your website is a possibility, but not all providers allow EPUB or MOBI files to be uploaded. You could use Smashwords and provide the subscribers with a code to get the book free, or you could use another platform like Payhip, where you can both sell your book or make it free.

Unfortunately, with all these options, which are free to use, you will get no end of questions about how people get their books onto their devices. By the time you've helped two or three people, you will be thoroughly sick of answering this question. You need something easier.

Helping people get freebies onto the device of their choice is exactly what Bookfunnel does best. It was set up with the specific aim to help writers deliver free books to their readers. It offers help files, an app and a response from a real human if your readers are still having trouble. No, it's not free, but it's worth not having to deal with the hassle.

TO DO LIST:

- Think about how you will deliver the free books to your subscribers.
- Get accounts at whatever places you choose.
- Upload the books, covers and descriptions.
- See what the download page looks like.
- Copy the links.

CHAPTER 62
FREE METHODS TO ADD SUBSCRIBERS

Some of the best methods to get people to sign up for your list are free. The catch is that they usually involve some work on your part, but they don't cost you any money either, so that's ideal for authors who don't sell much yet.

All these methods revolve around the same tactic. The landing page and sign-up form you have created will be your tools. Basically, you will throw these links out everywhere you go, and then make an effort to put them in places you don't normally get to.

You could ask a fellow author to feature you on their blog. In a guest post, you could talk about your books, some specific area of knowledge that you've gained through research, or anything that takes your fancy. At the end of the post you put a link to your free book sign-up page with the recognisable image from the cover of your book that subscribers can get free.

I hope you now see that getting this promotional image right and recognisable is important. The saying goes that people need to have seen an offer seven times before they act on it. Make sure they see it. Use an attractive image.

Of course don't forget to put the same image into your pinned post on any social media platforms where you are active.

You can ask other authors to display your free book offer for you, while you display theirs. You can ask them to feature you or your free books in their newsletter, while you do the same for them.

You can organise a Facebook party and ask other authors to take part in it. In this type of activity, you allocate each author a slot of time for the party, and you'll be at the party's site at your allocated time, talking to readers, giving away prizes, like free books, talking about your books, interviewing others.

By doing this with other authors you pull all your audiences together so that you have a better chance of attracting a good number of people.

Another free resource you can use is Goodreads, where there are groups especially for free books and promotions. Do not promote outside the allocated promotion areas, but you will find groups where it's OK to give out free books.

The same applies to Facebook groups. Some of these are incredibly spammy, and the value of posting in these groups can definitely be debated. It's probably something you'll stop doing as soon as you can, but if you're flat broke and a sale or two can really make a difference, these are options that exist that cost nothing. For one, looking at books in groups like these can make you aware of what is good—and what you need to improve—about your own books.

Here's a trick that helped me gain about a thousand subscribers when I first started my list.

Create promotional accounts on one of more social media platforms. Please don't do this on your regular personal account where you chat about the weather and your cat, because it will probably turn those people off.

At this virgin promotional account, you start interacting only about the subject of books in your genre, only with accounts that do the same. You follow those accounts. This means you target readers and reviewers far more than writers. There is nothing wrong with using social media to keep in contact with writers, but not on this account.

On most social media platforms, a significant number of people will follow you back.

Depending on the platform, you put the link to your free book signup in your bio, in your pinned post, or repeat it on a regular basis.

But please don't use DMs if the platform offers them. It's against what most people find acceptable and there is no need to annoy people.

I built my first thousand subscribers using this method.

It does take a bit of time, because you seek out the people manually. You don't grab an app that will just auto-follow everyone, because you fill your follow quota with junk accounts very quickly. You have to go to their profiles and read them. Spend half an hour or so each day doing this and you will find your list growing quickly.

But a time will come that you are simply too busy, or that growing your list for as little cost as possible is no longer an objective, and you may want to pay to get subscribers.

TO DO LIST:

- Put links to your sign-up landing page in your bio or pinned posts on social media sites.
- Put a link in the sidebar or header of your website.
- Consider using a popup form.
- Find groups on goodreads or Facebook that allow you to promote free books.

CHAPTER 63
PAID ADS

PAID PROMOTIONS WORK UNDER EXACTLY THE SAME PRINCIPLE AS THE FREE ones. The only difference is that you pay to display your ad.

This is where you're going to have to be quite careful because you can spend a lot of money for not much return.

As an author, you're going to be at a disadvantage. Paying for ads puts you on the same field as the large commercial companies. On platforms like Google AdWords or Facebook, you will be competing against the likes of Coca-Cola and Toyota. Because they are selling in much bigger volumes, or sell products that are worth a lot more, and have bigger advertising budgets, it's extremely important that you target your ad very narrowly.

Before you start advertising, you must work out how much you are willing to pay per new subscriber, or how much you're willing to spend on testing per month. Without this limit, costs can escalate very quickly. You also need to set a benchmark for performance of your ads. I suggest that this would be a certain number of new subscribers per month. You should also have a reasonable idea what these subscribers are going to be worth to you. Once they download your free books, how many books are they likely to buy?

Ways to determine this are:

- How many books have your current subscribers bought per person?

- What is the sell-through on your series on retailer sites?

Unfortunately, I've seen figures and formulas mentioned, but I don't believe any of them calculate this accurately. I don't even think it *can* be calculated accurately, especially if you're talking about attracting subscribers from a platform where you have never advertised before. These people will be different from those already on your list.

You can survey the people on your list to ask them how many books they've bought, but whether a statistically reliable number of people respond remains to be seen. I tend to think that this group will heavily self-select in the direction of having bought more books, because those who haven't bought any won't be filling out the survey.

Sell-through on retailer sites will be messed up by the fact that you give book 1 away to subscribers on a different site. It will also be clouded by the fact that some of those sales were generated by the retailer recommendations to people who are not on your list.

So whatever figure you arrive at, even if the hardness of the numbers seems infallible to you, will always be extremely rubbery.

I would simply determine a figure I'd be willing to spend as a promotional budget, a figure I don't *have* to make back, although of course if the ads are no good I won't be continuing them!

It's an experimental promotional budget. How much are you willing to spend for a look-see that may work fantastically, but, at least initially and until you figure out how to target people, may not work at all?

I would not recommend that you jump into these potentially extremely expensive ads uninitiated. There are a number of decent books and courses out there that teach you the ins and outs about ads specifically for authors.

We are unique, because our products are cheap and we need to be extra-careful about how much we spend.

However, I would not go into this unless I had a sizeable backlist to make back the inevitable cost of advertising and the increased cost of running a larger mailing list.

You may be better off writing another book. Maybe. That's up to you to determine. I definitely wouldn't be spending lots on pay-per-click ads if I had only a few books out. Unless, of course something started working really well. And that is why you try it regularly. Dip your toes in once every six months or so. Set a budget, read up on the latest tactics and simply test it.

Other than pay-per-click ads I would look carefully into paid advertising options that are specific to your genre. Not only are they often cheaper, but they come with the added benefit that they're already targeted.

For example including advertising in a conference goodie bag or specific websites or podcasts.

If you don't want to run your own Facebook ads, there are some companies that advertise that they can do it for you. Yes, it works. Yes, it's also very expensive, because you'll be paying for that person's time as well as the ads. And nothing is guaranteed about the quality of the subscribers. I know nothing is guaranteed about the quality of subscribers you get in a giveaway either, but they're likely to cost you less than $50 in total, not $50 per day for an entire month.

So: paid ads—tread with extreme caution.

To do list:

- Decide if you want to pay to drive people to your sign-up page at this point in time.
- Grab a book or course on how to do Facebook ads that's specifically targeted at authors.
- Or check out websites or other venues about getting email sign-ups through paid traffic.

CHAPTER 64
COMPETITIONS AND GIVEAWAYS

A very effective way to gain new subscribers is to do giveaways or competitions with other authors.

In a group giveaway, everyone in the group puts money together to buy a decent prize; and in order to enter and win the prize, people have to part with their email address and sign that they are happy to hear from the authors who have subsidised the prize. The authors then use their individual social media footprint to advertise the giveaway.

Often giveaway organisers will also advertise the giveaway in places where they have to pay for it; for example, they may run Facebook ads or advertise on other platforms.

At the end of the giveaway, the organiser distributes the list of email addresses to the participating authors.

Group giveaways like this will sometimes get a bad rap amongst authors, but they can be a very effective and cheap way of building your list, providing you understand a few things about them:

- By design, these subscriber lists are drawn from the aggregate of all the lists of the authors involved, so you have to make sure that you don't keep participating in promotions with the same people over and over again.
- In choosing a giveaway to participate in, it is very important that you take part in giveaways that are targeted to your genre and to readers, and don't just give away a monetary prize. You also have

to make sure that the person running it has a good reputation, because if you don't, you may get into a lot of trouble. In general I advocate that a couple of close friends in your genre are completely safe, as long as the giveaway states clearly what people are signing up for. In general also, people who sign up for these things know what they get themselves into.
- If this is your first time taking part, you will likely attract more unsubscribes than you have been used to. The people who take part in these gigs are usually savvy and they know the schtick. If they don't want to be on you list, they know how to unsubscribe and will do this. It's not the serial competition-entrants-unsubscribers you need to fear. They will take themselves off the list. It's the people who unwittingly sign up, and then fly into a rage because they didn't read the conditions of entry, and report everyone for spam. Unfortunately, you will always get one or two of those, so be prepared.

There are also companies that organise these giveaways commercially. They will usually pay for advertising of the promotion on their website. You do have to be a bit careful with these, because not all have great reputations. Unfortunately, there are no metrics that you can easily test. You can ask how subscribers are sourced, but the company can be as detailed, vague, truthful or evasive in their replies as they want. The best way to find out if a company you plan to use is good is to ask other authors.

Also many of these companies will also collect subscribers' email addresses for their own purposes as well as for you. And they will put your email address on their list and keep sending you reminders about their great offers once every day or so. So be prepared for this.

But overall, presuming you have the safeguards in place, competitions and giveaways are great.

There is, however, another method of gaining subscribers at a great rate.

To do list:

- Join Facebook groups for cross-promotion for your genre.
- If you don't know of any such groups, go to self-publishing forums and ask.
- Simply ask around, but be clear in what you want: you want groups for authors to coordinate cross-promotions, not groups where people come to spam their books.

CHAPTER 65
CROSS-PROMOTION TOOLS

Currently, writers have a few tools available that are extraordinarily useful for getting subscribers. I have no idea how effective they will remain in the future, or even how many of these tools there will be, but at the moment they are by far the cheapest way of obtaining front-end subscribers for your email list, using your free books.

These are promotions on the websites like Bookfunnel, Story Origin and My Book Cave.

How do they work?

Well, you open an account, upload your free books and their covers, and create giveaway links. The services are integrated with a few email list providers like MailChimp and MailerLite, so enter the list where you want the email addresses of people who download the free books to go.

Then go and join one of the many author cross-promotions. To find these, the sites list the available group promotions. Many of these promotions have a Facebook group attached where the organisers (who are usually just private authors) will post about the promotion and upcoming activities. When the promotion starts, the service will put all the free books with cover images on a page on their site and all participating authors will advertise that page to their audience.

At the time of writing, all these services are in constant flux and are always updating their range.

At the very basic end, they allow you to upload a book where readers can download it for free without you having to tell them how to sideload it onto their devices.

Cross-promotions are an extension of this service, because if you can attract a lot of people to a page with the lure of a selection of free books, more people will come.

Other than that, all the services are slightly different. Bookfunnel allows you to integrate their book delivery service with an online store on your website, Story Origin has a very wide range of promotion options. The promotion page can link to external retailers. My Book Cave allows authors and readers to rate their book for content.

Visit the websites to check them out.

Of course the new people who join your list via these services don't know much about you, but why would these people go to a website that specialises only in free ebooks if they weren't readers of ebooks? They're book enthusiasts, and you can't possibly find a better audience to advertise to. If they're at all inclined to spend money on books—and you have to accept that not all are—these are the people you want to reach.

In order to introduce yourself, you have your welcome automation sequence that kicks in as soon as the email addresses are added to your list. In a series of emails, you can give them more free books, tell them who you are and what you write, and make attractive offers to them. You can be entertaining and funny and review books and send them the things they like.

By giving you their email address these people have given you the mandate to entertain them. Do your best to make them your fans.

Another thing about mandate: if you have a mailing list that's primarily for back-end subscribers, and you normally send them chatty emails, start a new list with a new mandate specifically for advertising these promotions, especially if you do a lot of them. Your fans did not sign up for this, and they are likely to be annoyed.

To do list:

- Get accounts at Bookfunnel and/or StoryOrigin

- Join group promotions. Make sure you send the link to your newsletter on the agreed date.

CHAPTER 66
COMMUNITY

I want to say an extra few words about cross-promotions and the author community.

Community is extremely important in a solitary pursuit such as writing. Of course you don't have to connect with anyone, and you don't even have to leave the house, but often the writers who connect with some kind of community, whether in real life or online, do better than those without.

You need the community. Even a group of writer friends can be an enormous help. They will answer your questions, share your frustrations and understand your triumphs. These groups are where you find out the tricks and you find out where the cross-promotions are organised, because a lot of them are not found in a formal setting that you can search for. Quite often you may even need to be invited into these communities, which means that you need to know someone who is already in them, and need to have shown to these people that you are willing to commit and do the work required.

The self-published author community is particularly strong and the cross-promotions, whether for sales or for mailing list sign-ups, are proof of this. At any one time, in any number of Facebook groups, you can find promotional teams that you can join with your books. Some of them will use cross-promotion services, some link to retailers because they're group sales. Whatever the case, join some of these and be a good member of the community. Not only is the network between authors strong, reputation is a precious thing. If you show yourself willing to help others, others will help you in return.

Do the right thing by your fellow authors, and they will remember you.

If you give freely within the community, you will benefit from that later.

TO DO LIST:

- Consider your role in the author community and whether you are a good citizen.
- If you subscribe to cross-promotions, keep a calendar to make sure that you don't forget to honour commitments you made.
- Make sure that you read the guidelines of any promotion or group and stick to them, and don't ask for special consideration. Few organisers get paid for their jobs. They're just fellow authors. Don't punish their time commitment by being annoying.

CHAPTER 67
IMPORTING ADDRESSES

So you have taken part in a competition and the organiser has just sent you a list with a few hundred subscribers. What do you do with them?

It will depend a bit on how big your list is, and this is one of the reasons that I tell you not to take part in giveaways unless you have an established list. Most email providers don't actually like you importing lists of people, because the behaviour is so similar to someone buying lists illegally somewhere off the Internet, full of people who did not give their permission.

To your provider, your track record is going to be extremely important in determining whether to deliver your emails and whether they will even let you import the list.

Spam is huge, and the email list provider will do everything to prevent any of their servers being kicked to the doghouse of email delivery. This is what happens when they inadvertently let a bad spammer through.

So if this is your first time doing it, you have to be very careful. I suggest you do this only after you have been with your email list provider for a few months and have established a good track record.

I am going to assume that you have been careful how you determined which giveaway to take part in. Don't let yourself be lured by the prospect of getting thousands of addresses. At this point, it is better to get a few hundred and be cautious.

If you did happen to get two thousand addresses, you're happy that they were properly acquired, and your list is still small, I would split them into three or four groups before importing. Make the first group the smallest.

Certain email providers will already have a master list of banned email addresses of people who are known to cause problems. These will be fake emails, spammers, sellers of addresses and serial spam reporters. This is a game of give and take, and some people take way more than they give. There's no pleasing them, and it is in no one's interest to have these people on their list. They will filter them out for you.

I would suggest that you make a new list for your new giveaway subscribers. Usually, the organiser sends you a spreadsheet. Open the spreadsheet in whatever program you use to open spreadsheets. Then I usually just copy and paste the column with the email addresses from the spreadsheet. Unless you have asked for people's names—which I don't until people have been on my list for a while—there's no need to copy all the other information. Copying and pasting from a spreadsheet gives a more hassle-free importing of data than trying to get the program to import your entire file in one go.

You may consider giving the new subscribers a tag which tells you how they joined, either by putting them in a separate list that you name after the competition, or by adding a custom field to their addresses. However if you have done a couple of these giveaways, you will see that there are a lot of repeat email addresses of people who take part in these giveaways all the time, and keeping track of all the competitions can be very daunting, dare I say "too much information".

To be honest I just dump them all in what I call a competitions portal, which is a list that I use for people I have just imported, but are not on any of my other lists, and that I will need to sort into useful and less useful addresses.

Whichever way you do it, after you have imported them, start them on an automation sequence. I also make sure that this automation sequence doesn't start straight away, but with a delay of an hour, in case I make a stupid mistake and I need to reverse it. It may sound unlikely to you now, but I have definitely imported the wrong list of people into the wrong email sequence.

What is important, however, is that once these people are on your list, you send them something as soon as possible. Some of the giveaways stipulate that each author should send them something on an allocated date. In that case do as you have been told, because by being a good citizen, you will be invited to take part again.

If there is no such stipulation, send an email to these people as soon as possible. Remind them of the competition, why they are on your list, and then introduce yourself. At this point, most writers also find it a good idea to give away a free book, even if you haven't already started them on your sequence where they get the books you normally give out free to your list.

I would also suggest that at this point you make it clear to these people where they can unsubscribe. Yes, getting a bunch of unsubscribes may hurt a little, but I can tell you that you don't really want people on your list who don't want to be there. For one, you are paying for them.

Repeat this process with each of the list segments that you have made, until they are all in your list. Breaking up a large batch of subscribers potentially makes you aware of any problems with the group. If you got these addresses from a promotion between authors, you are not so likely to see a lot of problems. But if you have used a commercial company for your giveaway, you should be a little bit more cautious. If you see an unusually high percentage of unsubscribes or spam reports from the first group, I would advise against importing the rest. I would also make a note never to use that company again.

Importing lists becomes much less risky when your list grows, because by the time you have five thousand subscribers, importing a list of a thousand is not such a big deal. Also, by that time, you already have a history with your provider.

In general, the providers hate it when you open a new account and then start importing large lists of subscribers. This is for their own protection. If you import a troublesome list on a virgin account, they'll just shut you down without argument. If you've been a trouble-free customer of theirs for a while, you get a bit more leeway.

TO DO LIST:

- If it's your first time importing a list, divide it into a couple of batches.
- Send the first batch an email and wait to see what the reaction is.
- Send the next one when the first batch doesn't present any problems.

CHAPTER 68
WHAT NEXT?

So now people are on your list. What do you do next?

Here is where you should probably make a clear distinction between the people on your back-end list and the ones on your front-end list. The ones on your back-end list may have signed up just to get new releases. You will have promised this in your sign-up process. Most writers don't release something new every two weeks. The people on your organic list know that, and they are happy to receive something from you every couple of months. They're not going to forget about you in that time. Or they have signed up for a newsletter, a chatty email from you on a regular basis—as you promised them—and you write about project updates.

People on your front-end list however, have no idea who you are yet. And what's more, if you don't email them immediately, they are highly likely to have forgotten the competition they took part in that put them on your list. So as I said in the previous chapter, you should email them immediately, reminding them of the competition, where they signed up, and introduce yourself and your books. Leaving this too long will cause you grief. *Don't* just import them into your personal author list that you only email when you have a new book out.

If you're going to get front-end people, they will mean WORK for you.

You have to email them. You have to engage them. You have to sell yourself.

You should give them an easy way to unsubscribe. I know, it hurts to have 100 people unsubscribe from one email, having your ego crushed in 100 parts with each unsubscribe notice. Really, do all of you guys hate me that much?

One notion you should throw out of the window right now is that these people were yours to start off with. They never were. They took part in a giveaway. They didn't mind that a consequence of being in the giveaway was that you were going to email them.

They are NOT your fans. They are NOT your people.

Unsubscribes are part of running a list. Unless they suddenly spike out of the ordinary, you do best to ignore them. People unsubscribe for as many weird reasons as they subscribe. People are weird. Be prepared.

Actually, if your email provider sends you one of these cheery emails when people subscribe or unsubscribe, go in and turn off that feature right now. It's annoying and messes with your head.

I can assure you, getting a hundred unsubscribes is better than getting spam reports or carrying thousands of people on your list who have no interest in being there. In fact, I'll be even more blunt: once people from competitions and giveaways are on your list, you should view your list as a tree that you give a good shake every now and then so that the rotten apples fall out. Give the people who have no interest in you every opportunity possible to unsubscribe.

So that is a major difference between the two lists. You have to email a list from a non-organic sign-ups much more frequently. You have to do work to sort out the people who want to be there and are useful for you, and do your utmost best to get rid of the rest.

If you remember what I said in the beginning of this book about mandate, you'll have to admit that the mandate these people have given you is a little bit rubbery. They—sometimes begrudgingly—accepted the fact that you were going to email them because they wanted to take part in this competition. They didn't specifically give out their email address because they wanted to hear from you. So it's going to matter a lot more what you do and how you treat them.

The people on your back-end list are going to be happy to be emailed once a week or once a quarter, or however often you have promised them.

The people on the front-end list don't know you and have never heard of your books, but for the most part they are happy to be entertained. So you write a program to entertain them. And this is the major function of mailing list automation.

But first you must remember...

TO DO LIST:

- Examine your unsubscribe link and see if you can customise it or the displayed text.
- Can you put it in a prominent place?

CHAPTER 69
THE ULTIMATE FUNCTION OF YOUR LIST

Class, what is the ultimate function of your mailing list?

If you said, "To own your audience," you get 50 points, but full marks go to those who said: "To sell your books."

Oddly enough, this fact almost always gets lost in the discussion of mailing lists. Authors start mailing lists because other people say that you should.

Fact of life: never do anything because someone else says so if you don't understand why you should do it.

A mailing list is not an ego trip, it's not a subject to boast about how engaged they are—although power to you if you do have such a list.

A mailing list is an advertising vehicle, and a pretty powerful one at that.

Think about it:

If I gave you the choice between spending $100 to pay a company to send notice of your new book or special to 10,000 people, every month, or spending $1200 to acquire a mailing list of 10,000 email addresses to whom you can then send whatever you want, because they're yours, the choice would be simple.

But few people see it that way. They see the mailing list as a *service* to readers, not a vehicle to sell books.

You are creating your own sales vehicle like an book promotion service: over time you create an audience, a significant percentage of which will buy your new releases, if not immediately, often later. What is more, you can keep the addresses to use again for your next release, and the next one. And if you have no release, advertise a friend's book. The people on your list will email you to thank you for these suggestions.

The point of your list is to make money.

Your mailing list is for selling books. This is why I place more emphasis on front-end lists than back-end lists. A back-end list is a service, and a pretty simple one at that: sign up here and I'll notify you when there is a new book. Or: sign up here and I'll send you a monthly newsletter. Easy. Comfortable. We all get it.

But ultimately, in this business, we want to invest time and money into something because we want to sell books. And the front end is where you can sell the most, especially because few of these people will have read any of your books.

Supposing you had twelve books because you were following the Three-Year Plan and wrote twelve books in four trilogies. Supposing you gave new subscribers the first book in each of the trilogies for free, you then have eight books you can sell. Suppose you made $3 from each of those sales, a subscriber can potentially be worth $24. If you then decided that one of the trilogies was popular enough to warrant a second trilogy, all paid, that's another $12, all to people you know and control. Sure, you will send them to a retailer for the transaction, but where you send them becomes irrelevant, except you should probably offer as many different places as possible. It's not your business to dictate where people should buy.

I strongly hope that you can now see that dumping a list that you gained through non-organic methods into a newsletter that you run as a back-end service can end in a lot of tears. These people don't know who you are. Do you really think they will care about your work in progress when they haven't read any of your books?

Similarly, if you get a bunch of subscribers from a giveaway, dump them in your regular list and suddenly go all salesy in your newsletter, this will cause grief with your back-end subscribers.

You can deal with this issue in a number of ways, which we will discuss now.

CHAPTER 70
WHICH PROGRAM FOR WHICH LIST?

LET'S GET INTO THE BIG QUESTION: WHAT DO YOU SEND PEOPLE ONCE THEY'VE joined your list?

I hope that by now you can see that there is a clear distinction between what's suitable for a back-end list and a front-end list. You should absolutely not send them the same stuff, at least initially.

When someone joins your back-end list through a sign-up at the end of a book, they will want to hear what you specifically promised them. New releases, or a chatty newsletter, whatever it was you told them you'd send them.

But what about the front-end list?

These people may just have downloaded one free book, but not read it, by the time you send them your first email. Those people are not fans of yours, but they can be turned into fans.

You have a number of different options:

- You can send these people through an automation sequence that introduces them to you and your books, and then import them into your regular list.
- You can keep these people separate and develop a completely separate email strategy for them involving your books.
- They came to your list because they signed up for a competition,

so you can send them more competitions, cross-promotions and group sales.

Why would you choose any of these options?

You'd choose the first option for simplicity. If you are going to write just one newsletter to everyone and wanted to promote your own books, you would make sure that new subscribers are familiar with those books before you let them join your regular newsletter.

I'd consider the second option if I had a back-end list that I only sent new release information to. You can't import your front-end people into a new-release-only list. You need to engage them first, or they will unsubscribe en masse with your new release notices, because they have forgotten who you are.

The third option can be very powerful if you are going to take part in promotional events a lot. These events often require that you send information about the promotion to your list. Unless you set up your back-end list with this premise, you don't have the mandate to go promotional on them, so you make a list of the people you get from giveaways. Because people on this list expect to be sent giveaways and promotions, you can advertise your own promotions, too. What is more, you can advertise other people's promotions.

But, why should you advertise other authors' books on a list that you are paying for?

It seems counterintuitive, but in the world of reading and writing, I have found that the more you share and the more you give, the more you get back.

Another reason you may want to do this is to make back, through affiliate sales, the cost of running your list. But to be honest, the percentages are so low that this is not going to be a major moneymaking venture, just a way of defraying the cost of running a list of tens of thousands of people until you sort out which ones to keep, and while you're still not selling very much. Some people then, of course, discover that they like marketing and networking and that they happen to be really good at affiliate marketing, but that is another story.

TO DO LIST:

- Consider your email list strategies:
- How many newsletters do you want to send?
- Do you keep a new-releases-only list, or can you integrate your front-end and back-end lists after the front-end people have been through an introduction sequence?
- Do you want to start a separate competitions list?

CHAPTER 71
YOUR EMAIL STRATEGY

Now that you have determined why these people are on your list, and what sort of strategy will suit them, you must start thinking about how you're going to entertain them. In other words, what kind of emails are you going to send them?

For your personal back-end list, this is going to be fairly easy. They will be interested in when your next book is out and snippets from your upcoming work in progress and background information and things about yourself or your cat. Never underestimate the power of cat pictures. The Internet is fuelled by cats.

For any non-organic sign-ups, whether they come from cross-promotion services, through Facebook advertising or giveaways, it is a good idea to design an auto responder. This is a handy program that does all the marketing for you. And this is where email becomes really powerful as a marketing tool. There will be a lot more about email automation later.

You have to decide how often you're going to email them. As I already said, if people come from a non-organic source, they are more likely to forget who you are if you don't email them regularly. On the other hand, you don't want to overwhelm them; but I would recommend emailing them no less than twice a month.

There is another reason for doing this. Your first introductory email to a group of competition entrants is likely to attract the highest number of unsubscribes. But even after that first email, the next few emails are likely to report a reasonably high unsubscribe and spam report rate.

One of the metrics that your email provider keeps about you is the unsubscribe and spam report rate per email and it has targets for each. If you breach the target, you'll get a warning.

It may seem counterintuitive, but the more you email them—up to a point of course—the more this rate per individual email goes down. This is for the simple mathematical reason that if you give one group of people three links to click and a second group of people, the same size as the other group, gets only two links, each of the links in the group of three will have a much lower click percentage than the links in the group of two.

So if you have a big list of competition entrants and you want to weed out the ones who don't want to be there, make sure that you email them regularly. If you don't email them they won't unsubscribe. Silly as it sounds, when you import a large competition and giveaway list, from the moment the people are on your list, it is your task to get them to do one of two things: buy your book or unsubscribe.

TO DO LIST:

- Determine how often you want to email to which list.

CHAPTER 72
STUFF TO SEND YOUR LIST

Now you're stuck with having to send a bunch of strangers an email every two weeks. What on earth are you going to send them?

In the first place, it will have to be something sustainable. Something that you will be able to come up with every two weeks for the foreseeable future. It's not much good committing to sending people something when you're going to run out of ideas after a few emails.

In the second place, unless you've committed to a specials-and-giveaways newsletter, it will have to be something that's probably not too promotional. People are quite sensitive to being sold to, especially if they've already seen the same book pimped before.

If you want your book to sell, you don't tell people how great it is, you show them what's inside it. If you have written a book that includes research about an interesting fact, tell them about what you found, and at the end mention that it is included in the book. Then of course it would be stupid not to include any links to the book in question. Use your book's landing page for this.

Other topics that you can use would be interviews with other authors, descriptions of localities in your books, and photos of those localities.

You can include things about the writing process. People like to know what a writer does. If someone asks you "How do you get your ideas?" write a newsletter segment that answers the question.

If you're comfortable, add tiny bits about your personal life, especially as they relate to writing. You may answer questions such as: How did you start writing? And when did you decide to go full time? In my case, I have a couple of anecdotes about the traditional publishing industry. I love the one where some unnamed person in one of the world's biggest publishing companies told me "You will never sell this book," in those words, about a book I sold immediately after, and that is now part of my highest-earning series. People love that stuff.

People also love a little bit of personal stuff, especially if there is something special about where you live or your situation that will be alien to them. My subscribers get a kick out of when I mention winter in June and July or the fact that we're almost a day ahead of them.

Include things about the daily life of an author. Things that make them laugh. Animals. And never neglect to mention a different book of yours with each email. Always give them a one-click link where they can find all your books on one page. Use this link in your signature line or some other place with each email your send them.

You can already see that if you have only one or two books out, coming up with new and interesting subjects is going to be a real stretch. Beware of subject creep, where for want of material you start talking about—say—movies you watched. In that instance, you have metamorphosised your list into a movie review list, and the people who hang around do so because of your movie reviews. That's fine if you like writing movie reviews, but it detracts from your fiction.

So what do you do if you have few books out? In that case you are probably better off creating a competition list, to which you will send specials, giveaways, and new releases from other authors as well as your own. Because you probably don't have enough material to keep the list occupied and interested for that amount of time. And in turn those other authors may do something for you when you have a new release out.

Setting up a list is easy, but this sort of stuff warrants careful planning.

In fact, you are now editing a newsletter in the same way that news bulletins of old used to work. The editor had to find something interesting for the subscribers with every issue, something that fitted within the newsletter's subject matter and would not alienate subscribers or pull in people from the wrong target audience.

Target audience examples:

- People who read *your* books: write about you, about your books, give them snippets and talk about research.
- People who like your genre: author interviews, pimping your books as well as other authors' books, cross-promotions, book reviews, movie reviews.
- Other writers: craft, business of self-publishing, industry gossip, courses, podcasts
- Freebie and competition junkies: free books, competitions, giveaways, sales.

With each email you write, step back and consider if it addresses the right target audience. If you cross-target a few times, no one is going to bite you, but make sure you nip permanent subject creep in the bud. Because if people like your emails for their movie reviews, then you're going to be mightily disappointed that they won't buy your latest release.

A brief word here about email titles.

It is a fact that open rates vary between different titles. You can find many articles about the subject. For example, the MailChimp help files mention a list of words to avoid. One of the words that affects authors is the word "free". Apparently emails with the word free in the title are more likely to land in junk mail folders. As a personal antidote to the conventional wisdom, I—and I'm not the only author who reports this—usually find increased open and click rates if I use the word free in the email's title.

The bottom line is: don't believe what the all-knowing "they" say until you've tested it and found it so.

One "rule" I have definitely found to be true is that email titles that are plain and simply state what's inside the email have higher open rates than titles that try to be funny or clever. People don't have time for clever, and if you think funny is interpreted the same way around the world, I invite you to watch a show the Brits find funny and one Americans find funny, never mind the rest of the world. "Funny" only applies to a very narrow target audience. Your list is worldwide. People won't get it. If someone doesn't get it, they will feel stupid. One awesome way to disconnect from people is to make them feel stupid.

Also beware that you don't make your emails too long. People are busy and many of them read emails on their phones. Scrolling through pages and pages of stuff on a tiny screen is no fun.

Personally I have chosen to divide my emails to my author subscription list into a couple of sections. There is an introductory section with current news, often followed by something about research or locality or some other factual knowledge; then I will have a randomly chosen focus book out of my catalogue. This is usually not a first book in a series. I'll have an image of the cover and will include a small paragraph where I talk about the book in a chatty way: about how it was written or what my aim was with the book, instead of just repeating the book's blurb as people can also see it on the retailer sites. Then I often include a free book that's not mine. The people on my list who are still reading by the time they get to the bottom of my email are the ones who have already downloaded and read my free books. Unfortunately I am not a writing machine, and I only publish one book every three months. People can read much faster than that, so I keep them occupied by giving them free books written by my friends. This has proven to be a very good strategy for keeping open and click rates high in my emails. These people come from both back-of-book sign-ups and downloads of my free books.

I also have a mailing list that consists of people whose addresses I got through competitions and giveaways. I send them mostly other competitions, giveaways and group sales once a week, but I also include a focus book in this email. That book is usually mine, and I often advertise my own free books and my own author list to these people. Remember that they took part in a competition and they are not your fans. By advertising my own list to these people, I allow a more organic transition between my competition list and my author list. This keeps the engagement of my author list quite high.

TO DO LIST:

- Make a list of topics and ideas to write about.
- Make sure that you keep this list in a handy place (like, your phone) so you can add to it when you get an idea.
- Subscribe to a few lists from fellow authors in your genre to see what they do.
- Read up about email titles. It may be worthwhile deciding on a recognisable format; for example, mention the name of the newsletter each time you send an email.

CHAPTER 73
EMAIL DESIGN

At this stage, I probably need to say a few things about email design.

Your email list provider (MailChimp, MailerLite etc.) will provide a series of templates that you can use to design your emails. You can drag & drop boxes of text and images. Designs vary from plain white to really busy designs that look like restaurant menus or printed leaflets.

What should you use?

Personally, I'm in favour of a simple design. Remember that many people read these emails on their phones. The templates should be mobile friendly, but you really don't need garish colours and designs that look like you're selling the latest fashion.

But whatever you choose, templates or a simple design, absolutely do the following:

- Get rid of any standard images that come with the design and insert your own
- Get rid of the little graphic at the bottom of the email that advertises the service. If you have a free account on most of these services, you can't turn this off. Yeah, it makes you look like a cheapskate.
- Get rid of standard displays of social media icons, because every other writer and their cats will be using those same standard settings.

Some other design notes:

- Many of these email services use as their standard design grey print on a white background. A lot of people find this hard to read. Change the type to black.
- Don't use light text on a black background.
- Don't, on pain of death, use fancy fonts or Comic Sans in your emails.
- If you're going to insert images, by all that's dear, scale them down to a width of 640 pixels (MailerLite) or 500 pixels (MailChimp) first. Even if you use a picture taken on your phone, it will be 3000 pixels wide and the size is huge, eats up bandwidth, slows down the loading of your email (remember that people read on their phones?) and just annoys the crap out of people.
- Don't use more than 4–5 images per email.
- Make sure all your images are attractive. If you have zero design skills, pay someone to design promotional graphics. Otherwise stick to photographs.
- If you have no design skills, even if you have no money to spend on this, pay someone to make just the header that you will use for each email.

TO DO LIST:

- Decide on a template to use for all your emails. Adapt it with your settings and save it to use for your newsletters
- Clean up all things that advertise your list provider's website.
- Make changes to type, social media buttons and colours and save as a reusable template.
- Get a nice header graphic.

CHAPTER 74
INTRODUCTION TO AUTOMATION

AUTOMATION IS THE POWERHOUSE OF MAILING LIST OPERATION. IT ALLOWS YOU to send out messages that you have prewritten, triggered by certain events or actions taken by subscribers. Do you know those messages you get from Amazon about three weeks after you have bought a book, those emails that ask you if you want to review the book? Those are automated messages. So are the ones that you receive about books whose pages you have visited.

Often writers get excited about this. Amazon is sending out reminders that include my books! It's always a little painful to tell them the truth: they get the messages because they have an Amazon account and because they visited those books' pages. It's a simple thing operated through link tracking. Oh, oops. Maybe you should refresh your product page a bit less often.

But my point is that these emails are triggered by your visit to a page. With email automation, you can do that yourself.

Even the most basic email provider will have automation that starts as soon as a subscriber joins a list. You will need this, at the very least.

But there is much more you can do with automation, if given the tools.

For this reason, I recommend that you sign up with an email provider that allows you to trigger automation according to actions taken by the subscriber. For example if they click the link or if they opened an email, or a certain time after they joined your list. Unfortunately none of the providers handle automation and subscribers in the same way. Finding out how to do it in yours may require some lateral thinking.

If you have the option to let automation assign a value to a field in your subscriber's data, then you can do almost anything. It is a matter of finding out how to do it. Unfortunately I can't give a guide how to do this, so you will have to consult your provider's help files. If they are not good, or their help team doesn't respond to your questions, it may be a good idea to look for another place to host your list. Automation will greatly improve the value you get from your list, and there is no need to be hamstrung by crappy services from a crappy provider. Move your list now, before it gets too big.

A warning: automation is not easy. It requires some planning and thought. It may take quite a long time after a subscriber joins a list that it kicks into action. At times, you may need to think about what to do about the people in this queue if you want to change something else. You have to make sure that all the pieces go in the right place. I find that it helps to keep your automation sequences short, because if something goes wrong, you haven't lost a big chunk of information, or you don't have many subscribers missing out on something. It is better to have two automation sequences of five emails each than to have one of ten.

Keeping sequences short is not just a protection against mistakes on your part. Sometimes, a provider will change a system, and inevitably some subscribers will be left in limbo. If you keep your sequences short, this will affect as few people as possible.

In the next chapter I will go through different types of operations that you can perform, with some principles behind them. Unfortunately, I cannot give instructions for each email provider because they are all different, and because they change their systems all the time. I will, however, tell you what operations you should look for.

TO DO LIST:

- Design an email sequence of 3–5 emails for people who join your list through competitions and free book giveaways.
- Make sure you use the same header graphic for each.

CHAPTER 75
YOUR WELCOME SEQUENCE

The welcome sequence is the series of emails people first get when they join your list. In your automation menu, there should be a trigger that's called "when a subscriber joins a list" or some such.

It is a good idea to tailor the sequence to each list, especially if the subscribers come from different sources.

If, for example, you got a list from a competition or a giveaway, it's a very good idea to remind your subscribers that you got their email address because they signed up for the giveaway. I would make the welcome sequence a few emails long. More than one, but I wouldn't send them more than five. Just as illustration, I will briefly describe my process.

As soon as a subscriber joins my author list, they get sent an email which contains images of the covers and the links to my four free series starter books. I use the covers because people can tell the book's genre from them, and if they're not interested in fantasy, they will choose the science fiction ones and vice versa.

Each of those image links takes them to a page on Bookfunnel.

Two weeks later, they get an email that asks them whether they got the free books all right. Before I joined Bookfunnel, this was a necessity, because a lot of people would not know how to get the books onto their devices, and by not checking on them, I would lose a lot of readers because they downloaded the book, but then did not know how to read it.

But I've actually found that this email gets one of the highest response rates of all the emails I send. People will reply saying "Yes I got them, thank you very much". To which I will then reply "Happy reading".

Then in the third email in the sequence, I explain that I'm going to send them into another automated sequence which introduces them to all my series and that if they click on a button they can opt out of this. Under the button is another automation sequence that is triggered by the clicking of the button and that moves the subscribers to another list, bypassing the book introduction sequence. None of this involves anything I need to do.

Whatever process you decide on, in the first email you will typically introduce yourself and your books, and if you give away any free books for joining your list, the first email is typically where you put them. Typically, if people are on your list because they received a free book or they took part in a giveaway, this is the email that will cause the most unsubscribes. This is not a problem for you and you should not fret over it. Those people were simply there for the giveaway or the freebie. Let them be. The fact that they unsubscribed also means that you will not bother them again, no matter how many other giveaways they take part in, because your mailing list provider will not let you re-import people who have unsubscribed.

In this first email, mention how they came to your list. You may mention the name of the giveaway, but if it is an automation that's probably not a good idea, because you will have to change it every time you import people from a different giveaway. Then introduce yourself: who you are what sort of books you write. Keep the introduction fairly short, and add something that might prompt them to click or reply to you. This could be something funny, or a picture of your cat, because people love animals, and in case you didn't know this yet, cats are the driving force of the Internet. I'm joking, of course, but if you include something that people can relate to, they are more likely to open your subsequent emails. They like seeing that you're a real person and not some kind of marketing machine.

Keep the introductory email quite short. People are busy and will disengage if they are faced with a wall of text and too many opportunities to click away.

How long should you leave it before you send the second email?

There are several schools of thought about this. Marketing companies will advise you to email every couple of days. Other writers will be more cautious. I use as a benchmark the frequency Amazon emails readers. If you are on one of their genre email lists, you will know that they send you an email every second week. So my second email to my subscribers in my automated series goes out after two weeks. You can experiment with this, but I feel two weeks is probably a good enough time period.

So, as I said above, after two weeks I send them another email asking if they were able to download my free books correctly. I also like to tell them about how authors appreciate reviews. The point of the second email is to hold people's interest so that they will continue to open my emails, and as a result, my emails are less likely to end up in their promotions folder. People respond well to questions. They like being asked for their opinion. Be creative.

Then, after another two weeks, they get another email with my promise to them. I tell them that I will email them roughly every two weeks and I will give them news and updates on my books.

This is my basic welcome automation sequence. There are only three emails, but by the end of those three emails the people who are genuinely not interested will have unsubscribed already.

CHAPTER 76
ADVANCED AUTOMATIONS

The basic automation sequence I talked about in the previous chapter is the minimum you should have. Most email providers, even the very basic ones, will allow you to set this up.

But in order to have more advanced processes, you will need to be with a provider that offers a little bit more than just automation that's triggered when people join.

You want automation based on when they click a link or automation that can move them to a different group or a segment or give them different tags. Tags are data fields in the line that holds each subscriber's information. It's like a spreadsheet column. In the first column, there is the date that they joined, the next one their email address, then maybe their name. Most providers also offer standard fields for address and phone number and other things that we never use as authors. I don't even use name. But you can add custom fields: another column where you can put whatever you want. So I could make an automation that when a subscriber clicks a link, the software ads a value for a tag. Then you can use the tags to sort people who have clicked certain links and put them into groups or list segments. As I already said, each provider handles this differently and you will have to check the help files of yours.

Tags and list segments are enormously powerful and allow you to search in your subscriber base for people with specific behaviours, like when they downloaded a free book. You can send them to automation sequences just for them, for that particular series or even that particular book.

Remember the first email in my welcome sequence, the one that displays the covers of the four free books with links?

When a subscriber clicks a link, an automation sequence changes the tags to include the name of the books they downloaded.

And a set number of days later, another email goes out automatically, just like Amazon does, asking them if they enjoyed the book and would they be willing to review it? And then I also give them a bit of chatty information about the second book in the series.

All this happens without my involvement.

I do the same for new book releases. When a subscriber clicks that link, my automation sequence makes a note of it, and I can choose to do something with it later.

The more of the sales process you control, the more powerful automation becomes. It really shines for those authors who sell from their websites, because you can see who buys what. Does a reader buy book 1? Send them an email with an offer for book 2, or better still, an offer for all books in the series. Does the reader get the last book in a series? Send them an email for the next series.

Most systems will also allow you to send "abandoned cart" emails, offers to people who put things in their cart but do not buy.

As I said the opportunities with automation are endless, limited only by your own imagination, and the fact that automation tends to give you a headache just thinking about it.

TO DO LIST:

- Set up follow-up automations for free books people received when they signed up.
- Check your list provider's options to see if you can move people into different groups or give them tags based on what they click.
- If you have your own store, set up automations based on what people buy.

CHAPTER 77
OTHER THINGS

There are a couple of other things that you can do with the mailing list that I haven't yet talked about.

For example you can give out advanced reader copies, or ARCs. Some people will express their dismay about the fact that some authors, especially those who write Romance, will launch a book and immediately it will have 100 reviews. This while they struggle to get as few as ten reviews in the first year of publication. Getting reviews is not easy, but it becomes a lot easier when you dangle a free book in front of subscribers and ask them to review it for you.

You can recruit these people into a reviewer team. You remember all those people who said they only want free books? Well this is how you use them. Some people are genuinely short of money, they like to read and you help them in this way. They help you and everyone is happy.

Another thing you can do with your list is to hold your own competitions. You will do this as a promotional activity to draw attention to earlier volumes in your series, or just as a fun thing for loyal subscribers. Whichever it is, the notification that people can win something usually does wonders for your open rate of your emails. On several occasions, I have found that the people who win a competition have gone on to read all of my books, or I have maintained another kind of relationship with them. And on a very basic level, this is what a mailing list is about: building relationships.

Another fun thing you can do with your list is to use it for research. This may sound strange, but if you have several thousand people on your list, they will be from all walks of life. They will live all over the world, or have lived in many different places or visited them. There will be people young and old, and people from all different kinds of professions. So if you're writing about something that requires checking by a specific professional, you may just ask your list if there is anyone on it who knows about this specific situation. I have used this several times. For example, I needed to write about a court procedure, and I asked people on my list where I could find information that told me how to write this. I have also asked people on my list to voluntarily enter their profession and email so that if I ever have a question about a certain profession, I can ask them.

Many people are genuinely fascinated by the work of an author, and they are more than delighted to take part.

A very special thing you can do for your most loyal subscribers is to name a character after them. I did this in one of my novels, and it is a lot of fun. Yes, there really is a reader named Lenka Trnkova. There is also a real person named Mobashar Qureshi. People can suggest what kind of character they want to be, whether they mind being a bad guy or whether they mind being killed. It is amazing how many responses I got from women who nominated their ex-husband's name with the note that they want to see him killed as cruelly as possible.

Again, mailing lists are about engagement and asking subscribers. Questions like this, and having fun with their responses, is what it's all about.

TO DO LIST:

- Consider what other things you could do with your list—not just what you could do for them, but what they could do for you.
- Set up an ARC team by starting a new list and asking people from your existing list to join.

CHAPTER 78
BE CREATIVE, BE YOU

Once upon a time, a writer wrote a popular book about how to pick a genre on Amazon US that you were likely to be able to rank in, because there were relatively few books and a lot of readers. He described his methods in detail, but when people followed his advice, a good deal of them missed the step that said, "Find your genre." They wrote in the genre *he* had shown as example.

Once upon a time, another writer had success with Facebook ads. He is a very pleasant, kind dude and showed his successful ads and how to set them up. Lo and behold, a lot of people started doing Facebook ads. But instead of finding their own unique voice, they copied, almost to the word, the text from the example ad.

Seriously, they couldn't even think of their own genre and their own words?

What sort of paint-by-dots people are these?

Enter the reason I don't give out basic formats and templates. I do this for a very specific reason. At the level of designing automation, marketing is a creative endeavour. It is up to you to design a sequence and email format that is unique to you. If I gave out templates with guidelines, everyone would be copying them and every email sequence would look the same, because people are lazy and just copy stuff that they're given. I bet that if I gave out templates with tracking links embedded, many people would not even remove these. It's really shocking the degree to which people are copycats.

If there is one thing that I want you to take away from this book, it is: do not be a copycat. Make your stuff memorable.

TO DO LIST:

- Put on your thinking hat. Take a piece of paper into the garden or your favourite café and write down the sort of things that you could write about that are related to your fiction. Write down what sort of strategy you're going to use for your list. Write down what you may need in terms of graphics, or input from other people. Draw a diagram of how you want your automation to work. And then find your own way.

CHAPTER 79
LIST AND AUDIENCE SEGMENTATION

A QUESTION THAT COMES UP FREQUENTLY IS:

I write science fiction and fantasy (or two other genres). Should I have two lists?

My answer to that is going to be infuriating: it depends.

I write in two genres and I don't segment my audience. I've included both genres in my list ever since I started, and I can see no reason to separate them. Science Fiction and Fantasy are both speculative fiction. I read science fiction. I read fantasy, too. The two genres are enough alike that they will appeal to a broad range of the same people. What is more, across both genres, my style and voice and *brand* doesn't change.

My books tend to be realistic, gritty, and include political scheming. People who enjoy the Ambassador books might enjoy the Icefire books, too. They touch on a lot of similar themes even if one has magic and the other has space ships.

Don't assume that readers of one genre won't be interested in another fairly closely related genre. Assuming is self-rejection and the opposite of opportunity.

So I don't segment my list at the start, but instead I keep track of who clicks what. Remember advanced automation based on reader action? Well, this is where that comes in.

I group my readers according to the links they click.

The question is: once you've made these groups, what do you do with them?

Several things.

My newsletters are general. They include a bit of this and that about all of my series. I don't split them out according to genre or series.

But when I launch a new book, the segments become important. When you launch a book, you want most people arriving at your page on a retailer site to buy that book. You don't want them to leave without buying, or at least not at first. Retailer algorithms like it when a lot of people buy a book, so they are more likely to show the book to other people.

Working with your list's segments, a launch could look like this:

- Day 1: send to the list you gathered from sign-ups at the end of the previous book in the series
- Day 2: send to the people who have shown an interest in the series
- Day 3: send to the people interested in the book's genre, including the series in question
- Day 4: send to the rest of your list
- Day 5-10: ask your friends to send to their lists

A sequence like this will have the most powerful buyers first, and they will drive up the popularity of the book on retailer sites. If most people arriving at the page will buy the book, sites are more likely to show it to other people.

I also use the segmented groups to recruit people to send pre-release copies of later books in the series and to ask them questions about the series. This is especially useful if a series is ongoing.

So this is how I segregate my list without complete segmentation. It's based on what people click.

If, however, your genres are not terribly compatible, you may want two separate lists. For example, some of you received an email from me about the release of this book. That notice did not go to my fiction list or my competition list, except as a small one-line notice at the bottom.

TO DO LIST:

- Consider if you want to segregate your lists or keep them together.

CHAPTER 80
ABOUT OPEN RATES AND CLICK RATES

I OFTEN GET ASKED THE QUESTION: WHAT OPEN RATE SHOULD I AIM FOR?

And I'm going to be honest with you. I'll tell you that I think it's the most stupid question you can ask yourself on the subject of mailing lists.

Why?

Because people's useless fixation with the open and click rate metrics distract them from the important stuff.

In the first place, let's do a little exercise.

Author A has a purely organic list with 500 people. He boasts that his open rate is 70%. That's 350 people.

Author B has a list of 10,000. She has just imported a big batch of competition entrants, and her open rate is lousy, 15%. That's 1500 people.

Now they both have a new release.

For author A, half the people who open the email buy the book. That's actually too amazing to be true, but, let's just say, for argument's sake. That's 175 people.

For author B, only 11.7% of people who open the email will have to buy the book to achieve the same number of sales.

Depending on how attractive the book offer is, that may or may not happen. Author A is unlikely to get a quarter of his list to buy the book, either. There are many factors at play.

Again: now and forever into the future: it's always about the book. EVERYTHING comes back to whether people want to read the book. Do your utmost best to write a good book and make it look nice. Yes, I've said this before and will sound like a broken record (remember records?). It all begins and ends with the book. If the book doesn't work, then none of the rest of this will work either.

Right, and here is the magic of a front-end list:

Author B's large list is about *potential*. Author A has pretty much maxed out his audience. They may be wonderfully engaging, but there is next to zero growth potential in them unless he kills himself writing six books a year. Or unless a magical promotion suddenly brings in a huge influx of buyers who sign up for his list. But this relies on luck and stuff done by other people, and you may have noticed that I don't like to depend on this.

Imagine what happens if author B, through writing attractive emails with good titles, can lift her open rate to 20%. Imagine what she can do if she can write better emails to get a higher percentage of her list to buy her book.

There is also the fact that list B is unlikely to be static, because if author B has imported people from giveaways, she will likely do it again. So her open rate will be low, her unsubscribe rate high, but when she keeps adding people, the ones who open the emails and don't unsubscribe will eventually start to add up as a real audience. I will say a bit more about the list as moving target later.

Another exercise—if you ask 100 people: "If you're likely to get about 50 sales from either list A or list B, would you rather I sent it to list A of 100 people or list B of 1000 people?" I bet list B wins every time. Because of the potential.

This is what front-end mailing lists are about: potential.

So what about the dude who boasted about his open rate of 70%? In the first place I want to say that he can run his list in whichever way he wants. But that high rate is a sure sign he's not using mailing lists to their potential. Most likely, he has already decided that this book is not for him. That's fine. If he's happy, that suits me.

But as any politician knows, you don't increase the number of people who vote for you by preaching to the choir. In order to increase your congregation, you have to step outside the church and talk to people in the street.

This means you will not get wonderful engagement. Many people will ignore you. Some will even cross the road especially to avoid you. You are likely to occasionally piss people off. It's not about those people. It's about the people who are willing to go along with you and give you a chance to hear what you have to say.

In light of this, a high open rate means you're preaching to the choir. You're purely providing a back-end service, and if this is what you want, fine, but for crying out loud, don't boast about it as if it's somehow better than someone who is actively trying to increase their reach, OK?

On the flip side of the coin, a low open rate can mean a number of things:

- An unhealthy list, which may have been neglected
- A lot of non-organic sign-ups which still need sorting
- Obviously: room (and potential!) for improvement

Rather than staring yourself blind at the precise level of open and click rates (or even sillier: comparing them with other writers), study the steps you can take to increase them.

TO DO LIST:

- Keep an eye on your open and click rates.
- Take note of what increases them and what decreases them.

CHAPTER 81
CLEANING YOUR LIST

If you collect mailing list sign-ups from competitions or giveaways, your mailing list will grow very quickly.

It is natural that when people first join a list, they will open more emails than they will later on (see the honeymoon period).

This is part of a natural decay, and is normal.

However, if you import large numbers of email addresses, you will get some that the owners never check—because they use that address only to take part in giveaways—and your open rate will fall.

This matters because your provider rates all email list accounts. The deliverability of emails depends on this rating. Basically, your provider is interested in keeping their own rating high, so they will most likely favour email sent from accounts with the highest ratings.

For you, each extra subscriber is an added cost, so all of this is a roundabout way of saying that you may need to start thinking about culling some of these inactive people.

But who are they?

This is a very difficult subject, because the fact that your provider's statistics show that people are not opening your emails doesn't mean that this is actually true. There are situations when opens are not tracked, and people would show up as inactive when they have, in fact, opened every one of your emails.

You definitely wouldn't want to get rid of people like that.

I see authors send inactive people emails with the question if they still want to be on the list. The problem with those emails is that they annoy specifically the people we don't want to annoy: the ones who in fact open and read the emails, even if their opens are not registered.

It's a bit like something I'm sure we've all done: complained online about some habit, and the only people who felt that it was about them were the people who are your friends and acquaintances, and the people you were *really* talking about never even read the post. Long story short: don't annoy your regulars.

Then what to do, because you have a sizeable inactive group on your list. How to clean it up?

I advocate setting up some form of automation that cleans your list automatically as it grows. How you can do this will depend on your provider and what kind of tools they offer. They may offer an option in their automation sequence program to select readers who haven't opened certain emails. I don't know that any of them offer this as an automated process.

We will be using one metric that is a lot more reliable than opens: clicks. I have watched this across several mailings: the number of clicks reported in my MailerLite dashboard is virtually identical to the number reported on my website. Your provider knows the email addresses of the ones who click. You'll be using this.

The moment a subscriber enters my list, they go into two automations. One of them is the welcome sequence that I have described in basic automation, and the other only kicks into place about six months later. This automation sends them an email that says here is a free book. Now if they're on the ball and like free books, they will at least click the link. They may then realise that they already have the book. That doesn't matter because the email has fulfilled its purpose. I wanted them to open it. If they open and click, they're fine.

Then all the people who did not open that email will get a second email a month later with another free book and a differently worded title that does not include the word free. If they open that email, they get siphoned off back to the main group where they came from. So even if they already had that free book that also doesn't matter.

The group that matters is the ones who did not click either of those two emails. You can add more emails in the sequence if you want, or add one of these pinging emails every month and evaluate them after six months. It's up to you how you design it.

In any case, the people who have opened none of those emails are now sent a final email that asks them whether they still want to be on the list. At this point, when they get the email, the sequence has *already* unsubscribed them. The button goes to a resubscribe form.

Why is this better than the first option: sending all your inactive subscribers the same "do you still want to be on this list" email?

Because now you have filtered out your most active subscribers, and you're not bugging them with needless stupid questions that will only annoy them. I bet that the remaining people are your most inactive ones. They may include a few who only seem inactive, because they read on their phones where their opens may not be registered; and maybe they'll be annoyed by the question. But most of those people will immediately click the button "Yes, please. I would like to keep getting your emails." And at least you've annoyed far fewer of them than if you'd sent "Do you still want to be on this list?" to start with. The rest—those who don't open and don't click that button— they're already gone.

Of course this is still an imprecise method, and the subject of list cleaning is not an easy one. False positives and false negatives are common. I've certainly been on a number of lists where I get auto-unsubscribed every so often.

In the end, as list owners, we have to strike a balance between trying to catch them all and trying to be a good citizen in the big bad eyes of the Internet. The Internet doesn't care about the people who open your emails but whose opens don't register. It rates you according to the ones that do. It's always a trade-off.

When you implement a cleaning process, you should keep a very close eye on your list metrics, because if they do not improve over a couple of mailings, then it's obviously not working and you should stop the process immediately.

Yes, there is a risk that you will automatically unsubscribe some people who were still interested.

It is quite unfortunate, but needs to be weighed up against the cost of carrying a lot of subscribers who don't open at all. If people complain to you, it might be wise to ask them to use a different email address, since this often solves the problem.

Also remember that the honeymoon period also applies to subscribers individually. They are most likely to read and open your emails after they have just joined. After a while, they might find the next shiny thing and the next favourite email list, and will not open your emails as often any more. You might even get them to open again if they go through a resubscribe process. But even if people still say they want to be on your list, they may not read your emails. And meanwhile you're paying for them so maybe you are better off not having them. These are all things you can think about, and decisions you must make for yourself.

TO DO LIST:

- Consider methods to clean your list of non-openers.
- If you want to implement an automation sequence for this, it needs to be put in place when people join your list.

CHAPTER 82
THE LIST AS MOVING TARGET

I think far too many authors see their list and audience as a static audience.

While it is true that some groups, like diehard fans, will be a lot more static than, say, people who signed up to get a freebie, the truth is that *both* groups move. New people sign up and, sad as it may be, people leave, even on a purely organic list comprised of back-of-book sign-ups. People simplify their lives, people are too far behind with their reading, people didn't enjoy your new series because it's outside what they usually read, people move on, and yes, they die, too.

It's an email marketing ballpark standard assumption that the natural decay of your list will be 20% per year. That's quite a lot, and will obviously vary per list, but don't ever make the mistake of treating your list as a static entity. It's a constantly moving amoeba that not only gets shaped by your effort, but by the members of the list themselves, as they reply and ask you for certain things.

Moving and evolving is a good thing.

Why do you think websites of major companies change all the time, and every business does an overhaul of their presentation to customers every so often?

New things, and a change in presentation, attract new people. If you stop attracting new people, you start moving backwards, because people continuously leave at the other end. It's their right to do this, and you can't stop it. You have to attract new readers who are still in that stage that they will blurt to everyone who wants to hear it that they've discovered this great new author. The honeymoon period. It wears off for any relationship, personal, commercial or based on knowledge and learning. People have heard it all and they move on.

Plan for it.

TO DO LIST:

- Always be prepared to revamp your list, to redesign emails and landing pages, to start new lists and retire old ones (and ask people to follow you to the new list)

CHAPTER 83
RULES ABOUT MAILING LISTS

So here are the important take-aways about mailing lists:

Natural decay

People will leave, all the time. This may hurt, but it's mostly not about you.

Treat your list as a market stall where you're trying to engage people so that they will buy your apples. Some people will have no time and will move along even if you give them a free piece. Some will just want to chat, but have no money, and some decide that they'd rather have oranges. This is normal. Your list is *not for those people*, and you want to remove as many of them as you can. It's about the people who stay, the people who like apples.

In order to engage them, you must tell them about your apples, and give them free samples so that if they can at all be motivated to buy apples, they know that yours are great.

But you will fail with the majority of people. It's about the ones who stay.

Never assume

Assuming is the enemy of mailing list operation. Never assume what they want, ask them questions instead.

Don't assume that they don't want to be bothered. If they really didn't, they wouldn't have given you their email address. And those people who wanted only new release notifications would have signed up for this service at Amazon or Bookbub. These people want to hear from you, because they think authors are cool.

Don't assume that they have read all your books, even the ones who signed up to your back-end list.

Never assume that they are of a certain age, a certain gender or live in certain countries. Ask them. The results will probably surprise you.

TO DO LIST:

- Regularly survey your list (use Google Forms, it's free).
- Keep it anonymous.
- Ask them which books they've read.
- Ask them where they live, their age, their interests, the genres they read.
- Make decisions based on the answers.

CHAPTER 84
OF MAILING LISTS AND MONEY

How much is a mailing list worth? And how much should you spend on acquiring subscribers?

There are as many different answers to this question as there are writers. Some writers go into extremely detailed calculations. The problem is that although numbers, percentages and dollars and cents may look impressive, the resulting values are not worth much if the underlying assumptions are unsound.

You can ask how many books people on your list have bought, but because a survey is self-selective, people who have not bought any of your books won't fill it out. This will make your estimate too high. Also, investigating your current lists doesn't take into consideration all those people who you paid to acquire but who have since unsubscribed.

For this reason, I use a whole-list calculation for the value of my list.

I consider income from the list:

- How many books do you typically sell off the back of a new release?
- How many people then typically buy other books? (Sell-through percentage, which you can estimate from retailer figures)
- How many new books do you release per year?
- Affiliate income

And expenses of the list:

- Cost of running your list
- Cost of acquiring new subscribers, if they're Facebook ads, buy-in amounts for giveaways or cross-promotion services etc.

Calculate incoming and outgoing over a year to see if your list is costing you money or making money. If your list is new, I wouldn't sweat costs too much, but once you have a decent catalogue of books and your list is costing you money, then there is obviously something wrong. It could be a matter of time, but ultimately, you want your list to generate more income from a new release than if you got a Bookbub ad.

There are a number of ways to increase income from your list:

- Apply strategies to make more people open your emails and click links and buy books. Read some email marketing books.
- Release more books in series that people on your list want to buy
- Increase the price of backlist books
- Reduce the cost of running the list by cleaning it or using a different provider
- Increase affiliate income

Increasing your subscribers can be a double-edged sword, because they will typically cost you more and this cost is not always immediately set off by a corresponding increase in sales.

TO DO LIST:

- Tally income and expenditure from your list on a regular basis to gauge the health of your strategy.
- Make changes if you're not happy.

CHAPTER 85
SPAM IS MEAT THAT COMES IN A CAN

Spam reports, the bane of anyone with a mailing list.

They're pretty much inevitable. The occasional person will sign up, download your freebies and then report you for spam.

I know, I know, these people shouldn't be allowed to exist.

But they do.

Often people don't realise that a spam report can be generated by something that seems as harmless as moving an email to the junk folder.

But all of a sudden you happen to send an email that has a disproportionate number of spam reports and you're in trouble with your list provider.

This is especially a problem when your list is small. You compound the problem by not emailing your list frequently.

Why?

Well, as I said before, it's all about *percentages*.

If you email 100 people and two report you for spam (read: innocuously move your email to the junk folder), you have a problem. Email to 1000 people and those two don't present a problem at all. Even four people wouldn't be a problem.

Leave 3 months between one email and the next, and 50% of those 100 people have forgotten who you are. Many of them will go "who the hell is this?" and move your email into the junk folder. Bingo. Another spam report.

If you have only 500 people on your list in total, then this is a huge percentage.

So, to avoid spam reports, absolutely do these things:

- Import big lists in batches. Better still, if you're doing giveaways, use an automatic cross-promotion sign-up service like Bookfunnel, which trickles subscribers into your list.
- Don't leave it too long between emails.
- Use clear subject lines.
- In the first email, remind people why they signed up.
- Make it super-easy for them to unsubscribe. Put the unsubscribe button at the top of the first email. Frustrated people will make deliberate spam reports. If people don't want to be there, you really don't want them on your list either.
- A lesser-known option to significantly cut the number of spam reports is to use your own unsubscribe page. MailChimp gives you the option to redirect people to your own page once they hit "unsubscribe", bypassing their standard "why did you unsubscribe" questionnaire. One of the options in that questionnaire is "I never signed up", but if you've been diligent in collecting emails, this is patently untrue, and if they choose this option—because they can't remember that they signed up—it will result in a spam report.

MailerLite does not offer this option, but it does offer the option to automatically unsubscribe someone who clicks a link. Make a button at the bottom of the email that says "unsubscribe", make the link go to a page on your website that says "You are now unsubscribed" and unsubscribe them automatically as soon as they do this.

TO DO LIST:

- Make sure it's easy for people to find the unsubscribe option.
- If you can, direct people to a page on your own site rather than the provider-supplied "why did you unsubscribe" page.

CHAPTER 86
TOO MUCH EMAIL

Every now and then, people will complain that email marketing will fall down in a heap because "people get too much email".

There is no such thing as too much email. These days email is sent when parcels ship, when they're delivered, when there are statements in your bank account, when something you ordered is available.

Too much?

You *asked* for those emails. They deliver information you want.

There is only such thing as email that people don't find interesting enough to keep receiving. And the funny thing about this type of email is: people self-select.

So while it is wholly possible that an individual went on a downloading spree from authors who gave out free books in return for their email address, and this person is now dismayed at the quantity of email hitting their inbox, this is a receiver problem, and not a sender-induced problem.

But everyone is signing up for author newsletters!

Yes, they are. Chances are that any time in the past ten years, when you have bought something online, you've also been signed up to almost all of those sites' newsletters. Online stores have used email marketing since the beginning of email marketing. Authors are just catching up. If email marketing didn't work, why do you think major stores (like Amazon) would do it? They wouldn't.

But everyone is getting so many author newsletters!

Maybe, but as the discoverability of good books on Amazon has declined markedly, there are other ways readers find out about books, and author newsletters are high on the list.

Make no mistake, people who don't want to be on your list will take themselves off. That's what you want them to do from the moment they join: if they don't read your books, you want them to unsubscribe.

"Too much email" is about the receiver, not about the sender. The receiver can decide to simplify their inbox and get rid of newsletters they either don't need anymore or are no longer interested in. Especially the first type is something you don't hear mentioned a lot. If a newsletter is an automated learning program about a service, and I've been through it, I don't need the emails anymore. Does that also mean that I won't use the site anymore? That's a different thing. Email marketing automation sequences *teach* people things. When they've been taught what the company wants them to know, they can leave.

Which brings me to . . .

CHAPTER 87
BUT I DON'T WANT TO ANNOY PEOPLE!

OK, supposing you sent a mailing to 1000 people, and 30% opened the email. You also received two replies: one with a positive comment about the email you sent, the other complaining: "All authors are sending me email these days!"

Which do you think will bother you more: the fact that 299 people read the email and one even bothered to send you a nice reply, or the fact that one person (who, my guess is, probably complains about everything in life) complained to you?

I bet it's the last one.

It's ridiculous, isn't it?

Almost THREE HUNDRED people read your email, and you're going to worry about ONE email from someone who doesn't appear to have noticed that the email comes with an unsubscribe button. Wait, why don't you just engage it on her behalf? You don't need people like that on your list.

You should care about delivering value to those 299 people, because *they* are your audience.

This is why I said, at the beginning of the book, to lock up your sense of wanting to be liked by everyone, because it's impossible. When you start running a sizeable email list, you will find that there is no end to the supply of weird, rude and stupid people in the world. There are also many really nice ones, but strangely enough those don't tend to get under our skin so much.

A mailing list is about your mandate, sticking to it and pleasing the majority of your subscribers—most of whom will only complain if a download link doesn't work. And oh, then you will find out how many people really appreciate what you're doing.

Those people, that silent majority, are your people. Your audience. Your crew. They may not always be very vocal, but they're there.

CHAPTER 88
HELP, I'M F(L)AILING

Hang on a moment, I hear people say. I did everything you told me to do. I set up a website, started a mailing list, did some cross-promotions and I now have 4000 people on my list. There is only one problem: they don't buy my books! They're just costing me money.

I'm going to be asking you some questions:

Q: How long have they been on your list?

A: Two months.

Q: How many emails have you sent them?

A: Two, and each time I send them something, about a hundred unsubscribe! It's terrible. This list is useless.

Now hang on a moment. You make the judgement after two emails and two whole months? You don't recognise that unsubscribes are, in fact, a good thing in this case?

You have barely given people the chance to read your free book. Do you think it was the only free book they've ever downloaded?

The most important ingredient here is time. To turn a front-end subscriber from a giveaway into a reader takes time and effort. You have to send them interesting stuff. Talk about interesting research you did for your book. Show pictures of the locality. Talk about things relating to your book. Recipes, facts about medieval clothing, spaceship designs. Tell them anecdotes about writing. Tell them what you do each day, how you got into writing, why you chose your cover artist. Anything, in fact, that is interesting but didn't get included in your books.

Give them little things, like free short stories; tell them about your friends' books, let them know when one of your books is on special.

Do this on a regular basis. I would not leave much more than two weeks between emails. Don't give them the chance to forget who you are.

Most importantly: keep doing this. Also keep evaluating your results. Compare open rates between different types of subject lines. In general: more direct works much better than clever. People have no time for clever. If they don't get it because they're not in the right mind frame to think about it, they'll delete your email. Bam. There's another spam report.

CHAPTER 89
PATIENCE REALLY IS A VIRTUE

The mailing list strategy does not come on its own. There is not much point in developing a large list if you have nothing to sell them. I see people acquiring huge mailing lists, but all they have is one or two books and no complete series, or a couple of short novellas that they sell for 99c. It's virtually impossible to recoup your mailing list cost from that.

So the first thing you must always do is to keep writing. Because there is no point to doing any of this if you don't write. You must keep adding to your intellectual property, preferably in ways in which your readers like to consume it. Also think about different formats, and uploading to different sites. You must give your audience as much chance to buy your work as possible. And then you must keep them happy.

Writing new work is always the core of your business. Whether you write fast or slowly, as long as readers see that new material is forthcoming, they are happy to hang around and wait for it.

The mailing list is especially important if you don't write terribly fast. Because if you release nothing new for a couple of months, the algorithms on the retailer websites will have forgotten about you. Your books will no longer be recommended to other readers, because there are newer books available for people to buy. It is in the retailers' interest to always have the latest best-selling books on the front page. By using your mailing list you can redirect the focus to your books.

Building up a sizeable catalogue of books which you can sell to new subscribers takes a fair bit of time. This is the basis of the three-year plan.

If you write four books a year, and you do this for three years, you will have twelve books. This is a decent catalogue that you can play with. If you have much less than that, everything becomes harder. It's harder to make advertising work for you, it's harder to make a mailing list work for you. It's harder to get reviews, and harder to get and keep readers. So if you're at that stage, the best thing you can do is to double down and finish more books, finish series that you started, start new ones and simply put out more product for your readers to buy.

A recent survey done by the owners of Freebooksy showed that authors who earn six figures or more per year have an average of thirty books in their catalogue. A lot of them have no bestsellers, and most of them are not well-known names. They are what the publishing industry used to call midlist authors. It is well known that the publishing industry has been squeezing these authors out. As the size of industry advances has declined, it has become harder for those authors to make a living. Many of them have moved to self-publishing, and have taken their sizeable catalogue with them.

Another category of writers able to splash onto the scene quite quickly includes the writers who never sold a novel, but spent years querying agents and publishers. They might have gotten close to a deal, but never actually signed one. Meanwhile, they had lots of books sitting on their computers. When self-publishing came along, all they needed to do was pull out these old manuscripts, give them a light re-edit, send them off to an editor and a cover designer, and publish them. It might have looked like they were brand new, but they had been writing and honing their craft for years.

The main indicator for earnings of authors is the amount of content they sell. There are some authors who are lucky and hit with one book, but that is extremely rare, and has always been so. The power is in backlist. So you have to make sure that you have backlist. Yes, it's hard. This is not an industry for wimps and chickens. But you knew that already didn't you?

The same survey also showed that almost all of those authors pay for editing, and cover design, and that many of them employed people to do other tasks. I mention this here to illustrate that these people are committed to putting out the best product they can. As a new author, this is the part of their business plan you should emulate. Write a lot of good books, make sure they're connected, either because of your name or because they are series, package them well, and feed them into your catalogue.

Once these books are there, you can start doing interesting things with them. Use the first books as free content to give away in return for mailing addresses, use the first books in ads, do cross-promotions using those first books. But none of it works without the subsequent books to sell, where you make your money. So you must be patient and set this system up first. Write the books, publish some, start a list, increase your list, start automation, publish more books, then encourage new subscribers to buy from your backlist.

This is the basis of the three-year plan. Now get beavering!

INTERLUDE: MARKETING

CHAPTER 90
I WANT SOMEONE TO DO MY MARKETING FOR ME

Part one of this interlude on marketing starts off with the question that gets asked the most: where do I find someone to do my marketing for me?

I hate marketing, can I just pay someone to do my ads?

Yes, you can, and also, congratulations, you have now entered the prime territory on which the spammers and scammers and other lowlifes operate. Tread with extreme care.

The answer to the question of whether you can hire someone to do your marketing is going to be somewhat complicated so I'm going to talk about what drives people to ask this question. We delve into the things that authors should be asking themselves before engaging a company that claims to run your advertising for you.

It is not uncommon that people engage others to run their advertising.

And it may even be successful in some cases. But if you want the quick answer, in most cases it's going to be no, you can't get someone else to do your ads and expect to make money. Likely, the person you pay will be the only one laughing. All the way to the bank.

It's especially a question that's common with new authors who claim to hate all this advertising stuff.

The truth is, when you publish a book, whether you are self published or traditionally published, you will need to do some publicity stuff.

This is a myth that self published writers tell themselves, and even traditionally published ones, that traditionally published authors don't need to do marketing. They do. And if anything, it's much harder for them than it is for us.

The advantage we have as self-published writers is that we can run our own ads, and that we have control over our own budget and the activities that we do. Drop the price, book a few promos, submit to Bookbub, put some books together in a box set, put the book up on BookFunnel to collect email addresses. These are things we can do. We have control over our own pricing. There are no contracts that forbid us to sell in parts of the world. You only have to talk to a traditionally published author once to understand how big this is. Because we control our dashboards, we can see what is effective and where we can best spend our money that is best tailored to our books.

There may be a lot of advertising involved, or there could be a little. You may find that a particular venue works well and another doesn't. Through trial and error, you'll find what your most profitable audience is.

There is no one stop cookie cutter method for advertising that's going to work for everyone and every type of book.

So my first point just going to be that it's very hard to bring in a person with no knowledge of your books and your situation or your audience and pay them to do your ads without you being able to teach them what to do. Because "ads are too hard and I just want to pay someone to do them", right?

Even more than with editing, advertising is not a tick box in the self-publishing journey. Yes, you may well have to do some of it, that's highly likely, but how, when, where and how much is entirely related to your situation.

If you're doing advertising, you will need to have a tight control over what you spend and compare this with your income.

Two similar looking books can have very different responses to advertising in terms of effectiveness and target audience. How do you find this out? By trial and error. Supposing the person you paid found out things about your target audience, would you be happy not to know those things that they found out about your books?

Advertising involves a lot of learning in the beginning. You would want to do your own learning before you pay someone else to do it so that you don't pay for their time of learning how to advertise your books. You want to learn it yourself so that you can then teach them what to do. This is your best way of maximising the amount of money spent on their service.

Secondly, one of the big problems in self publishing is the same as in the proverbial gold rush, namely by the time everyone got in, the only people who were making money were those selling shovels.

People claiming that they will do your marketing are selling you shovels, especially if they're out and about touting their services in self-published writing forums. It is theoretically still possible to make money, but you don't make money in publishing by throwing unrestricted amounts of money at it. You're selling a low-value product and your margins are small. You need to be careful that the money you spend is spent on services that actually deliver return on investment.

An advertising service that says that they will take all the marketing off your hands is kind of like a black box. You don't have much control over what they do. They will probably treat your book in some sort of cookie-cutter process where they apply the same process to it that they also apply to other books.

I am not saying that these people are dishonest, because the large majority of them are not. I am just saying that if you pay someone to do a thing, you care most about the results of that thing, but they care most about how much you pay them. This is true for almost everything. Do you remember how I told you about editors who should be refusing your manuscript if it wasn't ready but needed to pay bills and took the money anyway?

Yeah, that.

Advertising services usually charge you monthly, and you are required to spend a certain amount of money with them. They are more interested in securing their income stream. They're a business. They are entitled to. But is this going to give a good result for you? You may have been recommended this advertising service by someone in a writers group, but did you notice that they required you to sign up for a certain period of time, like three months?

Wait. They have already presold you some shovels before you even know that it's going to work.

The added problem to this is that the people most likely to want someone else to do their marketing are at the beginning of their publishing journey. They are often people who have worked in a different career all their lives and are not short of this sort of money that advertising services require. They have got it in their heads that they need to advertise a lot, they have just published one or two books, they've decided they really don't like advertising and want someone to just take it off their hands so that they can go and enjoy themselves. Like housecleaning. Except in this case it is just like housecleaning. The only thing this is going to buy you is some time but it's going to be fairly expensive for a fairly limited result. Likely, your book isn't optimised to sell and has never sold well. In fact the prime target for these services is newer authors with a few books who are not short of that kind of money to spend on services. They've been professional in their daily lives and know that there is a cost to doing business. They feel that they need to treat their writing as a business and to them that means that they need to spend on contractors. They're itching to spend money just so they can see their book rocket up the charts.

Except the book doesn't (because it's not ready for the big time or misses the mark, or… just most books don't sell that well full stop), and then friction arises. The service is expensive. The results are (naturally) abysmal. The authors may explode all over social media. It's a train wreck.

I have been self-publishing for over ten years, and I have seen a lot of these services come up and then fall a couple of years, or as little as a couple of months, later in a big heap of ugly flames.

The problem with these services is that some would rather take your money than check whether your book or audience has some legs. So authors paid a lot of money. Then these angry authors start talking about how this company didn't work for them, which happens inevitably, then the shit fight really begins, and usually the company disappears, and the person who started it will quietly slink off over the horizon and may return a little bit later with some other service selling shovels.

The problem is that advertising isn't going to work equally well on all books. You cannot just pick up a book and apply a cookie cutter ad process to it with the guarantee that it will work or that it will bring in enough money for the author to be happy with the service.

Not at that level. There are some authors who spend significant amounts of money on advertising who do have someone to do their ads. I even know of some services that do these ads for them.

These services don't advertise anywhere and the authors are very hush-hush about it. If you were to come into contact with these advertising gurus and ask them informally to do your ads for them, they would probably not take you on. They only take people with a proven track record, people who already sell well and have been doing their own ads for a while and just want someone to either take it to the next level or to free up their time. They're likely to require a five-figure per month ad spend. The ad agencies will not take inexperienced authors, because they know that the whole experience will probably end in a heap of flames.

So, I implore you.

If you're new and you have just started, please do not pay anyone to do your ads for you. Learn what works for your books. This knowledge is yours and should be in your hands only.

Does this mean you have to spend all your time advertising yourself?

No, it doesn't. You can start selling with few listing ads. You can also do drip pay per click ads that run at low intensity for little money, which take a bit of time to set up and fine-tune, but you can then ignore. Also make the most of the list services that are effective in your genre and only require you to book them occasionally. All this is relatively cheap and takes little time.

This also allows you to gauge whether your book has legs. If advertising works, do more of it. If it doesn't, then fix what's stopping the sales first.

Always, always, always put the most money into your winners. Don't try to lift the losers. Back the winners. Once the winners sell better, this is likely to flow through to your entire catalogue.

If you've found some success and want to take it to the next level, I know a number of authors who have successfully taken in members of their family to do their ads for them. They paid for those family members to take the appropriate courses, and the family members are running the advertising presumably for a small share of the income. This kind of arrangement can work very well but you would probably still be quite involved in the process.

It would also work because both of you would be working towards the same goal which is selling more of your books which is the bit that brings in the income. There would be no agency trying to skim the cream off the top.

Is it absolutely mandatory that you advertise like mad?

No, it isn't. As with editing and the general presentation of the book, advertising can enhance a work. Advertising can give something a little push, but it is unlikely to be the sole reason that something sells. Or if it is, your balance between ad spend and sales profit is likely to be rather precarious.

If a book sells really well with a lot of advertising, it's quite likely to sell okay without much or any, minus the time spent and the money. You may even find your profit increasing when you stop advertising altogether.

If your book doesn't sell that well, you can do little promotions to get yourself to that stage that sales become self-sustaining at a low level. If that doesn't happen, don't spend ever-increasing desperate amounts of money on trying to push the barrow up the hill.

An ad agency really isn't going to be that magic bullet. It's just going to burn a hole in your bank account.

Write something else and move on.

There are no magic bullets. Quit trying to throw money at desperate attempts to find them.

Come back to the series later, try a different category, different cover, make book 1 permafree, give it away, and all of a sudden you might find that there is an audience for the book, even if it's not a huge one, that you never saw when you were so desperate for bestsellerdom.

You cannot buy success. You can only use money to enhance it. You must use your money wisely.

CHAPTER 91
WHY DO PEOPLE SELL SETS OF BOOKS FOR 99C?

THIS CHAPTER IS INSPIRED BY A QUESTION A NEW WRITER ASKED IN A Facebook group: why do people sell huge box sets for 99c?

Because, like, that devalues books, right?

On the face of it, it doesn't seem to make much sense to sell a set of 20 books for only 99c, but there are several tactics that could be into play.

Of course, you are familiar with the tactic to make your first book free. This is to decrease the barrier between the reader and your book. Once you have the reader ensnared in your series, it will be more likely that they buy the rest of your books.

It is similar with 99c box set. But in this case, you don't reduce the barrier right down to free, because people will say that if you give your books away, you attract a lot of bad reviews, because people who would otherwise never have picked up your book will download it. Some of those people are not your target audience. They don't read your genre and will punish you in the reviews.

I have personally never seen enough evidence for that to stop doing it, but there are other good reasons not to make your book free.

Many of the online retailers have special places for free books. And they're not good places. They don't include them in the rankings for example.

Amazon has a special ranking section just for free books. They don't advertise this on their site because officially books can't be free on Amazon and so we have to employ all kinds of trickery to make them free.

Free books are definitely harder to discover. On Kobo and Google Play they simply disappear down the bottom of the visibility ladder. Even if you search for free books, it will bring up an unsorted list full of garbage that will just make a reader shake their heads and click away.

Which is what the retailer wants. They don't like free books.

When your book is 99c however it is paid. Not only does the reader who buys a 99c book make a conscious decision that they actually want to spend money on the book, never mind that it's only a little bit, but the book will then show up in the paid rankings. So if gaining ranking through a promotion is your aim, then 99c is a very good way of doing this.

But it seems impossible to make money by selling a single book for 99c, let alone a bundle of them.

This is true, because a lot of retailers reduce their royalties for lower-priced books, including Kobo and Amazon, which pays only 35% for an ebook under the price of $2.99.

As is the case with free books, a 99c book is usually a loss leader. You don't expect to make a profit on that just that book, although it is possible in another way which I'll discuss a bit later, but by having all the other books in the series at full price, you hope that people will buy those afterwards and this is where you make the money.

As an author, I use 99c quite a bit for first books in the series, especially in promotions. Authors complain that 99c promotions don't work. I found that they do work, but not so much if you buy spots in the list services like Bargain Booksy or places like that. People on those lists have much more interest in free books.

I find that 99c promotions work quite well when cross promoting with other authors. For example in Bookfunnel promotions where you direct your readers to the stores instead of getting them to download on Bookfunnel. I have a couple of books that are permanently 99c for just this reason.

And then there is Kindle Unlimited.

Many authors who are in Kindle Unlimited or who are planning to launch in Kindle Unlimited are expecting to get at least half their income from page reads. Page reads are not dependent on the price of the book. But the price of the book does influence the book's ranking if you do a little bit of promotion. When the book has more visibility, the book will get borrowed more because people who see others interested in the book may be in Kindle Unlimited and prefer to read it there. Of course when the book is 99c, you get much more from a complete read than you get from someone who buys it for 99c. So if you see a huge collection for 99c and it is in Kindle Unlimited, the author is probably still making quite a lot of money from the page reads and promoting the book for a reduced cost at the same time.

It could also be that the author has just gotten a Bookbub promotion. There is a lot of talk about Bookbub promotions in author circles. I feel they're not quite as effective as they used to be, but for box sets, they are great.

They like taking full series or partial series box sets for 99c. Reduced price sales of box sets over single books do much better. You just have to make sure that there is something else that the readers can buy after they have finished reading it. And even if you are not in Kindle Unlimited, a Bookbub promotion for a 99c box can be profitable on just the 99c sales. You may get that many sales. And if the boxset is also out in audio this will be a huge boon.

If you see a boxset that's 99c and consists of many books by different authors that's riding high in the charts, then they couldn't have been pushed there by a Bookbub promotion because they don't accept those.

In that case the authors might be going for a bestseller list and are probably spending a lot of money and time advertising their books.

Making a list is not necessarily profitable, but could make it easier to sell future books or get future promotions.

I have personally never seen a lot of evidence of this.

But some people want their "letters" (like USA Today bestseller) and they just want the sales to fund the advertising they're doing need or are even happy to put money into it. In this case they don't really care about the profit. The sets will probably disappear again once the counting period is over.

These 99c box sets are purely promotional and don't need to make the authors money.

. . .

There are many ways in which you can use a 99c promotion, even for a huge collection of books. Making money is usually not the motive, but getting committed readers who are prepared to put money on the table for a book is. I hate labelling people freebie seekers, because I think it is disrespectful, but pricing a book even at a low price will keep away people who only download something because it's free.

The key to a successful 99c promotion tactic is that you have further material to sell, because that is where you make the money.

CHAPTER 92
WHY SELFPUBLISHING IS NOT MARKETING

I'M GOING TO DEBUNK A MYTH THAT GOES AROUND ABOUT SELF-PUBLISHED writers, that we spend all our time marketing and that marketing is somehow synonymous with self-publishing.

This myth has come into being recently and I'm not entirely sure where it came from. It is a myth, however. However, it is also true that there are writers who do spend a lot of their time marketing.

First of all, I'd like to point out that some self-published writers spend a lot of time marketing, simply because we can.

If you have a deal with a publishing company, they will hold so much influence over your book that marketing in the way that you see self-published writers do is nearly impossible. It takes heaven and earth to move a publisher to discount a book. They won't ever make it free, and even if they do so, they will not have control over all the territories.

I have watched several traditionally published authors try to take part in promotions just like the rest of us, but eventually give up in frustration. It's just too hard. Some publishers are learning, but even then they don't get what we're doing. What for example is the point of lowering a book's price to 99c to apply for a Bookbub promotion—which they can and do get because Bookbub loves traditional publishers—but then to reduce the price only in a few territories?

Of course publishers can't do anything else, because those are the rights they bought, but this just goes to show how incompatible the traditional publishing model is with our way of publishing. The traditional industry markets to bookshops and book buyers. We are trying to get the attention of the readers. Naturally, by doing this, we are going to be much more visible to the public. I think this is the source of the "self-publishing is marketing" myth.

There are also quite a lot of self-published authors who do very little marketing, or who do a type of marketing that is not quite as visible.

In order to start selling and to keep your catalogue selling, you will probably need to do some marketing, but a lot of this marketing does not need to be very visible or may not look like marketing. For example making the first book in your series free doesn't amount to screaming "buy my book" on social media. Marketing also includes choosing your cover and your genre and your keywords and writing a good blurb. It is true that you are going to have to do this. This is not strictly a writing activity, but it will affect your sales. It is true that the traditional publishing industry takes care of this. But then again, they are also unwilling to change it if a particular angle they've taken doesn't work. And what works in terms of sales is not a given, and whether or not a book does well is a matter of being in the right place at the right time and it's heartening to see that a publisher has just as little control over this as we do. But a publisher in general is quite immutable about things like cover design and categories. They make decision about this, very often don't consult you, and then you're stuck with it. Probably you have heard about some of the well-publicised cases, especially in young adult fiction, of covers being changed after outrage, but mostly these cases are very rare, and to be honest, the changes that were made probably didn't result in a lot of extra sales. It was more about representing the book accurately.

As a relatively well-known writer with a big publishing house, you do have some influence, but still, they probably won't consult with you over the covers you get or the genres you get put in.

These are marketing decisions that get made early in the process and that will influence sales.

The difference between beginning traditionally published writers and self-published writers is that—actually there is no difference. Most of the time when writers start out, they put next to zero thought into what genre their book will be in and how they are going to present it.

It's just that with the traditionally published writers, the writer doesn't actually need to do this, but the publisher will do it for them. With varying degrees of success, but that aside. Honestly, before you ever sign with a small press, look at their covers and presentation efforts, because a lot of them put out—what shall I say—less than ideal efforts.

A new self-published writer is likely to publish a book with a dreadful cover in the wrong genre, and then later realise they did it all wrong and the important thing is: they can fix it. They can change the cover and change the categories, change the blurb or even re-write part of the book if they really want to. These are all things you can't do as a traditionally published author. If it turns out that a genre didn't fit the book after all, they're unlikely to change it. But we can. Then we can re-launch the book and once again attempt to catch the public eye.

It may only look like we spend all of the time marketing, because we can actually do this. If we want to run a price promotion, we need to let people know. No one else is going to send it out for us.

Surprise, surprise, most of the traditional publishing companies don't have strong mailing lists either. They're not particularly good at selling directly to the customers, so they don't quite have as much influence as you think. Things are changing a bit, but they mostly still rely on the booksellers to do the selling for them, and of course booksellers, especially the brick and mortar variety, are much more interested in print, where discounting is much less effective and where selling books is a much more laborious process that involves huge backchannels and middlemen the average person on the street would never have heard about. It is a difference in marketing tactic.

We can actually run sales. You will very rarely see traditionally published authors talk about sales on their book. They're not allowed to talk about it. There are contractual limitations on book pricing. The sales don't flow through to the author quite as much. Promotions are going to benefit the publisher before they are going to benefit the author.

When you're a self-published author and you run a sale, you can see the effect by looking at your dashboard. Traditional publishers may let you know six months later how well you did. That kind of kills the incentive for doing this kind of activity.

I have only ever seen one traditionally published author who spent an extraordinary amount of time marketing his own books. He was very good at it too. He had it in his mind that his publisher would drop him if his sales dropped below a certain level. He became one of the better sellers of the genre for his publisher, but the publisher dropped him anyway.

This is what I really want to stress, we _can_ market our books in which ever way we choose, and indeed not all of us do, but we can do it because it is a possibility. We can do it, because we see the direct result of it and it is immensely satisfying. Or on the other hand, if it doesn't work we can work on our books and we can then change the presentation and try again.

I don't think this is a bad thing. This is actually a tremendous amount of fun. You get to think about your book in a way a reader would, think about the categories and where the book might fit, think about what the cover needs to represent and then see if it works. We can do that for relatively low cost. Changing the cover takes a couple of days until the image has filtered through on all sites. Then you can run some promotions to see if it works.

This can be immensely satisfying. This level of control is why you probably chose to self-publish anyway. But on the other hand if you really really hate doing all of this, it's a possibility that you can ignore all of it. You may not sell very well, but that's okay, if you don't really care and just want your book out there. I know some writers who write for fun, hardly ever market, have pretty mediocre covers, and the books really don't sell, but they just keep publishing because they think it's fun. I want to say in big screaming capital letters that THIS IS OK.

No one says that if you're a self-published author, you have to be marketing all the time. If you want a successful career, you probably have to do at least a little bit, but here is another thing, we can do the sort of marketing that actually works. If you sign a traditionally published deal, you may be asked to do book signings and readings and appearances at conferences. You may have reviews in magazines or newspapers or you may even have radio interviews and things like that. While these activities can be fun, there is plenty of evidence that most of these don't move the needle very much in terms of sales.

We can do the type of marketing that works. Book and run a promotion. Lower the price, make it free. Run pay per click ads to our books. Again, you don't have to do this, but if you do, you will probably see that it works, which makes it kind of satisfying to do.

The fact that so many people think that a traditional publisher will do all this for you is only partially true. They will probably do some marketing at the start, when the book is first published, but then they will drop it in favour of the newer titles. The model is based on pushing new content out the door. They are only just starting to wake up to the fact that backlist sales can be very viable and important. Many of us survive purely on backlist sales. Our latest published book might be the eighth book in the series, and you're not going to market that. You'll always market the first book. Again, we have the control to do that, but the traditional publisher will often sit on those books or would let them go out of print. Its next to impossible to find certain books in certain series and in certain countries. The traditional publishers have dropped the backlist and are no longer actively marketing it. With our model we can still do that, and indeed our model relies on loss leaders, first books in the series, to draw readers in and then make them buy all the other books.

You don't even have to discount those books. You can sell those books on your website and get a lot more money per sale. But you have control over your entire catalogue and can make a decision based on targeted discounts of specific books.

A newly released book is only new for a couple of months, but a book can be new do that reader as much as ten or twenty years later. Most books will eventually stop selling, but if you keep pushing them, some of them can keep selling pretty much forever. The self-published author who is continuously running high-level expensive ads to keep their sales going is only one type of self-published author. Most of the time, authors just do targeted promotions and, yes, you will see more of this happening with self-published authors, simply because it is within their power to do so and it's highly successful.

CHAPTER 93
BOOK LENGTH AND MAXIMISING EARNINGS

In this chapter I'm going to talk a bit about book length, about what is a novel and a novella, how long your book should be, and how you can optimise book length for sales.

First of all, let's have some definitions. I'm going to use the definitions as are used for the traditional industry by the Science Fiction Writers of America. According to them, flash fiction is anything under 2000 words. A short story is anything up to 15,000 words. They make a further designation between a short story and a novelette, which is the top end of that range from about 7500 to 15,000. A novella is anything from between 15,000 and forty thousand words. Anything over that is defined as a novel.

However, most novels that sell well these days are a bit longer. Especially in the print industry, and especially in science fiction and fantasy.

There was a time that pulp fiction was popular. Those were quite often fairly short novels at about 50,000 words and were designed to be quick reads. Something like the Lord of the Rings on the other side of the spectrum is probably 700,000 or 800,000 words.

When a reader buys a book that is marketed as a novel, they would expect at least about 40 or 50,000 words. In pages, this would be somewhere in the 150 to 200 pages range.

Most readers also don't look very much at how long a book is.

Also, if readers mention in their reviews that the book was too short, this could also be an indication that they enjoyed it and it was over before they realised it. If a reader complains that a book is too long, you might want to cut out some boring bits. The perception of length is highly flexible.

But in most genres, anything under about 50,000 words can be a hard sell, unless it's specifically marketed like that. Especially in science fiction, but also in romance, shorter works can do quite well. They can be placed in series of quick reads.

But a book that's 20,000 words along is not a novel, and should not be marketed as such.

So how long should your book be and then how should you sell it? The correct answer of course is that a book needs to be as long as the story needs to be, but if we're going to be less snarky, we might acknowledge that there are several strategic decisions that you can make that are about length.

In the first place, when you're planning a series, make sure that all the books are roughly the same length. If your first book is a novella, you better make them all novellas. If your first book is a novel, and you find the second is only a novella, you better beef up the second book or make the first book shorter or divide it into two books to keep the length even. The important part is that you train your readers on what to expect. If your first book was a novel, and the second book is much shorter, then you're going to get a lot of complaints.

If the first book was really short and then later books are much longer, you may have trouble getting the right type of readers into your series.

Novellas, short reads, and long novels have different audiences.

You don't want to mix them.

A book of course is as long as it needs to be, but that doesn't mean that you can't change sections of it to suit the length you have in mind.

You can add characters, you can create certain rest points in the book where you can potentially break it into two, tie up some threads so that it's a satisfying experience and then continue with the main story in the next book. This is a great way of hooking people into a series.

If you want to expand your book, you can add an extra point of view character or bring forward a plot point you were saving for a later volume.

The important part is that all the books in the series should be of similar length, because otherwise it becomes very hard to market and very hard to produce different formats. Novellas don't make very satisfying audiobooks if you are exclusive to Audible. A listener on Audible will look for a way to spend their credit, and they going to spend it on the longest book possible.

Short audiobooks can do quite well in libraries, but if you're exclusive to Audible, your audio won't be in libraries. If you have books of different lengths, people are going to be disappointed or confused.

A novella also doesn't make a very good print book. There is a limit to the number of pages you can put in a print book, and even before you reach that, the book is so thin, that you won't be able to put the title on the spine. It will just look silly.

In order to have a novella in print, you probably need to bundle it with another novella, which is great if you have a series of novellas, because you can bring them out in print as collected edition. But unless you also bring them out as ebook, this will confuse a lot of retailers and will mess up the recommendation algorithms. In my experience, it is best to have all books out in as many formats as possible and not to mix and match.

What should you charge for books of various lengths?

The price should reflect the length of the book and, in that case, you will probably run into trouble on the higher end of the wordcount spectrum.

You'll probably want to sell short stories for 99c at the most. I don't bother selling short stories at all. I give them away and then like to include them in collections, or use them for multi author anthologies.

A novella, I usually sell for $2.99. Some people may think this is too much and sell it for 99c. That's fine. You can do that, but it is at the $2.99 mark that you get the full 70% royalty on most platforms that penalise you for selling short works. And if you sell something for 99c, you can't ever discount it.

Anything from between 40,000 words to about 60,000 I will sell for $3.99. This is just an arbitrary figure that reflects the length because it's still a reasonably short novel.

Books between 60,000 and 80,000 I will sell for $4.99, and anything over that for $5.99. Now I stress that this is my pricing schedule, and you can do it differently depending on your preference and the genre you're in.

But what would you sell a book of 200,000 words for?

You could of course try to sell it for $7.99 or $8.99, and some people do this.

However, in the world of self published fiction, readers have become quite sensitive on the high end of the pricing range. Traditionally published books can be as much as $14.99 for the ebook, but Amazon also punishes us for pricing our books more than $9.99 by dropping our royalty from 70% to 35%. So it makes no sense to price books that high, because you'll get less money for a sale.

But on the other hand if your book is almost twice the length of another book you're selling for $4.99 and is, say, 75,000 words, then you may feel disappointed about not being compensated for the extra length and time you put in.

We frequently get new writers in writing groups who mention that their book is 180,000 words long.

Is that too long?

As I said, in traditional publishing, fantasy books very often go over much higher word counts than that.

But they are also sold at much higher prices. If you pay $14.99 for an ebook, it had better be worth it.

As self-published author, you're stuck with a book that's 180,000 words, and you feel the most you can charge for it is $5.99. The most you can charge is $9.99. That doesn't seem in proportion to people who are selling 50,000 word books for $3.99.

I have run into that problem only once before I realised what the solution was.

A number of years ago when I was still submitting to traditional publishing, I needed to quickly write a novel because I wanted to enter it in an application for a workshop.

I had this grand fantasy idea about an ice world in a dystopian setting where ancient magic is the result of an ancient civilisation and it will take the characters a fairly long time and a desperate to war to understand what is going on.

I started with the first book, but very soon realised that the story I had started was not going to fit into the allocated 80,000 words. At that time, I had not sold a novel to publisher, and it was highly recommended that your first book should be about that length.

Well, the solution was easy. I turned the story into three books.

I found some points in the story where a certain aspect of it was finished and where the characters moved onto the next part, often prompted by a change in setting. Think of the three act structure.

This turned out to be one of the best things I've done. Rather than trying to cram the whole story into one book, I got three books, and got to explore much more of the world and add more interesting characters. I could possibly have fitted the entire story in about 150,000 words, but instead it ended up being 270,000 and it's a much more satisfying story as a result of this. Because there are three books in the series, it is also much easier to market, because I can give the first book away for free, and then have two further books to make the sales.

So this is exactly what I usually recommend to a writer who comes to a group with a book that is 150,000 words or longer. Of course the first question needs to be whether the book actually needs to be that long, but books don't always get better if you shorten them. Sometimes you can also lengthen them, include more vivid description and a few more interesting characters and it becomes a better book.

So I tell those writers to find some points where they can break the book, potentially in sections of about 60,000, and then sell each of those for $3.99, and make the first one 99c or free. This also immediately gives you your first series. We all know that series are much easier to market.

There are some people who will tell you that fantasy books are always long and that readers have come to expect this, but I invite those people to look at the self published books that are available in the genre. Sure, you will find some that are really long, but you will also find many that are much shorter. All readers are different. If someone pays $3.99 for a book, they don't mind that it's not a door stopper. If someone buys the latest fantasy by a big name author and it's only 60,000 words, then they will be upset, because they've just spent $10 on it.

It is all about creating an expectation. If do you make your book into a trilogy, make sure that you make all the books roughly the same length and that you charge the same price for all of them except the first book. Then, they can't possibly complain about the first book that is 99c or free, and they already know that's in the first book and how long the series is so they can decide whether they want to pay $3.99 per volume for the rest. That will really depend on the quality of your book. Then you can also collect the books into a box set at the end and have another product to sell, for which you can jack the price up to $8.99 or $9.99, while still under the $9.99 price cap, and look like you're giving people a good deal at the same time.

CHAPTER 94
WHAT SHOULD YOU EXPECT FROM A PROMOTION

This chapter is about promotions: about what to expect when you're doing your first promotions, about how to do promotions on a budget, and how to make them work and not break the bank.

People always talk about the golden age of self publishing of around 2009 and 2010 where you could publish a book and it would just take off like crazy without having to do any promotion at all.

Well, that is a myth.

I was around in that time, and while there were a few well publicised cases of people where it did happen, it was still very rare and unusual. Most of us just published, sold a few copies and our books kind of languished. We couldn't advertise because there were very few places to promote. A lot of the commercial list services that we use today didn't exist back then. Many authors didn't even have mailing lists. Many of the companies that we use today to promote didn't exist or didn't offer the services that they offer today.

Conversely there are even people today who publish, do next to no promotion at all and make it really big anyway. This type of success is, and has always been, very rare and I don't subscribe to the mindset that it used to be so much easier. It was not. Quit thinking like that. It's not helpful.

Writers have always had to promote their books.

And the more actively you get involved with this, the greater the chance of success.

But at the same time, you also want to do this without breaking the bank and spending all your time promoting. You definitely don't want to do that.

But where do you start?

You've poked around forums a bit and have found the lists of email deals newsletters, but most of them charge at least $25 to promote your book, many of them are booked one or two months in advance, and how do you know that you will get your money back anyway?

The reality is that you probably won't. Most people who promote their books will sell a number copies, but you have to reduce the price of your book so much that it's pretty much impossible to make a profit, so people who make a profit out of promotions are those who have more than one book, especially if those books are in the same series.

This is the reason why you will hear the advice that beginning authors should wait with promoting their books until they have at least three books out.

But I think this is a little extreme.

You can start doing a few things and not all of them cost money.

If you are trying to build up your readership, and you don't mind investing a bit in your books, presuming you have a little bit of money, I would start to make a small budget of what you are willing to spend per month.

At this point in your career, the cost of promoting your books is very likely to be a loss, but if you have the cash, it will build up your readership and start building a fan base.

The first thing I'm going to recommend is not free, but it will pay off and is very much about building a long-term readership.

For about $10 a month, you can get a subscription to a wonderful site called Bookfunnel that I have mentioned many times before.

This is a site that delivers e-books in the hands of readers. But they also offer a venue to do multi-author promotions.

The promotions on Bookfunnel are generally of one of two kinds.

There is the type that gives out free books in return for people's email address and gets readers onto your mailing list.

Or there is the option to send readers to retailers where you sell your books for reduced price. If you make your book permanently free or permanently 99c, you can take part in as many of these promotions as you want for no extra cost.

You will however need to send emails to your mailing list or if you're super active on social media, that may also be option. Bookfunnel monitors how many clicks and downloads originate from your promotion link, and this is visible to the promotion organisers. Most of them won't mind if you're new and your share total is low, but after a while, your list should be growing, and you should get more clicks.

Doing these promotions also provides you with content to send to your mailing list.

Say for example you send your subscribers an email every two weeks, and you decide that you're going to put two promotions in each, one for free books and one for cheap books, you can take part in four of these promotions per month.

After you have paid for the Bookfunnel subscription, the promotions will be free.

Then there are the list services such as Bargain Booksy, ENT, Fussy Librarian and the like. Some are low cost, others are free or have a free, non-guaranteed option.

You can submit to these on a rotation, and if your book looks any good, and there is evidence that at least a few people have to read it, such as there are one or two or three reviews, then the chance is reasonably high to that the service will run your book.

Some of these services require a number of reviews, but these are mostly the paid ones.

Just put the services on a rotation and submit to a number of them every month. This tactic probably does require that you have one book permanently priced at a low price, and it will be much more satisfying if you have a second full price book for people to buy afterwards.

But then again, if you want to build your readership and you don't mind running the ads at a loss, you can start off with just one book at 99c while you write the second book.

Before you book, I would ask around to see which services are the best for your genre.

I don't recommend that you keep running the same book to the same services more than once a year. Some people say once every six months, but I definitely wouldn't want to go any more frequent than that. It would be great if you could offer them another book, and but now I presume you can hear the familiar refrain. Truly, everything does get much easier when you have more books. Not only is it easier to get promotions because you have different things to offer, but it is much easier to make your money back for the promotions you do get, and therefore much more satisfying.

Each of the promotions will probably get you a small handful of sales. Sometimes there will be no sales at all. Sometimes maybe 10 or 15, and that's really good, but until you have a second book to sell at full price, you're highly unlikely to make a profit on this.

So get writing okay?

What's next?

Personally I would wait until I had more books out, and was more in tune with who my audience is and where to find them before jumping into pay per click advertising such as facebook or Bookbub ads.

You can do Amazon ads, but if you're on a budget, I would either strictly limit how much you're willing to spend by setting a limit on your campaigns, and I would then also not listen to any of the advice that people give about running Amazon ads. Those people assume that you have the money to burn, and they are after the highest profit, but if you only have a discounted book, or you're giving away a free book, you want to spend as little as possible on your ads while also making sure that as many people as possible see them.

Pay per click advertising is quite an advanced strategy, and if you do it wrong, it can cost you a lot of money for absolutely no benefit whatsoever.

I run drip ads, which are ads that continue to run for long periods of time at a low cost and that you don't scale up but just run in the background. They generally go to books that feed into your main catalogue, such as the first free in a series.

The concept of drip ad is quite compatible with not spending terribly much on advertising.

The other thing I would also like to caution against is that when you start running promotions, it's inevitable that the first few are quite disappointing. This whole self publishing thing is all about managing expectations, and as beginning writers we have so many expectations that need to be crushed under the big foot of competition and the realisation that nobody is actually waiting for our books. So if you get the news that your book is being featured by a retailer, or you've paid $10 to be featured on a website or an email list, expect very little. It sounds quite depressing, but if you expect nothing, anything you get will lift your spirits. Your sales are not going to be any different, and it's not about "professional attitude" or anything like that. It's just that you will be so much happier if you don't hold high expectations.

But when do you continue to run small promotions like this, building your mailing list, selling a handful of books here and there, you're building your audience, which means that your readership is growing very slowly. It's probably growing so slowly that you don't notice it until you have three or four books out.

This is why it's important to set an annual budget, to determine what you can spend each month and then to religiously spend it, while finding better ways to advertise all the time.

It's just a matter of sheer persistence to start getting traction with promotions. If you do a couple of small ones and they have no effect, try something else. Try one of the other lists, try to get into some multi author promotions. If the right kind of promotion doesn't exist on bookfunnel, you can create your own.

But while you're doing this, always step back and compare your presentation with other people's. Does your book look as good as theirs? Do your promotional graphics look up to scratch? Are you perhaps trying too hard to push your book one while it's probably a better use of your time to write a book two?

And then just do the promotions every month and religiously book the newsletters and spend your budget every month even when you get discouraged. If you have done your homework, you will start seeing results. The first key word about self publishing is persistence. The second one is patience.

GOING WIDE UNBOXED

CHAPTER 95
TERROR AND TREPIDATION!

O.M.G.

You have unticked that auto-renew box for Select in your KDP dashboard.

After a few seconds of exhilaration—"I'm no longer a slave to a single retailer!"—the fear sets in.

What do I actually DO? How do my books SELL? There is so much stuff to do and set up and I don't get any of it. And I don't even get how people find books on these other sites and it's all so WEIRD.

Help!

Fortunately, you've come to the right place. I've been selling books "wide" since 2011, was never able to get any traction in Kindle Unlimited, through reasons that will become clear in this section. Non-Amazon sales have accounted for anywhere between 40 and 90 percent of my monthly income.

But, a word of warning: "going wide" is a mindset, and will require you to examine everything you do, from how you source your mailing list to where you advertise.

CHAPTER 96
WHO IS THIS SECTION FOR?

THIS SECTION IS A SERVICE TO MY WRITER FRIENDS AND ANYONE WHO IS interested in taking their books to a worldwide audience in many different stores as opposed to being exclusive on Amazon.

For some reason, "going wide" strikes fear in the hearts of many. It is the great unknown, the morass, and it looks like so much *work*.

Yet, at any one time there is usually some form of panic going on about declining sales on Amazon, about declining page reads, scammers in Kindle Unlimited, or any combination of those things.

This is a section for people who are sick of the fearmongering, who are sick of worrying about what happens on Amazon, who want to stop caring about rankings and that a single bad review will torpedo your career. This is a section for people who want to see themselves as global citizens and invest time in building a more solid sales base that can support a longer lasting career, without having to fork out big in stomach ulcer medication.

This is not about Amazon, or about any of the storms that are going on there at any time, and it's not about complaining how Amazon does the wrong thing by writers. This section is about everything that is not Amazon.

This doesn't mean to say that you should turn your back to Amazon, to the contrary. For most writers, but not all of them, Amazon is likely to provide the bulk of their income. Now this may change, but at this point in time, it is the reality we live in. And there is nothing wrong with that.

But it's a rollercoaster, and many people feel deeply uncomfortable with having their entire income in the hands of just one income source. It's not healthy, it's not productive and not conducive to reaching out to a worldwide audience.

This is not a section that tries to convince you to "go wide". It's for those who have already decided that they want to do it.

CHAPTER 97
STEP INTO THE WORLD

To go wide is to step into the world. This may seem a little frightening to people from the US, because in the US, the prevailing attitude seems to be that Amazon is the world. The everything store.

It is not like that in the rest of the world. Sure, Amazon exists in other countries, but it's often a latecomer on the scene, and not always the biggest one. Even if it is the biggest one for ebooks, it has a lot more healthy competition from the other stores in other countries.

If you're not from the US, you will probably already understand that not everybody buys on Amazon. You already know that in some countries books are quite expensive, and readers are used to these prices. Traditional publishing has a much stronger grip on the market in those countries. Some countries, like France, have a protective industry with laws that make it easier for local content to be sold.

You may already understand that some people in some countries hate Amazon with a passion and actively legislate against it.

Or you may understand that books are sold to worldwide niche markets that are big enough to allow you to make a liveable income from selling to just that market.

My point is: it is not always about the price, and it is not always about being a fish in the biggest pond.

While the market for science fiction books in Poland might be small, you could earn a handy income if for some reason your book takes off there.

This is not to say that your book will take off in Poland, but there are many other countries and many other small markets where it might. And readers in those other countries probably don't buy their books on Amazon. And even if they do, you give yourself more chance of being found if your books are available everywhere.

The frustrating part about your books taking off in Poland or Sweden is, of course, that you can't control any of it. You feel like you're just throwing wet spaghetti at the wall and seeing what sticks. You can't game it and you can't predict it, but there are definite steps you can take to make sure that something will happen somewhere.

An interesting byproduct of concentrating your sales efforts to non-Amazon markets is that you're likely to increase your sales on Amazon, too. More specifically, you'll likely increase your sales on Amazon stores that are not in the US.

The US is but one market. Quite a big one, but even so. The UK is one market. Germany is one market, and Canada, and Australia, and so on. By being in Select, you appeal primarily to people in the US, and a bit in the UK.

By being wide, you appeal to the entire world, no matter where they buy.

So, let's get started.

CHAPTER 98
THE FIRST STEP

First you face the unenviable task of creating files for all retailers and uploading them.

Yes, I can hear you groan.

I know this can mean a lot of work. I finally went direct with Apple a while ago, and took several days uploading all my books and filling out all the details. That was just one retailer. Of course, I had more than thirty books, but I understand why people are turned off, I really do.

How can you make this easier?

Make sure you have accounts ready to go and set up for all retailers. Make decisions about how and where you'll sell beforehand. You'll need the next few chapters to decide how to do this.

You need sets of files. Every retailer uses slightly different formatting requirements. Use Vellum, hire a formatter or learn to make them yourself. Draft2Digital has file creation templates for their file generation options. It's free. I say something about file creation in *Self-publishing Unboxed* but, in a nutshell, those are your options.

I strongly recommend using EPUB3 (Kobo, Apple, Google Play) and EPUB2 (B&N) files, and not to upload DOC files, even if many of the retailers allow it. I say this because the file generation sometimes produces strange stuff, especially if your DOC file comes from a program that's not Word (Pages, LibreOffice, etc.).

Divide the work into bite-sized pieces. Go by retailer, or by series, whichever is easiest for you.

However, don't make the mistake of taking a cookie-cutter approach to uploading your books. Before you upload to a retailer, have a look around on their retail site to see if it offers any clues how you might be able to optimise your listings. What categories do they offer, and how do you get into them? How much room do they allocate for book descriptions? Do they have different content for different countries? Are they curated by people? Pull up the top 100 of your genre. What books are in it and how are they priced? What does the site do with free books? If a book rises to the top of the rankings, how long does it stay there?

Those are all things that you can potentially use in tailoring your book's listing and your approach to various websites.

I also want to point out in a clear way that "going wide" only applies to ebooks. Even if you remain in Kindle Unlimited, you can do with your print books or audiobooks whatever you want. Those are independent of Kindle Unlimited and are not governed by the same rules.

CHAPTER 99
AGGREGATOR OR DIRECT?

THIS IS THE FIRST DECISION YOU HAVE TO MAKE.

At the time of writing, we have the aggregator sites Draft2Digital, Publish Drive and Streetlib. We used to have Smashwords, but they were bought by Draft2Digital so they are now the same.

For those who don't know, an aggregator is a service that takes your book and distributes it to other retailers on your behalf.

In *Self-publishing Unboxed*, I said that I believe that you should always go direct to sites that give you special promotional opportunities that would not be available otherwise, most notably Amazon and Kobo. Otherwise, it's up to you.

But in reality it's a little bit more complicated than that.

I think that your ultimate aim will be to use both. But it may take you a while to get there.

Pros of using an aggregator:

- Less work
- One account to manage
- One payment
- The aggregator has personal contacts with the retailer

Cons of using an aggregator:

- They usually charge a fee of 10% of the retail price. This may not sound like much, and it isn't when you earn $60 per month. But it becomes a lot more when you earn $600 per month. When you earn $6000 per month, you can pay an accountant with the money you save.
- When you're with an aggregator, you have much less control over your listings, especially your metadata.
- You may not be eligible for promotions on retailer websites, notably Kobo.

Think carefully, because when you go with an aggregator and then go direct, you may lose all your reviews for that book. Since people are more likely to review on sites other than Amazon, losing 900 reviews on Kobo just because you got sick of paying an aggregator $100 of your earnings per month is a difficult decision. If you intend to move your books across, it pays to email the retailers, because they may be able to migrate your reviews over for you.

The short & dirty:

- There is absolutely ZERO reason not to go direct on Kobo. Their dashboard is easy, you can get in-house promo and there are no restrictions on who can join.
- Although you no longer need a Mac to access Apple, you may still want to use an aggregator because Apple can be a handful to deal with. But the iTunes Producer software is much better than the online portal so if you sell a lot, it may be worth buying a small Mac. Macs are cool and most high-earning authors have one, even if only to use it for Vellum, a Mac-only piece of formatting software.
- You need to be in a limited number of countries to access B&N Press, so if you're not, you will need an aggregator.
- Google Play is not included in many aggregators and they require you to open an account anyway, even if you are going to use an aggregator. I advocate that you don't bother with aggregators for Google Play.

In general, it's better not to use an aggregator.

But, here is the rub, most aggregators have deals with sites that are not accessible to individual writers.

These are the library suppliers like Overdrive, which are owned by Rakuten which also owns Kobo, and are also accessible through Draft2Digital. There are subscription services like Scribd, now Everand.

Often you will see people in forums questioning whether listing there is "worth it". To be honest, I think that's a silly question. What, exactly, do you lose by making your books available there? I have no idea what half of these services are or where their market is. Dreame is a subscription-based platform in Singapore that I'd never heard of. But PublishDrive sent me a report that I'd sold $25 there. I'll take it. In fact, I'll take it along with the $25 per month from Overdrive and the $10 from Scribd and the $30 from the Smashwords retail site and the other small fry that adds up to $100 a month and $1200 over a year. Is that "worth it?" Well, if it's not to you, I'll take the $1200, thanks.

To be wide is to be wide. Make your books available on every available platform.

CHAPTER 100
KOBO

The Kobo Writing Life portal is one of the prettiest and easiest to use. Who can resist that awesome map that tells you where in the world you have sold?

Reporting is mostly real time, although in some countries it can take a while for the sales to show up. Also, Kobo's partner sites report in bulk, so sudden jumps in sales are quite common.

Official Kobo reports become available from their website once a month. The reports include data from their subscription service Kobo Plus, which operates in an ever increasing number of countries. The reports also include deductions for promotions that you have taken part in, since some of the promotions charge you ten percent of your retail price.

There is a $50 payment threshold, applied worldwide since you will only receive one payment. Payment is through Western Union into your bank account.

Kobo takes files in EPUB3 format, which is their native format. They run EPUB check on your document, and will flag issues. This sometimes puzzles writers who do their own formatting.

You have to make sure files don't contain links to competitor's websites, which is fair enough. Some people upload DOC files, but my personal experience with this has been terrible. I would recommend producing and uploading an EPUB file.

You can also upload audiobooks directly in your dashboard.

Kobo is located in Canada, but will take your local tax ID, and apply local tax.

The Kobo retail site displays its book offerings by country. This means that someone shopping in the UK will look at the UK site, UK rankings, and UK prices. The same is true for people in the US, Australia, New Zealand, Canada, South Africa, and a whole host of other countries. Kobo advises writers to set the prices in friendly numbers, ending in .99 for all their books in all territories. This is often necessary for taking part in promotions.

Kobo has no price point limit. This means that you can make collections of your entire catalogue and sell them for $40 if you want. The interesting thing is that these collections sell quite well on Kobo. In general, people on Kobo are much more willing to pay premium prices for the books they really want. If you look at the top hundred in the various genres, you will see that there is hardly a book under eight dollars. Free and low-priced books get pushed down in the rankings, and their visibility is poor. I recommend not leaving books free or cheap indefinitely. Kobo considers a price point of between $2.99 and $4.99 promotional. If you can, price higher than that, so you can take part in their site-run promotions.

One of the great things about the Kobo writer tools is the promotions tab. This is not a standard feature that you will get as soon as you join, but you have to ask for it by using the "Contact us" feature on the site, because it is supposedly still in beta. Once you have it, click the tab and scroll down the long list of possible promotions for you to take part in. Most of them require a ten percent reduction in your cut, which will get deducted in your spreadsheet. If your book is accepted, it gets put onto a page with specials.

These promotions can be quite successful, especially if you have a box set that you normally sell for $9.99 that is reduced down to $4.99. Kobo often runs these promotions by country rather than worldwide. Readers on the site get given a code, so the reduced price is not available in search engines, and thus it prevents price matching by Amazon.

One thing to remember with Kobo is that it is a truly international seller. Most of the sales are in Canada, but it is also very strong in Australia and New Zealand as well as France, Germany and South Africa.

The map in your seller's dashboard is awesome. It will show you dots in all the countries where you have sold books. After a while, when your sales increase, you will see that most of the sales on Kobo are not in the

US. In fact you will see sales in really interesting countries like Qatar, the United Arab Emirates, India, Malaysia, Malta, and a multitude of other countries. My claim to fame is that I've sold books in the Falkland Islands. Often, Amazon is not particularly friendly to buyers in those countries.

Kobo actively works with self-publishers through hand picking books for the promotions, and through the Kobo Writing Life blog and podcast.

Kobo also behaves a little bit like an aggregator. If you search your books and they come up in places like Bol.com, Chapters, FNAC and Dymocks, then this is through Kobo.

Kobo actively represses the rankings of free and cheap books. They do give promo opportunities for free books, but I would strongly recommend that you do not leave your books permafree on Kobo.

If you use more than one pen name, you can keep the names separate.

In short:

- Register here: Kobo Writing Life
- Open for: everyone
- File format: EPUB3
- Payment: bank account

CHAPTER 101
BARNES & NOBLE

You can get direct access to Barnes & Noble through B&N Press in a limited number of countries.

Nook gives you 65% on books between $2.99 and $9.99, but to make up for that, they pay 40% on books outside of that range. (Contrasting Amazon's 70/35 range)

B&N Press has a clean, pretty dashboard that's easy to use.

Payments are directly into a bank account. Payments are on the same schedule as Amazon, approximately two months after the close of the month. The minimum payment is $10.

You can upload a Microsoft Word file, TXT, RTF, HTML or EPUB manuscript file. Once uploaded, you can edit the text in the Manuscript Editor, invite collaborators to read your Manuscript, and preview the book as it will appear on Nook.

B&N Press allows you to schedule sales. They say price changes won't happen for 48-72 hours, but mostly the price change tends to be an hour or two at most.

B&N Press has a direct print function, where you can upload print books for sale in their stores. They require a virgin, never-before-used ISBN, but also provide free ones. Just grab one of those. They use the printing facilities of Ingram Spark.

They're very good about linking the print edition to the ebook edition on their website, even for print books published through another site. Their print books are quite expensive, though.

B&N Press' upload process is really easy to figure out. They allow up to five categories, they allow zero pricing (this is relatively new—they used to not allow this), and they allow for preorders. They will also allow you to upload editorial reviews, insert keywords, make it part of a series, etc. Each book also has an About the Author option, which is something Amazon doesn't have, which sounds great except the B&N site doesn't have author pages.

Nook will sometimes do manually curated first in series free pages. There is also a promotion dashboard.

You can keep pen names separate.

The main drawbacks of using them, if you're in a country where you can apply for an account, relate to the fact that their team is tiny and problems can take a while to be resolved. Especially if they relate to verifying your tax status and bank account. Most people eventually get it done, but I've also heard of people who cannot get the admin sorted and went back to aggregators as a result.

In short:

- Register here: Barnes and Noble
- Open for: people in a limited number of countries (check website)
- File format: EPUB2
- Payment: bank account

CHAPTER 102
APPLE

You now no longer have to own a Mac in order to upload to Apple.

You can do this through their online iTunes Connect portal. But if you have a Mac, consider downloading the iTunes Producer software anyway, because it's less buggy and offers more options.

Think clearly about how you're going to set up your account structure before you apply. DON'T use your personal AppleID to create your account, because it will take all your details from there. You cannot change this. Create an AppleID specifically for your business and attach all the appropriate business-related accounts, credit cards and tax IDs to it.

You may hear rumours about that Apple will reveal your real name when you write under a pseudonym. This is a bit of a mine field with Apple, and honestly a reason why you might prefer to distribute via Draft2Digital. If you own a publishing company, you can enter a publisher name, and this name will appear in the store. However, if you use more than one pen name through their account, they will appear under the same vendor name, connecting the two. In the name of European transparency laws, Apple also require you to make your business address and phone number public on your sales page. However, I'm yet to see examples of this on book pages. Maybe it's only displayed in countries that require it, but you definitely don't want your home address on there.

Apple is really the most confusing and infuriating retailer we deal with right now.

Apple takes EPUB3 files. One of the requirements is that the cover file is a flat file, not a 3-D image of box set, so if you have a box set or collection, you have to make sure the designer gives you a flat file in addition to the 3D set image.

Apple allows you to set your prices separately in a wide range of countries in a wide range of currencies. That doesn't mean that you have to enter them each individually. I usually enter one price—the one in US dollars—and apply it to all territories. Apple will automatically come up with a price point in all the individual currencies, and you can then use arrows to move that price up or down according to your wishes. For example if I want a book to be 99c across the board for a promotion, I set it to 99c in US dollars worldwide, but depending on the exchange rate it may go to $1.99 in Australia and New Zealand or Canada, so I then scroll down the menu and change the individual prices.

Apple does not have an upper price limit, and I recommend uploading bigger box sets, because people in general are accustomed to pay more for their books on Apple Books.

Because Apple displays sales per country, targeting ranks is not that easy.

You can use Facebook ads targeted to Mac users, but I am not sure how effective they are.

For readers who have Apple devices: The Kindle app on iPad and iPhone does not allow people to buy at Amazon. They have to log in to the Amazon website and purchase books there. This is because Apple demands 30% on in-app purchases and Amazon doesn't want to play that game. Apple wants Apple users to buy at the Apple store. They often do.

The Apple Book sales and specials are curated by real humans. You may get lucky and get featured, but because you have no control, this is not really a strategy, although the uploading menu gives you an option to contact Apple about your special or new release. I don't know that they ever do anything with these suggestions.

If you don't have a rep at Apple, and I don't, your best bet is to target users of the ecosystem.

This is the major drawback of Apple: their stores are so fragmented, and site so impenetrable, that it's hard for those not on Mac devices even to see your books. Hint: google "Apple Books [your author name]". This will bring up a list of your books. There won't be any rankings, but at least you can see whether the books are there.

In short:

- Register here: Apple
- Open for: everyone
- File format: EPUB3
- Payment: bank account

CHAPTER 103
GOOGLE PLAY

For a company the size of Google, getting your books into Google Play is a surprisingly (in my opinion, refreshingly), manual experience. When you apply for an account, a human checks that you're actually a real author.

A number of years ago, Google Play had a huge issue with scam books that were plagiarised books with the cover and title changed. They closed to all submissions while they cleaned up their platform and changed their application process.

Basically, they want to check that you're a real person and a real author.

Therefore, applying for a Google Play account is easier once you have a few books up. Being able to give them a website to check is great (they do check this). They will go to your Amazon page and look at your books.

Sometimes you will hear about authors failing their application and this is why: the real human person manually checking your profile did not find enough evidence that you're a bona fide author. You can appeal with more information.

The site is a bit onerous, but believe me, it used to be a lot worse, and these days it's reasonably easy to understand, and changes to your books and pricing are lightning fast.

You upload books on Google Play in the EPUB3 format.

They also allow you to upload audiobooks direct on the platform.

Just note that Google Books is separate from the retailer site. It's a search engine for books and allows readers to sample pages from your book. Your books are likely to end up on Google Books regardless of whether or not you list them on Google Play, especially if there is a print edition. They are not complete books and they are not a pirate site.

Google Play pays directly into your bank account.

I strongly recommend going to Google Play direct. Draft2Digital does not distribute to them and while PublishDrive does, they require that you have an account with Google Play direct anyway.

The book upload dashboard offers a lot of opportunities to make your books stand out. You can enter many different categories for different countries, and you can add links for print books and audiobooks. There are opportunities to offer series discounts or subscriptions. Use them, because Google Play displays these options on your customer-facing book pages.

On the site itself, you will find that free books are invisible. In fact, for a company that made its name with a search engine, their search function is terrible. They have only a few categories, and when you click them, all that comes up is a page of the bestselling books, and there is no way to see the rest of the list.

Terrible, terrible.

Except what Google Play displays to buyers is highly personalised and depends on the user's browse history.

And the Google Play Books descriptions are indexed and searchable.

Wait. I'll say that again: *the book descriptions are searchable.*

This is a feature not shared by *any* other retailer.

Now go use that tidbit of information to your heart's content.

In short:

- Register here: Google Play
- Open for: everyone
- File format: EPUB3
- Payment: bank account

CHAPTER 104
AGGREGATORS, DIRECT SALES AND DELIVERY SITES

Draft 2 Digital

Draft2Digital started as an aggregator but since their acquisition of Smashwords, they now also own a storefront. They distribute to all major stores except Google Play. They also distribute to a lot of library suppliers, including Bibliotheca and Hoopla.

The website is nice and easy to use. They host nifty universal links, where you can generate just one link for your book to use in advertising, taking the reader to their retailer of choice in their country. Beware, though, that those links can be a bit temperamental, especially for readers who are not in the US.

They also allow you to upload print books and audiobook distribution through Findaway Voices.

They pay through bank transfer or PayPal.

They have templates for ebook and print formatting that you can use for free regardless of whether you use D2D for distributing your titles.

One very handy feature of the site is that they allow income-splitting, which means that if you publish a book where more than one person needs to be paid, you can do this and everyone will get paid automatically, without the need for one person to take care of the spreadsheets to do it manually.

. . .

Publish Drive

Originating from Hungary, Publish Drive's international focus is clear from the moment you enter their site. They distribute to a lot of outlets that are not covered by Draft2Digital. Their focus is Asia.

Unfortunately, unless you want to use them to distribute to the major players, their subscription-based system will probably make it uneconomical for you to use them for those smaller retailers.

But if you have a lot of books, want to use an aggregator to distribute them everywhere, and you have halfway decent sales, their top subscription tier is absolutely much cheaper than any other option. On top of that, you can include audio and print. For roughly $60 per month (2024 price) that is a steal.

Visit the site for more details.

Other services they offer are: getting you into promotions at retailer sites and running your Amazon ads via their site.

Free book delivery services

If you want to give your books away and collect email addresses, you may want to get an account at Bookfunnel or Story Origin. There is more about these in *Mailing Lists Unboxed*, because these services integrate really well with your mailing list.

Despite the fact that these services both distribute free books when people sign up for your mailing list, they are not the same.

Bookfunnel concentrates on getting the book onto people's devices with the most ease possible. You will realise that this is an important function once you give your book for free to list subscribers and start getting "How do I get this on my Kindle?" emails. Their promotions are also very good and useful. They integrate with the major direct sales platforms Payhip, WooCommerce and Shopify.

Story Origin concentrates on author promotions and giving out copies for review. They integrate with the ecommerce site called Lemonsqueezy, which is a platform to watch because they handle taxes worldwide.

CROWDFUNDING

I briefly mention these platforms here, because crowdfunding has become quite popular with authors since Brandon Sanderson's $46M Kickstarter.

The best site for authors is Kickstarter. You can, but do not have to, make special editions or simply sell your newest release prior to putting it up on retailers.

Backerkit is trying to invade on this space.

The premise of both is: I'm going to make this cool thing. Here is how you can get it. It is not: I'm broke, give me some money to pay for editing, which is the type of funding you'd angle for on Gofundme, which I don't generally recommend for fiction authors.

If you want to know more, grab one of the excellent books available on Kickstarter for authors.

DIRECT SALES

There are a number of platforms that allow you to sell direct to your readers. Most will handle ebook, audio and print in some capacity. These are the most popular, with a few comments:

Payhip

Super easy to set up. They handle your taxes. They integrate with Bookfunnel for ebook and audio delivery and Book Vault for print delivery. They charge 5% + Paypal/credit card fees.

WooCommerce

For those who run wordpress sites, WooCommerce is 100% free. It's more hands on, but the possibilities and integrations are endless.

Shopify

Super easy, but quite pricey, and may not be worth the cost, especially if you're not selling huge numbers. Also not terribly customisable.

There are many other options and more coming up all the time and what you may want to use depends on if you want to offer limited time or bundle offers from just one page or you want the full shopping cart experience. An increasing number of tools now offer direct integration with payment platforms like Stripe where, once you have an account—for example through a Kickstarter that requires you to set up an account—you can also integrate it with Mailerlite and use email to sell directly without a full webstore.

If you want to know more about direct sales, there are great books on selling direct for authors. Look for ones that offer a balanced overview of all different options over those that push a particular platform. All platforms allow you to do similar things. Direct selling is about the strategy and tactics much more than it is about the tools.

CHAPTER 105
WHAT IS NEXT?

So now you have your books up on all the sites.

How do you tell everyone about them?

This is one of the questions I get asked most often. Writers want to know the magic pill that gets them selling on other retailers. They probably forgot that in their first months on Amazon, they didn't sell much either.

So the first ingredient to getting people to buy on other platforms is time. You need to give people time to discover you.

Then you will need to advertise. How?

Many of the so-called rented lists like Bookbub, Ereader News Today, Book Barbarian and such offer opportunities to enter links to other retailers. Use them. In fact, I suggest that from now on, you try to step away from the lists that advertise only on Amazon. You want to advertise your books everywhere. Not just that, you want to advertise *the fact* that your books are available everywhere. Even if people buy on Amazon right now, you want them to know that if they decide to buy elsewhere, they can.

Next, you need to realise a very important point about wide sales. When you sell your books wide, you are the main driver of discoverability and sales. You, not a retailer. You don't sit back and let the machine do its work (or as it is, let the machine let you sink). *You* promote your books. *You* own your audience. *You* send people to retailer pages to buy.

So yes, ads are good, but you can probably see what I'm going to say: your own mailing list is better.

But.

If you have been exclusive to Amazon for a long time, your mailing list will be populated by people who mostly read on Amazon; after all, that's the place where they found your books. So you are going to want to recruit people who read wide. How do you do that?

In the first place, you advertise where those readers are. As we have already seen at the beginning of this section, they are quite likely to be in other countries, and they can be targeted in Facebook ads through their locality or operating system.

Reaching wide readers may also require a bit of lateral thinking. I'll address a few points about wide sales.

In the first place, and this is an utterly important fact that often gets overlooked in the KU vs. wide discussion: *you won't be leaving Amazon.* You'll just be targeting a different type of reader on any platform, including Amazon. In fact, it is 100% possible, as I did, to significantly increase your sales on Amazon by unticking that exclusive box. People will buy instead of borrow. You are likely to get more per sale than you get per read. People may borrow (propping up your ranking) but won't read. When people buy, that's money in the bank. When people borrow, they may not get around to reading. Most importantly, the reader who will buy books they really want is a different type of person than the one who buys a subscription and samples. Not saying either is better or worse, just different.

Many readers like free books. The Three-year Plan methodology relies on giving away free books to readers in the hope that a percentage of them will buy the rest.

We have to look at where people get these free books.

People in Kindle Unlimited are less likely to download free books from free websites, because once they paid for their membership, they can get any number of books for free from Amazon. They have more books than they can ever read.

Readers who do not have Kindle Unlimited, and still like to get free books to sample new writers, have to go somewhere else. They will either download free books available from retailer websites or Amazon, or they will get their books in other ways. One of those other ways is book giveaways and cross-promotions at sites like Bookfunnel and Story Origin.

I already mentioned Bookfunnel and Story Origin in *Mailing lists Unboxed*, but they warrant special mention here. Since I started using the sites, I have noticed that my sales at other sites and outside the US on all retailers have increased. I can only conclude that people who get free books at these promo sites do not in general have Kindle Unlimited, because, if they did, they would be getting their free books there. These promotions work on the premise that people leave their email address in return for a free book, so it's a good source for mailing list subscribers who don't have a Kindle Unlimited subscription at Amazon.

A wide audience is much more international, on Amazon or off, and therefore it makes sense to promote internationally.

If you don't live in the US use your local contacts. Go to a local con, or organise a cross-promotion with local writers of the same genre. And if you do live in the US, try to swap mailing lists or blog posts with people who have an international audience.

One word of caution: first make sure that your fiction appeals to international audiences. If your fiction is very US-centric in setting or subject matter, then you may be better off staying in KU. Do your research. Have a look at what is for sale in the target country. Which genres do well? What sort of books do well?

In general, humour translates badly, pop culture is likely to be different except for the very famous references, and anything based on hot subjects in particular regions also does badly.

You can drive readers to your books by using the free drawcard. To make your book permanently free on Amazon, it needs to be distributed to other sites, notably Apple or B&N, and then you need to let Amazon know that the book is available for free elsewhere. If your book sells reasonably well, the price match will be quick. If your books needs a bit of a push, send an email to KDP support via your author dashboard. Give them the links of where the book is free.

Beware that if you want to use Bookfunnel or Story Origin, you cannot have that book in Kindle Unlimited.

CHAPTER 106
DRIVING SALES

So how do you drive sales?

First of all, you need somewhere to drive them to.

In *Self-publishing Unboxed*, I already mentioned the importance of your website. I told you that the function of your website is only partially to display your books. More importantly, your website is a place where you host your landing pages where you can send people.

And while those people are there, you can find out who they are by asking for their email address.

Before you start advertising your books everywhere, you need to update your website with all the retailer links where you want people to buy. This can be a major pain in the behind.

There are WordPress plug-ins that will make this process easier, but there is no denying that adding four or five links for each of your books can be a headache, especially if links change or you make a cover update.

If you're not afraid of a bit of simple code, turn to the next chapter for an easy and free way to do this with a minimum amount of hassle.

CHAPTER 107
BEST HACK FOR WEBSITE CONTENT

ONCE YOU HAVE A COUPLE OF BOOKS ON YOUR WEBSITE, YOU HAVE TO maintain those pages. Every time you make a change, the potential for errors increases. For example, when you change your blurb or your cover, or one of your book's links changes, you need to change it in a number of different places.

This may mean that you need to insert the same image, links and the same text in a number of different places. It is easy to make a mistake, and you might not find out until your readers point it out to you, because there are just too many places to check all at once.

What you really need is a content management system. Most people will think about some sort of database when I say content management. You could indeed use a database, but if that sounds too technical for you then I've got good news, because it need not be.

A web page for a book typically consists of a framework of elements in HTML code and the cover image and blurb for a book and links to retailer sites.

Web code is only visible if you use the "view source" option in your browser.

The user will see a title, the image of the cover, the book's blurb and maybe a sample, and then links to all the retailers where the book can be bought. It is more than likely that, in order to create uniformity on your website, you made the design of each page the same. This makes it ideal for automation.

A content management system is simply a system that merges your data for each book with the code that needs to be on the page that controls how the text and images are displayed.

Since the code is always the same, you can perform this merge function with a database, but everyone has a piece of software that can perform this task and it is free. It's a humble spreadsheet.

Most people think of the spreadsheet as software that calculates data, mostly financial. It will be used for accounting, for keeping your books and for making financial statements.

Spreadsheets also have a number of very powerful logical and text operation functions.

I said earlier that a website has very simple code. Using the spreadsheet's functions, you can merge the code with your book's data and produce your book's pages off-line, so that if you need to update it, you only need to copy and paste a single cell.

You can use any spreadsheet software, but I prefer to use Google Sheets, because it's platform-independent and stored on the web. This is important for backup purposes, but also because you can use either a Mac or a PC or both.

You can export your spreadsheets to back them up and share them with other people. You can use the spreadsheet to produce more than one different type of page from the same data. When you now need to change your cover, you only need to change it in one place and all your updates are done with.

Moreover if you ever have any problems with your website, like it is hacked or becomes damaged, all you need to do is delete everything and copy your book pages again from your spreadsheet. No expensive restores or finding of data required.

I suspect that for many of you, this will still come across as abracadabra. Therefore, I have produced a spreadsheet so you can see how it works for yourself. You can see an example here or in the notes for this book. You can copy this sheet to your own Google Drive account and insert your own books. The instructions are all on the sheet.

CHAPTER 108
THE POWER OF HIGH

IF YOU'RE DOING YOUR HOMEWORK AND YOU'RE GOING TO ALL NON-AMAZON retailer sites to look at the way they list books, you will very soon notice that the prices of the top 25 books are likely to be a lot higher than on Amazon.

There are several reasons for this.

In the first place, other retailers tend to be dominated by the traditional publishers. These sites often have relationships with traditional publishers. Not only that, they make a lot more money from selling a book at $10 than selling one for $2.99. So it would make sense for them to push the more expensive books harder. Some of the sites even give better rankings to higher-priced books and repress the rankings of free books entirely.

For them, it makes a lot more sense to have a top 100 filled by the biggest names than one filled with cheap books by authors no one has ever heard of. That just does not look good for the site.

Now that we know this, what does this mean for you?

Well, you could price your books higher.

But, you will say, the site terms and conditions mention that you can't price higher than on other sites and I have my book set at $2.99 elsewhere and I'm happy with that. I don't want to price my books at $6.99 on one site and $2.99 on the other, because that's not fair.

The easiest way to play the high-priced game that can make wide listings interesting is to make a large set of your books that is not available on Amazon. I have a couple of complete sets of series that I sell at these websites for over $15. I don't put these books on Amazon.

In fact, Amazon would penalise me for charging that much by taking an extra 35% of my earnings, so I refuse to list my books there. I just think that's nonsense. Besides, box sets don't sell much there unless they're on special and really cheap.

So: bundle your books into really large sets. Charge more than $9.99 for them. Leave them off Amazon.

Enter these sets in Kobo promotions. Offer them for sale on your website for a discount. Advertise them on Facebook. Advertise them to your mailing list.

CHAPTER 109
THE PRICE MATCHING MONSTER

When you upload your books to Amazon, they remind you that "pricing is at our discretion" and hoo, boy, do they mean it.

There are a number of things about Amazon that really put the boot into how we can run our business. The worst one of these is the tendency to match the lowest price available anywhere automatically.

Because Amazon does not allow us to make our books free, we misuse that capability by making it free on the other sites, and waiting for Amazon to price match.

But there are also a lot of situations where price-matching works to your disadvantage.

If they find your books for cheaper elsewhere, they will price-match.

It could be that you forgot to put your price back up after a promotion, but it could also be that Kobo promotion you took part in last month. They don't tell you.

Even after your book has been free or discounted for a while, Amazon doesn't always raise the price again, even if your instructions clearly state that they should do so. If you raise it with support, they will mumble some generic comment and remind you that "pricing is at our discretion". Sometimes you find why they kept your price low, but sometimes you don't.

Tell me, how are we supposed to run a business if the partners we pay for their service don't stick to the price we set?

This affects our ability to run promotions. Most of those need to be pre-booked and pre-paid.

What can we do about this?

Besides taking care not to leave cheaper prices on other retailers, not much.

But because Amazon has become such an unreliable partner, I don't tend to meddle with prices anymore. I set the price for the first book in the series either discounted or free and then don't touch it. It's not ideal, but you do not need to have a limited time price point to run promotions.

CHAPTER 110
THE RETAILER AS CONTENT DELIVERY SITE

An interesting article I read recently stated how people are becoming less loyal to brand and more loyal to retailers. People prefer to go to one place and do all the shopping in that place, rather than chase around finding certain brands. This meshes with a society in which people are less willing to spend time shopping, because they can have purchases delivered to their door. They may have accounts with certain retailers and it is just too much of a bother to go somewhere else for specific things.

What does this mean for the authors selling their books online?

Sales are becoming divided into pillars of retail. The retailer has great influence over people's buying power. If I have an iPhone I am likely to shop for my digital content on Apple; if I have an android phone I will shop on Google Play—unless I have an Amazon account, and then I may shop for everything on Amazon. Except I can't buy books from Amazon on my Kindle app on my iPhone (because Apple and Amazon are toddlers who can't play nice in the same sandbox). So I may buy on the Kobo app instead. I may have both Kindle and Kobo apps, and can't be bothered to download yet another app where I have to open an account.

Each of the major technology companies is trying to create their platform to hold onto their loyal users.

The world is fragmenting into thousands of smaller and larger pillars of retail. The boundaries between going from one retailer to the next may well be stronger than buying one brand over another. We already know that many of the brands are made in the same factories, so there often isn't that much difference between them anyway, except status. This is very obvious with ebooks: they're exactly the same across all retailers.

Yet the boundaries for people to set up an account, to enter their credit card and download an app are bigger than just buying another book. People live within the retailer ecosystem and are reluctant to venture outside.

We're in the last chapters of this subject, and you may wonder where I'm going with this.

I mention this here to illustrate the true independence of being wide.

Loyalty to only one platform means a certain short-sightedness to all the other pillars of retail that don't happen to be important to you, to your country, or even just the area where you live.

A smart author uses the retailer as a content delivery site.

The retailer is not proud to sell your product for you. Instead, they are merely a place where you can send your readers to get the book. It is their task to collect payment, process delivery and deal with complaints.

The reason I mention this is that I highly encourage you to see retailers in this light: they are pillars of retail whose function it is to display and sell your book, collect payment and deal with delivery.

The retailer doesn't care about you. The retailer doesn't owe you anything other than the agreed percentage of your sales. You definitely don't owe the retailer anything—least of all complete loyalty.

The retailer is a content delivery site. The content is yours. You should put it on as many different retailers as possible, so that people loyal to those retailers can get it where they want it.

CHAPTER 111
THE RIGHT MINDSET WINS

If you listen to or read any interviews about the successful careers of long-standing midlist writers, you will notice that one thing stands out. They may have relied on a major source of income for short periods of time, but not for their entire lives, and in fact they strongly advise people against relying on a single income source. Diversification is key to a long-term career. Believe it or not, today's giants are tomorrow's have-beens. Companies go broke, break up, get bought by other parties with visions that send them in a different direction, or just plain fail their target audience and die. This is the reality of a creative freelance career, which is what you're doing as a self-published writer. So, either straightaway, or not too much later, you have to look at some form of career diversification. You have to make sure that if one of your boats sinks, even if it is the major one, you still have other boats to keep you above water.

But, you will say, I'm only a small time writer. I will worry about things like that when I sell more.

I think that is wrong.

Not only do you have no idea what is going to take off, and where, but if you start on all platforms, you start building your audience on those. There is no worse time to start building an audience than when you're desperate and there has been a major industry shake-up and many other people are desperate, too.

You hear all the time that people find it so hard to get away from Amazon. This is because they have spent their entire career selling books on

Amazon, attracting an audience that buys mostly on Amazon, and not on any of the other platforms. In a world where content is king, Amazon is just a single content provider. You need to make people want to read your books, which are not interchangeable with any other writer's books, and offer them wherever those people are. If the world is a pie, you want a bite of all the different sections of the pie. You can't make a reliable living by just putting yourself on only a slice of the market, even if that slice happens to be the biggest right now. This is a major mistake people make. They ask who is the biggest, and then only focus on the biggest, forgetting that a slice consisting of 30 million different people on a different platform can generate a pretty solid income.

There are many stories of freelancers who have been saved by the foresight to put their material in places that they never thought they would rely on. When you're into freelancing, you simply have to diversify to survive.

There is no secret, and it is a lot of hard work, and success is not guaranteed. However, when you diversify, your sales will be more stable and ups and downs on any one single retailer will not affect you as much.

INTERLUDE: THE WORRIED WRITER

CHAPTER 112
COMPARISONITIS

This chapter is about a subject that makes happy writers very unhappy, namely the tendency to compare ourselves to others. This can be a problem early in your career when you simply need to be more patient, or later on, when you see other authors who are having much more success than you despite having fewer books and having been published less long. It can be very debilitating, and frankly sucks the life out of your enjoyment.

It's called comparisonitis.

Don't think that just new writers suffer from this because I don't know a single writer who does not suffer from it at least occasionally.

Some writers are able to channel that angry energy into production or other positive energy, but for most of the normal people like the rest of us, it just kills our enjoyment.

Other people make warm and fuzzy statements such as _I don't look at these things_, or _I'm just happy for other people when they do well and cheer them on_ but it is impossible for most of us to either avoid all author gatherings where this type of news is shared, or to pretend we're endlessly enjoying the success of others.

I mean—come on, don't be such a sanctimonious you-know-what's it.

You're having feelings you can't repress, and can't deny, and to be honest, you shouldn't. It's not healthy.

So, short of having a good rant to your best friend, or using a punching bag in the garage, what to do?

In the first place, it's always a good thing to educate yourself. If you see someone else having a lot of success doing a particular thing, realise that this is only one aspect of their career. It is impossible to see what someone else's author business looks like from the sidelines. You don't know how much time or money people are spending on certain tactics.

You have no idea how much advertising they do. You don't know about all the things they don't have time for. And you don't know about the places where you sell and they don't even have their books up.

But the reality is, there will always be someone who is more successful than you. When you're around for a longer time, you will also see that a lot of people burst onto the scene like a flash in the pan and are gone a few years later. They burnt out, couldn't repeat their success, or simply didn't enjoy it any more.

Maybe they suffered from comparisonitis as well.

I think the best way to look at your career is to concentrate on things you can change and consider your lifestyle, rather than the amount of money or success you want to have.

If you can keep publishing, and you keep making your books better, and you work at becoming better at advertising or build up a stable of activities that work for you, then eventually you will have some success. Unless you lose the enjoyment of writing and you stop it altogether, but in that case you've probably found something else to do, and that is okay, too.

Many of the people you're enviously watching are on completely different pathways. They have a lot of time, they have a lot of really good ideas that just pour out of them, they have a particular gift for telling a particular type of story and have hit the market really well. You can't repeat that and you shouldn't be tempted to try. It is pointless trying to be someone else. You can only be yourself.

Writer income is only half of the story.

Even if it is your aim to make a living with your writing, keep in mind a backup plan that you could pursue instead. Making a living with an artistic pursuit is not easy, and you may luck into something that is easier. I have seen people start as writers and then become successful editors, podcasters, or cover designers. Some people found that they are very good at marketing but don't like writing so much, and they went on to publish other people's books. The best thing to do is to view your career as a moving object to find out what works for you. If you have something that is working quite well, you do more of that.

When a new trend comes along, have a look at it to see if is something you would like to do. Above all, it has to be something that you enjoy doing. Jumping into a trend because people say they're making a lot of money is probably not a good idea. In the first place, you don't have a full picture of what is involved.

How much time do they spend on various activities?

People think that being a writer means sitting down all day and writing. The truth is, that after you have a couple of books, you will probably have to do more marketing. There are writers who keep their careers alive through writing a book a month, but I would find that extremely mind-numbing. I couldn't do that. There are others who barely write and keep their books alive through marketing. I couldn't do that either.

So instead of allowing yourself to be jealous of other people and their success, try to learn something from what they're doing. Try to see if it is something that you like to do.

For example a number of years ago when authors started to talk about having mailing lists, I knew straightaway this was something I wanted to do. When I was a kid, I had pen friends in a lot of countries. I was always very much into writing letters or emails and enjoyed that sort of thing. I had also seen, in a different business, how successful a mailing list can be.

It is no use for me to compare myself with people who do loads of advertising, because I am not ever going to be the person who spends $40,000 a month on ads in order to earn $60,000. I don't mind if you are, but there is no point for me to become jealous towards people who need to sell $100,000 worth of books a month so that they can pay their advertising bills and have some money on the top. I would much rather earn less and not do so much advertising. I'm not that good at it and hate it.

There is also not much point either for me to try to compare myself with authors who write a book a month or who write in very popular trends.

I know I'm not wired that way, and while I sometimes lament that I don't have anywhere near the success they do, there is not much I can do about it. I have tried writing fast, but it just makes me miserable.

If you're going to have a career as an artist, you have to do something that you enjoy and that you can sustain long-term.

How well you end up selling is guided by the way you write and a decent dose of luck. But most of all it's guided by persistence. You can slowly build a readership and cater to just your audience, or you can chase after trends in order to catch that elusive bestseller. You might be lucky, but by the same token, and much more likely, you will not. Then you will give up in frustration, die from comparisonitis and be unhappy.

Fame is not something you can control. Aspiring to it is not really useful. That doesn't mean we shouldn't try, but you should be mentally in a place where it is okay if it doesn't happen.

Fame is also highly relative. It's extremely unlikely you'll be a person everyone knows. I'm not sure if you'd want that either.

But you can have your own bubble of fame in your own audience, even if that audience is very small.

Derive your satisfaction from interactions with readers you already have and who already like your work, rather than the readers that you don't have, the readers that other people have, and that you may never get.

Knowing yourself and accepting the way you are is the key to keeping the enjoyment alive.

CHAPTER 113
THE SURVIVAL MINDSET

Here are some thoughts about the mindset necessary to survive in this ever-changing world.

After more than ten years of being a writer, I see a lot of people struggling with this. They don't seem to be clear on what sort of writer they want to be. They may not have settled on their personal writing schedule, yet they want their writing to be everything they dreamed of and more. And some of those dreams are fairly attainable and realistic, but others are not.

Self published writers have been somewhat sheltered from the truth that traditionally published writers have known for a long time, namely that this is a fickle unpredictable and difficult industry to survive in, that euphoric highs are followed by depressing lows, sometimes in the same year, that having success is by no means repeatable, and that the market shifts and changes all the time.

And sometimes that change is beneficial to you, and sometimes it is not.

In traditional publishing, there is the saying that you are only as good as your last book. In self publishing, that fortunately does not need to be the case, but it is still a game of ups and downs, and unfortunately you cannot always control either.

There is only one thing you can control, and that is your own attitude towards all of this.

. . .

I know, you thought I was going to say something about the quality of your product or something equally uplifting, right? If your product is good, then you'll be fine.

Nope, not really. So much of what determines our success is not in our hands.

You need to know what you want from your writing, and it needs to be something you can achieve.

Of course, it is perfectly fine to say I am writing just for the sake of it, but there are not many writers for whom this is genuinely the case. Most writers, even though those who say that this is true for them, secretly hope for some financial success. People paying money for your work is the only validation we have left, having eschewed the traditional industry and its gatekeepers. Awards are not often open to us, and because most of us write genre fiction, awards are not terribly important for our success anyway.

So what do you want from your writing? Answer that question first and foremost.

The key to a realistic mindset that will keep you happy through the ups and downs of your career is that it has to be satisfactory to you.

I know this is not very helpful to those people who hate their job and hope to replace it with writing income one day.

But hoping for that to happen is sadly not going to make it happen, and it may even make you miserable. The best way to get started in a long-term writing career is to have some income from somewhere else. Whether that is a job, a spouse, retirement, a redundancy payout or a combination of these things, and making some life choices about expenses, that is up to you. If you're at the beginning of your writing career, and you desperately need money to survive, writing is probably not going to give that to you.

Of course, you'll hear stories of writers who were writing like crazy when they were down to their last dollar and their book made it big, but they're very few and far in between, and none of us will ever know how much those stories were embellished for dramatic effect.

Most people find that stress about paying your bills is a very bad motivator for making good art. Supposing you were that stressed and you did make a good income from writing one month, it would still take two months before the retailers paid it out. Even though self-publishing is immediate, getting the money is still quite slow. You need money to tide you over. A steady income preferably.

For most of us, the first years were extremely lean. We probably had to invest some money into getting covers and editing and other services set up for our first books. The time when you first start and you're finding your feet is when self publishing is the most expensive. You may make a mistake and pay for a nice cover which ended up not suiting the book, or you might have spent money on an editor who didn't do such a good job after all or you booked some ads that didn't work.

When you look at the Written Word Media annual survey of self published writers and their income, one thing the higher earners have in common is that they have a large back catalogue.

If you want to get a sustainable income, you have to keep writing, and to keep writing at a pace that is sustainable for you, and to do this while the process of writing remains exciting to you.

You're trying to leave a stressful job you didn't like and you don't want to end up in a similar situation, with lots of stress about too-tight self-imposed deadlines.

So consider what you actually want from your writing. This doesn't have to be an either or situation like it is often painted. That if you are in it purely for the money you've got to write drek. That if you're not in it for the money, you can't make money. This is a continuum where you have to find your own space where you're happy. Except if you're in it purely for the money, you're probably better off getting a job where that money is guaranteed.

Even the writers who make the most money are still in it because they enjoy writing stories, and many of them dread the moment they no longer enjoy writing those stories. Writing stories is important. Enjoying writing is extremely important. You have to do everything in your power to protect your ability to enjoy it.

All of this means that you have to find the right combination that works for you, and you have to find the right communities that speak to your way of thinking. Some people truly thrive in a very competitive environment. Some people enjoy having the pressure of constantly writing more books. Some people really enjoy jumping into the marketing and seeing success in this way. This becomes an option when you have a larger backlist. Some people continue to chase after big money and can really make ads work for them, but many people are not like that. They might enjoy publishing off-beat projects to a small but loyal fanbase. They might get into related formats. Audio, audio plays, screenplays, graphic novels, selling books at cons and markets, Kickstarters, having their own store, partnering with visual artists, music, the list is endless.

But somewhere in the gamut of options, you need to find a place that makes you happy, and where, if something didn't go as you had planned, it doesn't crush you.

Life becomes a lot easier if you don't have the constant pressure to earn ever more and you don't view your fellow writers as competitors.

At times you do well, put away some of that income in other investments. Many people also make lifestyle choices. They consolidate any debts or move to a cheaper place so they don't have such a huge mortgage to service, all in the name of taking away the stress.

Get rid of groups and people in your social writing circle who make you unhappy and anxious. That includes places where bestsellers boast their socks off and you're made to feel like a failure unless you hit a certain income level. There is nothing "inspiring" about a goal you're not reaching. About goals that are for a large part out of your control.

That is toxic stuff that is likely to lead to disillusionment in the long term.

It is never wrong to listen to a lot of different voices in publishing, but you shouldn't feel the need to act on any of them, unless you can see that something is going to be interesting or beneficial to your situation.

Rather than one magic button, a successful writing career is built up out of the building blocks of having a solid catalogue, continuously working on your audience, continuously working on your discoverability, in whatever way you choose, and a share persistence and tenacity.

Over the more than ten years that I've been in this industry, I have seen many people disappear.

The vast majority of them never sold very much.

A small subset of those people were looking for the one magic button that would make them rich, and made this desire known in many of the writing groups. Some of these people even declared openly that they were going to be a success because apparently acting like you're going to be successful turns you into a success. Or schmoozing with super-successful people does, like it's going to rub off or something.

While this sort of bluff may work in the workplace, writing is a surprisingly egalitarian world, where in order to have success, you have to produce the goods, those goods have to be liked by the people who buy them, and only by having fans do you have some means to expand your audience.

If you think you can bluff your way into this, that you can turn your book into a success while it lacks one of the ingredients that makes audiences want it, or you think that there is some kind of magic button and you're desperately looking for it, then you're not only highly unlikely to succeed, you're making yourself miserable in the process.

If you feel unhappy about the way your career is going, stop to think about whether you are really looking for the magic button, and if so, just stop doing that, because it's not helpful, it distracts you from what you should be doing, and most importantly, it messes with your satisfaction in life in general.

Most writers, including myself, are not guaranteed best sellers. Sure, I make enough money to keep it interesting. Of course, I would like to earn more money, but at this stage of the game, I am not willing to sacrifice my happiness for that. I could, in my current situation, live from the money I make, and that it's a relief, but I have also built up non-writing income.

It is possible to live purely off your writing, but when you're starting out, and this is the only thing you desperately want, trying to attain it is a recipe for a lot of stress and unhappiness. There are much easier ways of getting a reliable income than writing.

Within publishing, there exist two very unhelpful stereotypes. On the one hand, you have people who assume that all writers are poor and that you can't make money from writing. On the other hand, you have people who assume that making a lot of money from writing is easy.

Writing is not a secure or guaranteed career. So much can happen that can either supercharge it or torpedo it, and these things can happen in close succession.

Therefore, the most important thing is that it satisfies what you want out of life. Most writers who do this long-term enjoy being able to write what they want, when they want, where they want much more than chasing ever-increasing levels of income.

Don't give up a stable income too quickly, sock away money during the good times to tide you through the bad, diversify your income and at all cost, protect your ability to write like a hawk. Make sure you don't lose the enjoyment. That's my advice for keeping your career alive.

CHAPTER 114
DOES A ONE STAR REVIEW SINK YOUR BOOK?

IN THIS CHAPTER, I'M GOING TO BE TALKING ABOUT REVIEWS, AND SPECIFICALLY about the question whether one bad review is going to sink your book.

Of course it hurts when your very first review is a bad review.

But bad reviews are going to happen no matter what you do, and the best thing you can do with them is trying to drown them in other reviews.

But let's have a look at the reviews themselves. Is the single one star review going to sink your sales, as some people claim?

Let's first look at the reason why people leave one star reviews. This can literally be for all kinds of reasons but they fall broadly in a couple of categories. In the first place, of course, they hated the book. This doesn't mean they read the book, it means that they may have hated the book's premise or the fact that it contains a certain thing that they don't agree with or that other people said they hated the book, or it could mean that they read the book, bought the book, and wrote a long review about why they thought it was a waste of money.

Sometimes people give one star reviews because they disliked the author's behaviour in public places.

Readers also leave one-star reviews for all kinds of other weird and wonderful reasons.

Remember that we are mostly talking about reviews on Amazon here, and Amazon sends readers a reminder a couple of weeks after they have bought the book that they should review it. Some people don't like writing reviews and they don't appreciate the reminder, so they give the book a one star rating because they hate being asked. Amazon no longer requires readers to actually write a review so it can just be a rating. This can be infuriating, but on the other hand, they didn't write anything bad about it.

It could also mean that they read a lot of books and use the one star rating to indicate books they haven't read or books they would like to read. This is also infuriating, but there is nothing stopping them from using the review system like that.

So if you get a one star rating, look at whether there is actually a written review attached. Then look to whether that review makes sense. It could be that Amazon has prodded them and that they wrote in the box I haven't read it yet. And then they posted the review, because they didn't know how else to make Amazon's reminder go away, or they are of the opinion that every bit of correspondence, no matter how automated, needs to be replied to.

This is the first rule the Internet, by the way: the secret to a be a happy writer is choosing your battles and choosing what to engage with. The vast majority of stuff that gets sent your way does not need a reply.

If the reader has written something in the review box and it is about your book, it may be that they are just having an angry day, and their review might not even make sense. It might not be about the book. It may be about having bought the book but being unable to find it, or that they don't understand how to get it onto their device or sometimes that the book is about a subject that they don't like, or that there is swearing that they don't like or that there is sex that they don't like or there is no sex and they were expecting it.

There are all kinds of really weird reasons why people write these reviews. Some of them are barely literate. If these kinds of reviews are not your first review on your book, I would not worry about them.

In fact, from the reader's point of view, they're probably a good thing. Honestly, a rambling rant with a one star review will probably do more to draw eyes to your book then a bunch of glowing comments.

Since authors are always trying to goose their reviews with glowing accolades, a reader who cares about the reviews, will often only read the one and two star ones. If there are none at all, that might be a reason not to buy the book. If there is a one or two star review, and it's a barely literate ramble, or it is from a reader going on a particular crusade about some subject, then that new reader is going to be satisfied that all is okay with the book. This is presuming that you have other, normal reviews for them to look at.

Give the reader some credit. If a review makes no sense or is for the wrong product, they won't attach any meaning to it.

If it is your first review, then it's a good idea to get it couple of other reviews on your books. But also don't dismiss a one-star review if it points out issues with quality and these issues are repeated in other reviews, good or bad. Then you may have a problem.

I would look at whether the reviewer has a point, and if so, if you need to do something about it.

Do other reviews mention that the plot is confusing, the ending is not satisfying, the characters are wooden, it's not clear what is happening?

Do other reviews mention errors? Are they specific? Do they mention what the supposed errors are?

It is virtually impossible to never have "errors" mentioned in reviews, no matter how much you spend, and how many people edit your book.

Especially if you write international English, readers will encounter spellings they are not familiar with. It's not as bad as it used to be in 2010-ish, when publishing became international, but still happens.

Dialects of English also inform different word choices and some readers have big bees in their bonnets about their form of "correct" English.

If the comments are specific and they are real errors, fix them.

In my view, there are only two types of books: those with a handful of typos, and those which haven't attracted enough readers to spot the typos.

If you're getting a lot of comments about confusing plot, wooden characters and stuff like that, then you may consider using the comments to improve your next work. Don't go and and unpublish the work in a huff, especially if it is still selling.

Some reviewers have a bee in their bonnet about things that most people won't even notice.

They're not always right either.

What you absolutely shouldn't do, and please disengage from your reviews and stop reading them if you are the kind of person who might think this, is that these reviewers are out to get you.

Often you will hear authors complain that they looked at the reviewer's profile and that they wrote one star rants for all books and this reviewer just hated everyone and hated authors and hated you in particular.

No, not at all. There are just people who like writing ranting reviews for the entertainment value. They have a band of followers who enjoys seeing them rant about books. The followers might even buy the books based on the rants. What you should absolutely not do is engage with these people, because they can be like a pack of angry dogs. Just let them be, because they will find another book and another author to poke into making unfortunate responses. These people are not out to get you. These reviewers are doing this to entertain their own circle of friends. It is a kind of miserable thing to do, and you may wonder why these people don't get a life, but there you go.

Ultimately, reviewers don't owe authors anything, and then there's nothing in the terms and conditions that says that they're not allowed to do this.

It is not about you, and while the review may be about your book, and maybe even they're mocking everything you've written, the audience for the review is the reviewer's band of followers.

Most people who buy only skim a handful of reviews, that is if they look at the reviews at all. They are more likely to look at how many reviews there are, because the number is indicative of how many people are reading the book.

In summary, a one star review is not malicious, no matter how much it might hurt you. A one star review just by itself won't mean your book sales will tank. Especially if there are already a number of other reviews. Reviewers give books star ratings for all kinds of weird and wonderful reasons. Other potential readers are not stupid and can see this for themselves.

Don't worry too much about it and move on.

CHAPTER 115
HOW MANY BOOKS DOES IT TAKE?

In this chapter, I'm going to be talking about a question that you hear quite a bit from beginning writers, and that is how many books does it take before you see success?

I honestly wish that new writers would actually listen to their gut because they know how to answer this question for themselves.

The answer, of course is: no one knows, it depends.

Even the fact that the question gets asked displays a certain level of wishful thinking mixed with despair, and a desire for there to be a paint-by-numbers formula to success.

Well, there isn't.

So I'm going to be talking about what I think is the best attitude to this question.

It is now a number of years ago that I set out a post on successful writing careers on the Kindleboards which was then the most popular community to hang out as a self published writer.

It was where you learned about what to do and not to do, about the effectiveness, honesty or otherwise of the plethora of service providers that were springing up like proverbial mushrooms.

These days, the Kindleboards are not a tenth as good as they used to be, because through various reasons most people have moved on to different communities.

This is what tends to happen to good communities. People hear that it is good, more and more people join in, so that the weight of the community is strongly favouring people who are just starting out, and if you've been in the community for a while, there is only so often you can answer the same beginner questions.

Anyway, a few of us are still around, and the archive is also still available and searchable and you can still find that post. I've even based a book on it. It's called the three year plan. Four books a year, four series, make the first book free for mailing list subscribers.

So that would make twelve books a kind of benchmark for success.

Well, it depends. The Written Word Media annual survey indicates that people in the top earning class have at least twenty books out.

But you don't need these surveys to know that more books means more chance to have one that sells well and drives sales to all your other books. It could happen to someone with one book, and someone else might have written fifty books and still doesn't make coffee money. It really depends.

It's about the kind of books, about your craft, and yes, also about your ability to sell them, but not as much as it is about the attractiveness of the books themselves. The stories.

The newbie asks: but how many books, really? I've written one and I feel nervous about another one because I want the current one to do well first.

There are two things wrong with this question.

In the first place it is the thought that success would be a universally defined concept. In reality success means a lot of different things to a lot of different people. If your idea of success is to make more money than you're spending, then you will probably spend a book or two or maybe 3 to get to that level, given decent craft and an average ability to market. If your idea is to fund the occasional family holiday, or other fun things, then it probably gets a bit harder, but it's still very doable. It's likely you'll need more books.

If your idea of success is to quit your day job then it will completely depend on what sort of job you have at the moment and how many people you're supporting with that money and also how much of a cushion you have from other activities or other members in your family. And where you live.

If you live by yourself, don't need to spend that much money, if you can easily move to a cheaper place or cut certain expenditure, then it's going to be much easier than if you have a family, a mortgage, kids in schools that you need to be paid for and your family depends only on you. Sure enough, there are people who have done it, but you will need a very secure and strong income that doesn't fall below a certain level, or you need to have secured some backup income from other sources. I might say a little bit more about this later.

If your idea of success if that people will know your name and you will regularly inhabit the front page of your Amazon categories, then I still don't think it is impossible, but obviously a lot harder yet again, because the measures by which you gauge your success are not in your hands and it all depends on how you can catch lightning in a bottle.

(By the way: Yes, you heard that right: being a full-time writer is easier than being a famous writer.)

Now there will be some people who say that success has nothing to do with catching lightning in a bottle, that you just have to study the market, write in what they call hungry genres and then keep doing it, but there are several issues with that proposition.

You have to be wired to understand or to distill the right aspects from books that you're studying. You have to be wired to want to do that over and over again. You have to be wired to not want to introduce random aspects to the story just because you like them. And you have to be wired to repeat this again and again. I cannot tell you how many writers I have seen hit huge success, then tell everybody that it's all about hard work and nothing about luck, and then a few years later, you hardly hear about them any more, because they cannot replicate the success they had.

If your definition of success includes bestseller status, a lot will hinge on how well individual books sell, while I prefer the income generated by the aggregate, your entire catalogue. Single-book successes are even more temperamental than catalogue successes and failure is likely to make you more miserable, because the wreckage of dashed hopes is so much more painful.

This goes into the second definition of success, which is to lead a lifestyle you aspire to. I wanted to write because I wanted to be creative. I have always liked creating things much more than I like consuming things, and an office job is terribly non-creative.

I wanted to make enough to cover my publishing costs and some extra.

The level of sales for lifestyle happiness has two aspects: the money earned, yes, but also the money spent. Lifestyle decisions can mean moving somewhere cheaper and it can also mean making decisions about your finances that will aid your career in the future.

A writer's sales are terribly fickle. Genres go in and out of fashion, life happens and mistakes happen.

I've learned that over a longer term career, say ten years, many of the following are true:

What goes up must come down. If you have success with a series, plan for what you'll do when inevitably sales wane.

Always spend less than you earn, especially in the times that you earn a lot. I've only ever heard one writer podcast mention this tactic. Investment, baby! Put any money you don't need away in a place where it will earn you an income. Interest, real estate, dividends, whatever.

Never stop writing. You know how they say that a writer is only as good as their last book? Yeah, that.

Also, look after your herd of little book sheep. Even if sales are low, a bit of promo, a mention here or there or inclusion in a newsletter will keep the sales going.

Keep learning writing and storytelling skills.

Explore new formats. Don't have all your books in hardcover yet? Release them! Audio? Special anniversary edition on Kickstarter? Those are all options that don't require you to write a new book and will extend the long tail of sales.

I have been doing these things throughout my career, but I've never made millions. My goal is to be happy. Surely, to be happy includes making money, because money is a great validation of what you do.

So this is one aspect of the question. Define your definition of success and be realistic about it. If you start with a small aim, and you're happy when you make more money than you earn, when the pursuit of writing and creating something is a large factor in your enjoyment and your reason for doing it, then success is highly attainable. If you're wanting to go all out and say: I'm not aiming for something so mediocre because that just sets you up for mediocrity, it very likely that you'll have disappeared off the scene within a year or two. I've seen those people as well. They don't hang around, even if they have a level of success that most of us would envy. What they get is never enough and they're never happy.

Okay, then now we get to the how many books part.

It is also to do with the concept of catching lightning in a bottle. Some series or some books will just completely flop. You had high hopes, you studied the market, your marketing and imagery was all on point, but for some reason it just doesn't seem to sell as well as you hoped. Sometimes a book does sell better than you hoped. I hate to say it, but this is never the book you expected to do well.

Because playing this game is so frustrating, I prefer to not really play it at all. Just make sure that your books are sitting comfortably within a genre, and then do your own work to get steady sales.

In order to do any promotional work, you have to have at least some books that you can use as loss leaders, and you probably have to have a completed series of some description. It is probably better if you have two series or if you have three.

Adding new books to your catalogue is very important, probably the most important thing you can do in the beginning of your career. But adding books becomes much less important when you already have a large back catalogue, at which stage some writers can live just off marketing the books they already have. Where is that line? Who knows.

Much has been said about the very interesting court case against the merger of Penguin and Random House.

One of the articles about it astonished people around the world where the director of Random House admitted that the company was called Random House because publishing is so random. I have seen several articles in the news exclaiming that after 100 years of publishing the publishing industry admits that they have no idea what they're doing.

But we all know that is true.

It is impossible to predict success, to catch lightning in a bottle. If they spend a lot of money acquiring a book they really don't know whether it's going to do well, they just hope that they can recoup that money for having attracted a big name author or a concept that they found particularly interesting. Whether the public agrees with them, well, nobody really knows, and anyone who tells you otherwise is blowing smoke out of their rear end.

Nobody knows what drives the massive successes. For every Harry Potter, there were already many books like it. How many large scale epics fantasy novels were there already when Brandon Sanderson took off? How many psychological thrillers before The Girl On The Train? A lot of these types of books were not particularly unique, it's just that they happened to catch a vibe and a lot of people caught on.

And to hear the publishers admit that they also have no idea what causes this was shocking to many.

How can these publishers who have done this for many years not to know what they're doing?

But for me, and probably many others, it was just a great vindication of what we already knew. That this industry is completely random. You can't game this type of success. It is extremely hard to predict whether a new project will do well, and this is why so many franchises keep rehashing old things or keep adding to series because they know there is an audience for that particular thing.

But what does all this mean for a beginning author who has just got one book and is asking the question of how many books do you need to be successful?

Well I think it shows that expecting that books will take off if you follow certain rules is just a waste of time and not a productive use of your time and energy.

There will be people out there who are saying that this is terribly defeatist, and they want to stay positive because positivity wins the world, and I don't think so.

I think it pays to be realistic.

I'm starting off with the proposition that you are unlikely to ever see any kind of really huge success. Instead, you should spend the energy and time you would spend worrying about mega-success on building a catalogue that earns you more than you spend while having fun.

So if you have only one book out, you obviously haven't got enough books. Get beavering.

But if you have a number of series out, and at least some of those are complete or have more than three books in them, they're all in the same genre, and they're all branded well, then the issue becomes much more about selling those books and increasing your audience. It becomes about finding where your readers are. If you keep banging your head against the same wall, like trying to break into the Amazon top 100, step out of it and try something new. Your books might catch a completely different reception on the different platforms. There are also fundraising projects you could try like Kickstarter or Patreon. Change up your advertising, find authors to cross-promote with, the options are legion.

So in the end, the question of how many books it takes to see success is one that no one can answer. We all knew that, right?

It is also a question that's not helpful, that is like literally due to frustration. Like, I'm in a prison, how many more years of this?

A better question would be, am I enjoying this?

Making more money than you earn is very important to your enjoyment, and maybe look at either your expenditure or look at the way and the places you are marketing your books.

Be bold. If you're spending a certain amount of money on a platform and you feel that it isn't really getting you anywhere and you also feel that you can't stop because otherwise you'd sell even less, be bold and just cut those ads to see what happens.

Regroup. Try something different.

Your definition of success also needs to be tied up with your definition of enjoyment. You can be successful while also not being a full-time writer. Writing is a terribly isolating experience, you might enjoy your day job, you might need the money, and you might also like the security it offers you. There is nothing wrong with being successful while also being employed in the workforce. I know many writers, especially traditional writers, who have jobs.

Define what you want out of your writing. Define what success means to you personally. Keep other people's opinions out of that equation. Be realistic, because if you're inflating your expectations, the further you inflate them, the harder the bang when the balloon bursts.

This is a hard business, nobody knows what they're doing, not even Penguin Random House, and personal satisfaction of the job is the most important thing. Without it, you can't do anything else. How many books does it take you do that?

Well, if you like being a writer, that question is irrelevant, because you will always write another book and start something new. That is just the nature of it. Don't worry about how fast these books are published. It is about your fans waiting for those books, and they will wait however long it takes you to produce them. They do not really care if you don't write a book a month. They care when there is a book in their favourite series, and they will easily wait a year for that.

So my answer to the question is that it's not productive to ask the question in the first place. You've got to find out a way to enjoy what you're doing and then keep doing that while learning about your audience and the best way to market your books.

INDIE WRITER UNBOXED

CHAPTER 116
THIS IS A SECTION FROM MY HEART

THE RUSH OF EXCITEMENT IS OVER.

You've published a book, and you're working on the next. Maybe you've published a number of books. They might be selling fine (what "fine" means will depend on the individual), or you might be unhappy with sales.

You are now a self-published author. Your books are out there for all to see.

But inevitably questions of doubt rear their ugly heads: is this all there is? Do I really have to spend so much time marketing? Is it meant to be so hard? What's next? How do I advance my career? How do I even make a career out of this when my books don't sell as much as I'd like to? How do I get out of this rut?

Don't worry, this section is for you!

In this section, we will join four writers who are just like you, and follow them through their trials and tribulations as they learn to cope with life as self-published author.

So what sort of project is this?

In 2017, I published *Self-publishing Unboxed*, *Mailing Lists Unboxed* and *Going Wide Unboxed*. I always had thoughts about a fourth part, one that took a holistic look at what goes on in a writer's career post-publishing. It would be a project that attempted to make sense of the cycle of elations and frustrations, the ups and downs you can only understand once you've published.

Many self-publishers and their communities focus on targeted, practical subjects that you can act on immediately. A lot of these projects are incredibly short-term, concerned only with immediate profits or gains. To be honest, this is the entire nature of the industry. Fed up with waiting for someone else to take months (or years) to decide about their books, writers take matters into their own hands. Of course they're a little impatient.

When you're wondering what to do for a book launch, you don't exactly feel like thinking about the things you do now that can influence your career next year. You want an easy path to as many sales as possible and you want it now.

Not that I'm immune to the short-term trend.

We're consumed by publishing schedules, deadlines, return on investment and mailing lists. It's about efficiency. We like that. Solving problems is our thing. Hands on is the way we like to do our business.

But sometimes, it's worth taking a step back and thinking: where is this all going? Am I on the main line or the sidetrack? Am I making the type of progress I want to make, and what is this life doing to me, to my finances and my happiness?

So this is about you, the writer, and all the different ways you can tackle your progress—or lack thereof. It's a project that discusses the options from the point of view of the person who has to do all of it: you.

Because the most important ingredient in your writing career is your ability to keep writing books.

The path you take in your career is a reflection of your personality, your writing speed, the way you like promoting, the way you interact with readers and many other factors related to writing or to your life in general.

Do you want to be full-time but it seems forever out of reach? Did you go full-time, but are you not happy? Do you suffer from crippling self-doubt? Do you feel burnt out with the ever-increasing pressure to produce books at a faster and faster pace? Or do you feel that everyone else seems to have more luck and better sales than you? Do you worry that making money seems to become harder every day? Do you feel you can't keep up? Did you have success early on but your sales are slipping every day?

THIS IS A SECTION FROM MY HEART

If you current situation makes you unhappy, it's time to reconsider your processes and habits. You need to look at yourself and decide what sort of career you want. You need to cut out a new space for yourself. Most importantly, you will need to discard some of your activities that cause stress or that don't deliver results.

You may need to re-examine your definition of success.

Not looking after your emotional stability or trying too desperately to keep up with the Joneses can send you down nasty rabbit holes, where you will meet with the many different ways in which you can sabotage your career. Self-doubt, self-rejection, envy are all emotional states that can seriously affect your ability to write, as well as damaging your general happiness.

Sitting down for hours at the computer can be quite detrimental to your health.

When all those things—your workspace, your financial security, your home space, your mental space—are not aligned, your productivity drops and your morale falls.

This section is about how to navigate the right space, and how to determine whether something is or isn't going to work for you. It is about how to avoid difficult situations and how to keep yourself happy and writing.

It's a section I've written because I've lived many of the situations or have seen them happen, time and time again, in front of my eyes.

So let's dive in.

CHAPTER 117
IN WHICH I RAIN ON YOUR PARADE

I don't like being a Negative Nelly. That said, some things about writing careers need to be talked about. The self-published writing community is one of great positivity. It's full of can-do people with plans and hopes. The sky is the limit; the world is your oyster. That sort of thing.

No more gatekeepers. We can be our own boss. We don't need to conform to publishers' narrow definitions of genre or wait for their OK.

It's liberating.

It's exciting.

But it can also be scary and depressing.

It's not going to be an easy ride for everyone.

It's probably not even going to be an easy ride for most people.

Yet those negative things can be kind of taboo in the community. No sales? Easy. Change your cover; change your blurb! Run some ads; write another book. Those are all things you can do. But the truth is that it's unlikely to have the desired effect. And what then? You spent a lot of money ordering new covers for your books and pinning your hopes on a rebranding, but they still don't sell in great numbers.

So in the next few chapters, I'll go on being a Negative Nelly for just a bit. It's all in the name of tough love and managing expectations. And a little tough love never hurt anyone.

IN WHICH I RAIN ON YOUR PARADE

I will spend the next four chapters raining on your parade, so that I can get the raining over with and can talk about what to do about these issues later.

It's now time to meet our four imaginary writers to illustrate a couple of bad places you can find yourself in after having written a few books. Likely, you'll find a bit of all four writers in your own situation.

A note: these people don't exist. I've cobbled them together from writers I've met in the real world. They're not real people, but they might as well be.

CHAPTER 118
TOM: UNICORNS FARTING RAINBOWS

Tom (62) has been reading his chosen genre for a long time, and has been writing for quite a long time, too. He submitted to a few agents and magazines years ago, even got some encouraging rejections, but has never sold anything.

Tom feels disillusioned with the state of current publishing, being unable to find any books he likes on the shelves of recently published books. So he has decided to write those books himself.

Tom writes Science Fiction.

Tom is semi-retired. He is a trained chemical engineer, has worked for a long time, and is confident in his abilities.

After his wife Helena was diagnosed with a debilitating illness that's slowly killing her, he took a redundancy package to enable him to look after her. But since that's not a full-time occupation, he's been motivated to do something about his long-held dream to write.

He chose to self-publish this time, because he read about other people making good money doing it.

Tom has published four books. Because Tom is a thorough fellow, he read up on publishing before he pushed the button, and he had his books edited and supplied them with nice covers. His books are even in a series: three in one series and one book in the next series.

Except the books don't sell very well. Early on, he sold a few hundred copies of the first book, less than half of that of the second book, and less again of the third. For a beginner, this is actually quite admirable. He must be doing something right. But Tom is not really happy.

So he did the right thing and started another series. To his dismay, the first book of that series sells even worse.

What gives?

He's done all the right things, and look at his books! They're so much better than the stuff that inhabits the top 100. The fellow who ran a workshop that Tom attended before publishing told the students that all you needed to do was make sure you put out a quality product. He did that, and now the books are ranking in the telephone numbers.

He doesn't get it. They're all just selling unicorns farting rainbows.

Tom hates marketing because none of his ads ever seem to work when he tries. He detests book spam.

He doesn't like spending money. He has a website which he built himself, doesn't like newsletters, although he's got one which he uses infrequently, because people don't really seem to connect with him there.

He feels dejected and reluctant to continue his second series, and even more reluctant to start something new. He knows the books are good because he's got good reviews, and cream should rise to the top, right?

CHAPTER 119
EMILY: LET ME OFF THE HAMSTER WHEEL

EMILY (32) IS A WRITER OF COSY MYSTERIES AND PARANORMAL ROMANCE.

She's newly divorced, without children. When she found herself without work, she started writing.

Her first cosy mystery book sold really well by a kind of fluke, because she'd never written anything before, so she wrote a second book in the series, that also sold really well, so she wrote a third book and then her series really took off. After six books, she was heartily sick of the series. There was nothing more to tell.

So she started another series, which seemed to do fine for a while.

Emily noticed that each time she released a new book, her sales would jump, so the answer was obviously to write more. She followed some productivity courses to the point where she could comfortably write a new book every couple of weeks.

Emily doesn't market much, because she doesn't have the time for that. Besides, bringing out a new book is the best marketing, right?

But it's starting to catch up with her. She's running out of ideas, she feels like she's repeating herself and, if that wasn't bad enough, her sales per book keep dropping. With fifty books, she is now earning the same as she did with twenty-five.

Should she change tack?

She can write quickly, so she tried a different genre, paranormal romance, under a pen name. Emily can write, so the sales were encouraging at first, but then tailed off. Then she discovered that having two pen names means doing two lots of keeping up with everything. The obvious route seemed to let someone else take over one of the pen names as ghostwriter or collaborator. That worked for a while, but Emily still needs to generate the ideas. And she feels she is fast heading for that wall where either she's going to run out of ideas or the amount of work she has to do is going to put her in hospital.

She can't write any faster. In fact, she would love to write a bit slower. She would like to write in a different genre, but her fans keep asking her for books in the same series, including the series she now hates so much she can't stand the look of it. In fact, every time she opens those books, she cringes with the clunky prose and overall terrible writing.

Emily lost the enjoyment of writing, and she wants to find it. She wants her life back, where she could do other things at night, take time off and, heavens, even go on a date.

She wants off the hamster wheel.

CHAPTER 120
JACK: FEEDING THE BEAST

Jack (35) was trained as a graphic designer and worked for a web design company for a while before quitting his job when his third book sold really well.

He writes a couple of books a year. He writes crime fiction and mysteries.

Early in his career, he sold two books to a medium-sized press, but his other books are all self-published.

Jack has a successful crime series, which is not finished, and is working on a police procedural series, also not finished. He also has some standalone books, a psychological thriller and two spy thrillers, and his earlier work with the publisher is detective fiction. He has since managed to get his rights back for these books.

So he has a decent stable of books, even if they're disjointed.

Through some fluke, his third book—the police procedural—sold really well, but it didn't spill over to his other books as much as he hoped. And the time when you can just publish a book and have it sell well is over.

Jack understands that in order to make money, you have to spend money. He got involved in pay-per-click ads early, and he considers himself quite good at them.

The problem is, the cost keeps increasing. He's spending 50 cents out of every dollar earned in advertising, which, when combined with the production cost per book, doesn't leave him much room. His sales might be decent, but he's spending more and more on ads, leaving him with less and less income.

He's also spending more time looking after his ads. At one stage, he paid someone else to do it, but that also grew too expensive, so he's gone back to doing it himself, which gives him less time to write. Meanwhile, readers keep asking him for the next book in those series he plans to write and some he doesn't.

Jack is fearful that his costs will keep going up and his income won't keep pace. He's worried about the time he spends marketing, but he's afraid that if he does less, his sales will collapse.

Jack lives with his partner, Tony, who has a low-paying job. Between the two, they can pay for the rent of their reasonably upmarket apartment, maintain their old car, and pay all the bills. But there is no money for extras, including the dog they dearly want.

CHAPTER 121
LUCY: READY TO QUIT

Lucy (45) has written a number of books, some of which have sold quite well. She writes romance and has written both historical and contemporary romance.

She's not a huge seller, but makes a decent middle-income wage.

She is a very social person, who runs a reader group on Facebook with an active community focus.

Lucy also has a lot of interests and she runs a Facebook group for animal rights activists. In this capacity, she has clashed with a few people, and now she is convinced that those people are trying, in her words, to "tear her down" by leaving one-star reviews on her books. She has complained to Amazon numerous times, and has been ignored. After this happened, she asked her readers to support her. Then another writer in one of her groups told her she was seeing fairies, and now her friend group is split, and people are arguing with each other.

On top of that, her husband is making snide remarks about the time she spends writing, even though he likes the money she brings in.

All this is affecting her ability to write. She feels like she is continuously putting out fires and she is simply not enjoying it anymore. This seeps through in her writing, and the last book wasn't as well received as the one before that. She's still making money, but the time she spends stalking reviewers on Amazon pages and Facebook groups makes her sick.

Sooner or later, she'll come to a public page where someone will have called her a hack and a fraud. She never took any formal writing training, so she is a fraud, but she wonders why people need to be so mean and punish her through her books. Don't they understand that she works hard, and didn't their mothers tell them: If you can't say anything nice, then say nothing at all?

Lucy lives with her husband Sam and has two school-aged girls. She hasn't worked for about ten years, and started writing because she needed something to do with herself.

CHAPTER 122
WHAT IS SUCCESS ANYWAY?

Early on in his career, Tom did an online course by a well-known self-published writer whose name is Luke.

Attached to the course was a Facebook group in which a couple of other writers were vocal. They all seemed very knowledgeable and businesslike, and all sold very well. They talked about hiring assistants and going to events overseas.

Tom saw this as an encouragement for what he could achieve with his hard work. He saw "do this and this and then you will earn this much". He was not afraid of a bit of work, and he did the work.

He hired an editor and cover designer who both came with recommendations and made sure his books looked good.

But they still didn't sell half as well as the books of those writers.

He put the question why to the group.

Some people talked about the covers. They looked nice, they said, but how well did they reflect the genre?

Other people talked about the blurbs. They were a bit dry, they said. There wasn't a character to sympathise with.

The books are old-style science fiction, Tom replied, it's about the ideas.

One person said it was all down to luck. The moment you put out a book, you have very little control over how well—or how poorly—it will sell.

And a whole bunch of people jumped onto that commenter to say how wrong that was. That if only Tom had a big mailing list and this dreadful thing called an *audience* or, even more dreadful, a *platform*, he'd have no trouble selling his books. He just needed to find his readers.

But Tom doesn't have a big audience. In fact, he doesn't really like mailing lists and abhors social media.

He's not into list-swapping or giving free books away, because he wants his fans to be genuine, except he can see that if no one reads his books, there won't be any fans.

Then one writer pointed out that Tom's books had sold a few hundred copies, and that this was much better than hers had sold, and she pointed Tom to a reasonably recent survey by Freebooksy, which showed that the vast majority of authors who earn six figures a year have more than thirty books.

This put things in perspective for him.

Those writers who were so vocal in the group, being helpful about sharing their sales and methods? They were flukes.

Most group members were the silent majority, neither as successful nor as keen to talk about their (lack of) success. Tom is, in fact, perfectly normal.

He feels a bit stupid, because he should have known that. Every so often, articles come out saying how little the average author makes. Self-publishing shortens the odds somewhat, but that is because of the lack of layers and layers of middlemen taking their slice out of a book's cover price.

Even when Luke started the course, he said that it was a hard industry and that if you wanted to be certain about making money and making it quickly, you should take a paid job.

After all the other things he talked about, like his success and the success of his friends, the reality check was so easy to forget. The talk was so tempting. Write a book, give it the professional treatment and watch the cash roll in.

You must spend money to make money.

If only it really were that simple.

But first maybe Tom needs to examine his definition of success. What does he need and want, and what is his dream?

Some people consider success as simply having published a book.

Many people never finish the book they started, so it's a kind of success, but Tom thinks that's lame. There must be a more ambitious definition.

Having a bestseller is success. That's Tom's dream: being able to say that a book was a #1 bestseller or made it to the USA Today bestseller list, even if a lot of people say readers don't care that much about those things.

But Luke also said that getting a bestseller is a fluke, especially very early in your career. He said it was much better to produce a number of books that sell at a consistent level that respond well to advertising and slowly chip away at this whole success thing than to have a flash-in-the-pan and then be at a loss as to how to repeat it.

But Tom glossed over all those words that Luke said in the course. He heard, "You can be a bestseller," and forgot about the "can" part. Looking back on it, it's almost amusing how he fell for this clever advertising to sell the course. It was useful, to be sure, but the course was still being sold to him with the promise of success. It taught him tricks of the trade. About success, it said little.

What Tom really wants is some extra money for him and Helena to visit Helena's brother before she becomes too ill to travel. He will settle for that as a short-term goal.

Other people may want to quit their job and some seek to supplement their income. Some may simply want a little extra on top of a pension. For some people, publishing is not about money at all.

However, Tom now understands that he has poor control over how well his books sell and how they rank, so he should quit feeling bad about the writers whose books do better than his. Of course it's easier said than done.

He would love to earn some money and he has a dreadful time constraint.

Tom would be much happier if he took measuring success in small, month-by-month steps. Has he earned back the cost of producing the books yet?

When he has, he might look at the next step: can he afford to pay for covers for his new series in advance? Does he have the money to take a short course, attend a workshop or con, or ask advice from an advertising expert?

Tom should try to budget a percentage of his income on ads. He makes a few hundred dollars a month, but even if he only makes $40, he might spend $10 on a promotion. He can spend it on a smaller site or save it for something bigger.

But he can also try to reduce his spending. If I were him, I'd keep the editor, but rather than go with the really expensive cover designer, I'd look for someone who still does really nice work but is a bit cheaper.

If he and his wife were younger and healthy, he might also have liked to move to a cheaper place. Why do you think that quite a few writers live in rural areas or low-cost countries? Why do you think people sell their houses and decide to live cheaply for a year?

You can control your expenses much more than you can control your sales.

You can budget yourself into being a full-time author.

Unfortunately, that's not a viable option for Tom and, besides, he has some savings and only needs to bridge three years until he can access his retirement income. He's not terribly worried about surviving.

But he feels like he's treading water, and time is ticking.

CHAPTER 123
KEEP LEARNING

JACK IS A PERFECT EXAMPLE OF HOW MUCH A CAREER IS A MOVING TARGET.

He started off as a graphic-design professional, got a deal from a publisher, self-published, and sold really well for a while before moving into heavy advertising.

Jack knows that he has to keep learning or he will grow stale, and before he knows it he will have been left behind by everyone else.

Learning involves a good amount of keeping track of methods to write better stories. Learning also involves the latest trends in your genre and the most effective marketing methods.

He's a member of the same Facebook group as Tom, and he sees a comment by Tom that disturbs him.

Tom says about learning marketing: Marketing is all rubbish. It doesn't work for my books anyway.

Jack challenges him to state what he's tried and what he's been learning.

A good book markets itself, Tom says.

Yes, if only that were true. Jack pulls up an example of a book everyone can see has issues that is better-ranked than Tom's. That's marketing right there, he says, and goes on: I'd hate to know how much these people spend on ads. You can absolutely advertise your book to rank well, at least for a short period. You only need to learn how.

An intense discussion ensues.

Jack says:

The more you get into commercial publishing, the more you will understand that even writing craft and marketing are intertwined.

The type of story you tell, the type of sentences you use, the type of point-of-view character you choose, will influence major choices such as what genre you put your book in, and that determines how well you can market it.

But, Tom says, those genres are just rubbish perpetuated by publishers. I'm free of that. You can't classify my books.

And Jack says:

Nope, Tom, mate, you write science fiction, and I don't think you understand the concept of genre as shorthand for a type of book readers want to read.

Readers don't want to have to read the blurb to see what they're getting. Neither do readers want to think they're getting a space opera, only to find that the story is a family drama with a very strong literary bent.

Your craft and familiarity with other books in your genre is of vital importance. Craft is storytelling, and it ties in with genre, including established tropes you can break, and ones you can't without upsetting readers in your genre.

You have to learn to let your readers know that your story is kind-of the same as one they've read before, but different. It's not as easy as it sounds.

At this point someone makes a very cutting remark about Jack's scatter-shot catalogue that gets deleted by the group's moderators, because it's a "personal attack" and Jack had not asked for advice.

But he gets angry anyway, because the maker of the remark really doesn't know anything about his situation, about how much time he spends researching his books and improving his writing. He's taking his career seriously, and he sells better than the upstart writer, so what does he know?

But the remark burrows under his skin. He *knows* that he should write book 2 and 3 in the series of the book that still sells well. But, he says, you have to consider your ability to keep producing books at a rate that is comfortable for you, and find a way to measure success that is not going to leave you feeling depressed.

At this point, he leaves the discussion, because he has work to do, and doesn't want to draw his own work further into the discussion.

All this talk about not feeling depressed is not easy, Emily says. The rest of the publishers are moving at a ridiculous speed. How can you keep up when groups of people are publishing a book a week?

A book a week? That's ridiculous, says Tom.

Others confirm that there are groups of people doing just that, and not just in romance either.

Lucy says: The answer is you can't keep up, but you can find your own audience.

She is very good at that. Her readers are loyal, even if they sometimes also make her feel stressed out.

Talk to the readers, she says. Send your fans a survey to ask them what they want. Give them a choice of two books to download, by other writers if necessary, and see what they choose. And then go and write in that subgenre.

This makes Tom feel more depressed, because he doesn't want to talk to anyone. He just sends new releases to his list—if he remembers.

Emily doesn't even have a list, so she feels even more depressed. Yet something twigs with her. She really doesn't know much about the people who read her books. Not that she needs to know exactly who they are, but it would be useful to know where they hang out. For example, she hears that Facebook attracts mostly older folk today and that the young crowd are all on Instagram. Do her books appeal to older or younger people? She's always assumed she was writing for "people like me" but she could be completely wrong about that.

Before signing off for the day, she makes a note that she puts on the pin board on the wall above her desk. She hasn't used the board in ages. It still displays some pieces of paper with plans for books she published years ago and outlines for other books she never ended up writing.

On the bright yellow note, she writes KEEP LEARNING, with underneath the points: craft, advertising, mailing list, and her bugbear: research.

She never does enough research. There just isn't the time, and cosy mysteries are not known for their factual correctness. It's all about the story, right?

But it does bug her that sometimes reviewers find issues that she really should have checked. Peanuts grow under the ground, not on branches. Even in her paranormal romance—a genre where everything is made up—she managed to screw up the moon cycle. That was embarrassing. If you write about werewolves, you should know about the moon phases.

Someone else said something to her the other day. He said: if they see something that annoys them, most people will just close the book and never say anything. The ones who write reviews are only a small percentage.

What if her flubbing is catching up with her? It was easy when she started, because her first book caught the wind. But now there may be other, newer, less formulaic and overall better-researched books for readers to buy.

Tom is pretty certain that he's already done a lot of learning about his subject and his time submitting to traditional presses has prepared him well for writing. He just needs to learn how to market.

Jack only feels he needs to learn how not to put his foot in it. He's a real Jack: Jack of all trades, master of none. Except maybe advertising, but without a good product to sell, advertising is going to be extremely expensive. Maybe that's what's wrong with his books. They plain suck.

CHAPTER 124
EVERYTHING GOES WRONG

After that embarrassing discussion, Jack is annoyed with himself. He really needs to write books, not faff around in Facebook groups.

But after seeing off Tony to his boring menial job, he sits around staring at his screen. He ignores his ads. He makes coffee, he does the washing, makes more coffee, decides they need milk and goes to the shops and before he knows it, only an hour remains before he expects Tony to come back.

He knows he needs to write more books, but it's just so easy to set up a few ads. But those ads deliver an ever-thinner margin and he's not sure how long they will continue to be successful. His rankings are slipping all the time. It's not a long-term strategy. He needs to write something new.

So he goes back to the group.

He writes: For writers who write more than four books a year: how do you do it?

This is right up Emily's alley. Even though she's sick of writing so many books, she has some advice.

Plan your books, she says.

Jack is not a planner.

I wasn't a planner either, she says, but if you want to increase your production, you need to plan, take it from me.

OK, he wants to know: how detailed?

She says that she writes a short paragraph for each chapter and then fills it in. She says she also knows people who make more detailed outlines.

Jack struggles with an outline for the next hour. He's never outlined, hated writing a synopsis for his traditionally published books, and he knows that when he's writing the story, it will go in directions that are irrelevant to the outline. Writing the outline feels like a giant waste of time. But he completes it anyway, and hates it, so he writes another, which he also hates.

When Tony comes home, tired from filling shelves, Jack is about ready to fling his computer out the window.

Tom has heard Jack's comments that learning about the competition is part of marketing. He has his next book mapped out, but he doesn't want to start writing it for fear that he's wasting his time.

So he spends the day looking at the Amazon top 100 in Science Fiction. He reads through the Look Inside samples of a lot of the books and hates most of them. They're neither well-written nor interesting. He does find some books to buy, but none of them are written by his self-published colleagues.

Then it's time to take Helena to a medical appointment. In the car, he talks about his frustration. He doesn't like the fiction that's being published.

She says, "You always said that the moment you stopped enjoying your job, you'd retire."

That's true. He had said that, and in the end the choice had been made for him.

He asks her why she brings this up.

Helena says, "It seems to me that if you don't enjoy what you're trying to write, maybe you need to write something else. You can't change those books that are in the top 100. If you want to be there, you need to write in that style, or whatever those writers are doing, or if you really hate today's science fiction so much, write something else."

That shakes him, because that's not what he means at all. He doesn't hate science fiction; he just . . . doesn't like what's being published.

But even he and Jack are doing better than Lucy.

She is supposed to be writing a new book, but two months ago, she agreed to organise a giveaway and now she needs to set it all up and communicate with the writers who are taking part.

Have you ever tried organising a group of writers? It's like herding cats. And some of them are so rude. She's still having an argument with this woman whose book she rejected for the giveaway, because the cover was amateurish and ugly. Lucy told her she'd be accepted next time if she got a more professional cover, but the woman is complaining about not having money and Lucy discriminating against her.

So while arguing with this woman, Lucy emails the other writers, collects the money for the prize, sets up the web page, and then needs to get her children from school. They've run out of bread so she needs to get that as well, even if the shops are on the way back home for her husband, and they won't need the bread until tomorrow morning. She asked him once before, and he was most miffed.

When she comes back, there is another whiny email from the slighted woman—seriously why don't these people get a life?—and now someone has left a one-star review on her best-selling book.

It's only one line and says, "Couldn't get into it." That is surely another one of those troll reviews. It doesn't even come from a verified purchase, so it's just someone who read the sample online. Why do people do this?

Emily sits in her living room at the dining table. She can sit there because no one else uses it, and she doesn't need to cook because no one is eating at home, except her cat.

She is in the middle of her most recent book, and she hates it. From having written so many books, she knows it's common to hate every book when you're in that horrible middle. Usually it all gets resolved at the end.

But this time, she feels different. The story feels stale. It feels like she has written this book before. It feels like the readers also know this, and they're deserting her.

Emily checks her sales figures once a day, and when she finally does that, her sales are slightly better than yesterday. Still not a figure she is happy with, even though her last release was two weeks ago.

She picks up the cat and carries him to the window. From her third floor apartment, she can see into the street and into a cafe and fruit and veg shop across the road.

A couple walks hand in hand over the footpath. A bus stops, letting out a few people in business clothing.

Emily feels detached. She made her 5000 words for today, but it no longer feels fresh, or even like an achievement. She doesn't understand why people have so much trouble writing that much. It's easy. It's the rest that she has trouble with.

CHAPTER 125
NEVER MIND THE JONESES

Lucy has been worrying about that review all during dinner. Her book has a 4.7 star average and she doesn't want that to go down any further. She's sure that the person who posted the latest review belongs to a group of trolls that's been bothering her in her animal activist group.

So after dinner, she sifts through a few thousand members of that group to see if she can find anyone she disagreed with recently.

At any rate, she files a complaint with Amazon, but knows—having complained before—that they never do anything. She doesn't understand why not. It's clear this person never even read the book. Going back through their reviews, Lucy can see that the reviewer has been posting lots of short reviews, most of them one or two stars.

She asks for advice from the writer group.

There is nothing you can do, they say.

One or two people even suggest that she should forget about it and stop looking at her reviews.

How can you just conclude this is a troll? Another writer asks. I can't see anything that points that way.

But she didn't even read the book, Lucy says.

They reply: people write these reviews all the time. People are entitled to say what they want about your book. You can't stop them.

Lucy asks: So you think I should just let them abuse me? I won't stand for it.

It's not abuse. It's the reviewer's right to say this, a number of members tell her.

But it's unfair, Lucy says.

Yes, if they haven't read the book, it is, says one of the bestselling authors in the group. But I try not to let it affect me, because if I do, the reviewer wins, because I spend my time obsessing about their words and not writing. I won't allow them to have that power over me.

And that, finally, is something that strikes home. In the last few days, Lucy has done little except worry about reviews and trolls and keeping all the people in that giveaway she's running happy. She should be writing.

Jack is watching the discussion in the group. In another browser tab, he's checking his ranking, as he has done a few dozen times today.

Tony can see from Jack's face that the news isn't good.

Jack feels ashamed to tell his partner that his expensive ads are failing, but Tony isn't dumb.

He tells Jack: I don't really care what ranking your books are at.

Ranking is money, Jack says, without taking his eyes off the screen.

Tony holds a cup of coffee in between Jack's face and the computer.

No, he says. Money in the bank is money. Ranking is comparing yourself with other people. If you were second to the best crime writer in the world —what is the dude's name again?—you'd gladly be second. It wouldn't matter. What matters is what they put in your bank account.

Jack insists: But that's related to rank.

It stresses you out, Tony says. I don't like that; it makes you grumpy. Like it's so important that some so-and-so all the way in Canada ranked better than you. Who cares?

But Jack cares. He knows that people out there are watching him. People from his days of traditional publishing, who said that self-publishing would finish his career. People who would gloat over every point his rank slips as a way to prove that his writing sucks and he's a hack.

But he knows there is no point in this race.

No matter how well he does, there is always someone who does better. Ranking is a snapshot in time, and while he can see his own ranking at all times, the people around him can't, and who these people are changes all the time. Another writer may have had a successful release or a big mailing list, and this is why their book suddenly surged past Jack's. Or they may have had a successful ad campaign.

He doesn't know what goes on in these writers' lives, and therefore it's pointless to worry about it. The only one who worries is him. He shouldn't seek approval from those writers who disapproved of his step to self-publish. He will never get it, even if deep in their hearts they're jealous that he was able to give up his job and they're still struggling to make more than a few hundred dollars per year.

It's not about them. It's about him.

He finally shuts down the computer and watches a movie with Tony.

CHAPTER 126
MARKETING THAT'S RIGHT FOR YOU

Tom started asking in the author Facebook group about marketing. Soon, it was clear to him that the other group members thought his questions ranged from ignorant to clueless. Never having done any marketing, he was just not familiar with the lingo.

A lot of people jumped on him with suggestions even he could see were out of his league. When he said so, a helpful person in the group said that older writers needed simpler solutions because they couldn't be expected to be up to speed with all the technology. Tom replied that he was happy to face her off in the use of mathematical software any time. And then Emily jumped in to defend Tom, because she felt just as clueless and she was young, and it was absolutely unfair to make the judgement that old equals technologically challenged. It almost broke out into a flame war.

Isn't the internet wonderful?

Fortunately, one of the moderators came up with the idea for the group to tailor marketing plans to specific writers. First, the group went about determining all the different types of marketing. Tom copies everything he learns into a single document:

Your book's listing: passive marketing

The best marketing starts with the book. If you don't have a book that looks attractive to the readers, they won't buy it.

Marketing starts with your book cover. Make sure it stands out, and make sure it communicates the genre and tone of the book.

Marketing is simply presenting your book in places where people are able to buy it.

This means that your listing at retailer sites is a form of marketing. More retailers equals more marketing.

It means that having your book in your email signature is a form of marketing. Even having an image in the header of your Facebook page that shows all your books is a form of marketing.

You want people to be familiar with what your book looks like so that when they feel like something new to read, and they happen to come across your book, they will be happy to give it a go.

You will want other writers to be familiar with your books, so that when they have a lull in their publishing schedule, they might be able to suggest that their readers try your books.

You want to make sure that when a reader gets to the end of your book, they find a link on what you want them to do next. In most cases this will be to buy the next book.

These are all very important tools for marketing your book. All of them are passive ways of marketing and every author should do them.

By this point you haven't spent a cent on ad sites. It is entirely possible to do successful marketing without buying a single ad.

Free books: passive marketing

Free books are an excellent way of advertising your catalogue. If you have written a number of books, make sure that you use a permafree book at least some of the time.

Much has been said recently about the supposed effectiveness of free books. People are saying it doesn't work any more, and that the readers are just freebie seekers and only want books for free. People will say that we're training readers that all books should be free and are devaluing fiction.

But how is that going to work, when all you ever make free is your first book, it ends in a cliffhanger, and there are two more books in your series?

The people who want to read the rest of the series will buy the other books.

This is a form of advertising that doesn't cost you anything, but you will need to put some effort into it.

You can just make your book free on all retailers, sit back and do nothing.

At first you get a number of downloads, but this starts to peter off very quickly.

You have to advertise.

You can do this by entering promotions, by buying ads, most specifically on the list sites like Freebooksy, or you can use pay-per-click ads, and some people have been using these to great effect. You can also cross-promote free books of other authors (and they promote yours).

Free book bundles

It can be quite effective to bundle your first-in-series free book with a number of other free books from other authors and make it a box set. These big bundles get more attention, because they represent great value to the reader, and a number of authors work together to promote the title.

It also has the effect of populating the strip of also-boughts on your book pages with the books by those other authors (and vice-versa), in which case you will be linked for more free cross-promotion. If one author in the collection has a successful release, everyone else benefits. It goes without saying that you need to carefully select the other authors. These opportunities exist in closed-door Facebook groups and amongst groups of friends. If you can't find a bundle to join, start your own. Get a couple of authors with similar books, get a nice cover and join all the books into a collection with Vellum (Tom makes a note: find out what Vellum is, because like a true geek, he hand-codes his own books, but doesn't know where to start with bundles). Upload and make it free everywhere. Then ask all participating authors to post to their audience staggered across the first few weeks. Buy some ads. Put it on Facebook and ask people to repost it.

Social media

You should set up an author page, and post there regularly. You can also get your fellow authors to like and share your posts. The constant struggle with many social media outlets is visibility. It will be reduced unless you get engagement on your posts. Learn to use hashtags for searchability.

Posting in Facebook promotional groups is generally pointless. Most of those groups are filled with authors. However some people have found limited success advertising free books there. It doesn't cost anything, so why not?

But the downside is there may be better uses of your time.

Social media is not a priority. Do it when you enjoy it and you can see that it works. Otherwise, it's a waste of time.

Rented lists

These are websites that send links to free and discounted books to subscribers, where authors can pay an amount and have their books advertised to the site's audience.

The cost of taking part in these can range from free to a small amount of ten or fifteen dollars to hundreds. The cost will depend on the size of their list and the site's reputation.

The effect of a listing is limited to the day that the ad runs. But if you advertise the first book in a series, it's highly likely you will get further sales at a later stage.

Other than the limited duration, the disadvantages of using these lists repeatedly are that you can wear out the audience, that many of them aren't hugely effective, and that it may take quite a lot of time to keep making submissions.

Pay-per-click advertising

If you want to try pay-per-click advertising, it's probably a good idea to read up on it thoroughly before jumping in. It's possible to blow through a lot of money with not much to show for it. Sites like Facebook will eat your money very quickly if you give them half a chance.

You need to start conservatively and learn how to use the platform, where your audience is on it, and which are the most effective ad types.

Most of the courses and books mention that it is likely to cost some money before you have worked this out.

If you are not prepared to spend this money or time, you're better off not embarking on this type of advertising at all.

Tom doesn't like spending money, so he probably thinks this is not a good fit for him.

But someone suggests that he might be able to set up a couple of ads for very low budgets that keep running continuously. If he checks on the ads every few days, they can keep things ticking at a low level for a long time.

On Amazon, you will have to advertise a book, but on Facebook, you can advertise whatever you please. Some people suggest advertising free series starter books for people willing to sign up for an author mailing list. There are many different ways of using Facebook ads. Direct book sales is only one of them.

Pay-per-click advertising is a game of percentages. You don't earn big until you spend big.

Yeah, Tom is not sure that he has either the will or energy to do that right now.

In the end, Tom concludes that he should start with the passive advertising: make sure that his books are presented in the best possible way, and set up a mailing list (and actually use the list!) and optimise listings across all retailers. He can also see himself getting together with a group of authors to do something together. He might be able to find another author who has this magical Vellum thing.

Emily looks at Tom's document with a sense of dread, but if she really thinks about it, she can see herself buying some regular ads for her KDP Select free days (she should actually start using those!)

Jack and Lucy already do quite a lot of advertising, but they may still benefit from a regular re-jig to consider whether their current methods are still the best.

Since Jack was worried about the rising costs of pay-per-click advertising, he should probably change his strategy. Some of his audience may have shifted, or he might have burned them out.

Lucy might once have been happy with a lot of direct communication with her fans in Facebook groups, but she is feeling a bit vulnerable and fears that her books are being made a target. Maybe she can get some peace of mind with some simple paid ads.

CHAPTER 127
SOCIAL MEDIA: DO YOU HAVE TO?

When hearing the words "social media", Emily's courage sinks.

Not so long ago, she was searching for information about marketing online and she found an article that gave reasons why authors should have a Facebook page, and post something on the page every day, and "like" replies, because if you didn't do that, no one was going to see your posts. And do the same on Instagram and TikTok and…

And you had to be chatty and not talk about your books all the time.

It sounded all very sensible. After all, platforms like Facebook want their users to talk to each other, not be bombarded with quasi-ads.

But Emily doesn't "do" chatty, and she hates the idea of schmoozing fans because it's not her style.

The words social media are the subject of dread for her. She is an introvert, and the idea of selling herself on a platform where everyone can see it strikes fear into her heart.

She sees other writers go all out on social media. They download lists of must-dos on social media, and follow them religiously. TikTok videos at least three times a day, make two posts on Facebook, upload pictures of your book covers on Instagram, make boards for your books on Pinterest, and so on and so forth.

But do you know what?

None of it looks genuine. They're following a script, a checklist of things to do, that has been developed with someone else for a different purpose. Maybe the person who developed this list was a non-fiction author, or maybe the originator of the list was a marketing teacher who merely rattled off things you could try, and other people took the list as a must-do scenario.

Emily can never see this working for an author of fiction.

The people who developed those lists are not authors of fiction. They're people who sell courses on how to sell books. They like giving lists of actionable advice. The part of the advice that says, "Try these things," gets lost in translation.

They will say that you must be on Facebook or you must be active on TikTok, because that is important to them as a marketer of courses for authors.

So what should Emily really do?

Is it really necessary to do all that stuff?

Another writer, someone Emily respects a lot, says:

The thing that marketers forget about social media…

Is the word "social".

Social media has taken the position of the phone and letters as a way people communicate with each other. It's taken the position of magazines as a way to connect with people who share similar interests.

In some cases, you can sell things to these people, but the social aspect always comes first. It must be real, and it must be genuine. If it's not, it's better to make sure people understand that it's advertising: buy an ad.

If you feel forced when posting updates on social media, you are never going to sound genuine. Not only that, but nobody is going to want to follow you, because your updates read like automated garbage, and people are on social media to interact.

So if you consider which social media platforms you should be on, consider first which ones you want to be on. These are most likely the ones that you're on already and the ones you use as a social being.

If your answer is: I hate social media, then don't. Simple as that. It's all about your fiction anyway. If people want to buy it, they'll buy it because they want to read it, not because you bombarded them with spam on social media.

So, Emily wants to know, I don't have to do social media at all? Her sigh of relief is almost audible.

It's not quite that easy, people in the group say. Because readers will still look for you on social media, and if you're not going to be present there, where do you want them to find you?

Emily says: Um—how about only on Amazon?

Sure, an experienced writer tells her, but I heard you say you were unhappy with the direction your sales were taking. You have to do something.

Yes, she has to do something.

But Emily is quite certain that being active on social media is not going to be it. On the other hand, she can see that readers who like her books would want to know when the next book is going to be out, and they want to find this out from her. She puts "set up website, mailing list and Facebook page" on her to-do list.

Lucy is doing social media very well. She runs a number of very active Facebook groups. One of those is for her animal protection interest.

The other is a group of readers whom she has befriended over the years she's been writing. They include her beta readers and her most ardent fans. This group can only be accessed from the back of her books, and every time she has a new idea or she's starting on a new book she talks to her readers about it. The group is active and friendly.

If you're reading this book in some unimaginable future where Facebook no longer exists, don't worry, because something else will have replaced it. We humans like to talk to each other, and we will always find ways to do so. Facebook is forum software. There will be a replacement that is also forum software.

In the author group discussion, Lucy attributes much of her success to her reader group.

But, Tom asks, is Lucy marketing on Facebook?

It's true that her group of fans rushes out to buy her new book as soon as she publishes it. But she has not courted these people to be part of this group with the intent of selling to them. She runs the group as a service to her fans.

At this point, Jack gets a bit annoyed with Tom. Didn't he just read through the entire discussion where people outlined all the different kinds of active and passive marketing? Of course keeping up with your fans is marketing. Marketing is not just buying ads that you spray into the ether in a hopefully somewhat targeted way.

But the discussion circles back to Lucy's huge commitment to Facebook groups.

The focus of the second group she runs is very broad, and she doesn't mention her fiction often, although many people there will realise that she is an author and that her fiction represents her views on the subject.

The people in this group are a completely separate audience from her readers.

Well, that's not rocket science, you might say, and Lucy completely agrees with that.

But an author comes up with an example of another author who established a Facebook community about learning to write well. It became very popular, but the author was disappointed that the members of the group then didn't go on to buy his fiction. The question he raised was: can an author establish a community around anything other than variations of "buy my book" for people who will actually, you know, buy the books? And if not, why should writers start or take part in these communities?

It's about paying it forward, Lucy says. You can certainly sell to these people, but their primary interest is going to be the reason they joined the group. They want to be better writers, they want to market their own books, they want to know about this particular period in history or, in my case, they care about the well-being of animals. In short, they are not there because they want to read my books.

It's pretty hard to find an interest group where the population of people who join is directly related to your fiction. People don't like being marketed to on social media, except when it's clearly an ad, and many people don't even like those. They're on social media to be social. We all know Facebook groups that have been completely ruined by book spammers.

The only place where I can put up promotional material about my own fiction (and even then not all the time) is the group of fans I've built up who are there specifically for this reason. And at this point we circle back to the quality of and engagement with your fiction. Such fans are there because they read and liked your books.

In other words, trying to collect a huge social media following and expecting to sell to them before people have become fans of your fiction is putting the cart before the horse. And because, although the horse may be willing to push the cart, it will still require you to do a lot of steering and pulling to make sure it goes in the right direction. There are much better ways of doing this.

Be on social media because you like it. And if you don't, then don't.

Lucy admits to being an extrovert who is happiest when talking to other people, organising and directing stuff.

So, what is it that we can or should do on social media?

Apart from Lucy, none of our other writers have a huge presence on social media. Tom distrusts Facebook, but he doesn't mind Instagram because he follows two of his cousins who post pictures from their world travels there. Emily forgot that she already has a Facebook page for her fiction, which is indicative of how much she posts there. Jack has a Facebook page (because you need one to advertise on Facebook), but also doesn't do much there.

As self-professed haters of social media, what should Tom and Emily do about it?

Jack says:

Think about it from the perspective of a reader who has enjoyed your books. They may not be willing to sign up for a mailing list (because many people don't), but they still want to know when the next book is out. Of course they can sign up on Amazon, but not everyone buys there, or Bookbub, but not everyone even knows what that is. The Facebook site has pretty good SEO, so when a random reader types in your name (providing it's not John Smith) or your name and the title of your book, the sites that will come up are: your website (if you have a self-hosted one where your name is in the URL or title), Amazon (but they don't want that, because they already bought the book) and Facebook, if you have a page there, and any social media where you have an account where your name is in the bio.

So even if you never plan to do anything on these sites, at the very least open an account, make a Facebook page and make sure that your first post and/or bio mentions where people can contact you instead. Do the same at all major social media outlets.

It costs nothing.

And when Emily goes to her neglected Facebook page, she finds, to her great embarrassment, that readers have been trying to contact her there. One message is from a mother who tells her that her sixteen-year-old daughter went missing six months ago, and she found a copy of Emily's paranormal romance book on her desk in her room, tied with a pink ribbon, so she must have been enjoying it very much.

Now Emily feels extremely embarrassed.

Writing is not the one-way street she has been acting like it is. Your writing affects people, and you owe it to those people to give them an outlet to contact you, and also to respond to them.

She adds to her list: talk to at least one fan every day.

CHAPTER 128
YOU MUST WRITE MORE BOOKS

THROUGHOUT THE LIFETIME OF THE AUTHOR GROUP, THERE IS ONE PIECE OF advice that keeps coming back: if you want success, you must write more books.

Tom wants to know: how many, and is that always the answer?

Yes, it's a loaded question, because he doesn't really feel like writing more books that won't sell, and ever since Helena's health took a turn for the worse, he's spending a lot of time in the hospital. Frankly his mind isn't in the right place to spend so much time on something he isn't even sure will sell.

So he asks the question, but what he really wants to hear is: no, you don't need to write more books. You can fix the ones you have.

But the group crushes that thought pretty quickly. It's almost always true that more books is better, until it isn't.

When is it true?

In general, if you have few books, if you have series that are selling reasonably well, if you have a plan to use book 1 in a series in a giveaway or a free box set, or give it to subscribers to your mailing list, you should write more books as quickly as you can.

It's also true if you want to try another series, another pen name or a slightly different genre.

It is not true when you already have a lot of books and each new book you write does little to increase your overall income, or when you're sick of a series and hate the thought of it.

Tom says that the release of his last book did little to increase his income, and one of the group's bestselling authors came back pretty hard on this: Tom, mate, you have only four books. That's not a lot. The first three sold reasonably well, so the seed of something good is clearly there. The fourth book doesn't sell, because the cover says Book 1. Where is Book 2?

Emily is quiet during this discussion. She realises that she's running on the escalators in the wrong direction, putting out more and more books, while her overall income is staying the same at best.

So in her case, it's not so much about *more* books, it's about *what kind* of books will get her out of the rut. She wants books that keep selling for longer.

Jack says that the major difference between Tom and Emily is that Emily's books kind of accidentally discovered a market, and Tom's didn't.

But clearly the market is shifting away from the type of books Emily writes. She hasn't spent any time learning about her audience, and has no mailing list to speak of, so she has to start over from the very bottom. That is dispiriting and a shame, because Emily's books were well loved by the readers, if only she could follow to where these readers are.

Writing more books with more of the same isn't going to help Emily. She should step back and figure out a new direction, but writing more books will help Tom.

And with this remark, Jack again puts his foot into it. He's just so good at diagnosing other people's issues without ever following up on his own advice.

Let's look at Jack.

CHAPTER 129
COMPLETING THINGS

THE BEST WAY TO DESCRIBE JACK'S CATALOGUE OF BOOKS IS "SCATTERSHOT". He's written in a few genres, has some standalone work and unfinished series.

He's been pretty much like that all his life: flitting from one thing to the next. Jack of all trades, master of none.

Because he tends to shoot off at the mouth in the author group, he only has a few people he can trust with the truth. The bestselling author who started the group, Luke, is one of them.

Luke says: look, mate, it is hard to decide whether to continue something that's not doing well, but what does this say to readers? It says: this dude never finishes anything. Don't bother waiting for the next volume. In fact, why should they bother at all?

Luke is not known to mince his words.

Jack finds it hard to pick which series he should continue. He enjoys writing one series much more than the other, but it sells less and it's not as clear-cut in the genre.

Luke says: leaving series unfinished looks untidy and scattershot.

We all know the one or two authors who never seem to be able to finish anything. With every new volume of their series they dig themselves deeper into a hole from which it seems to be almost impossible to come to a satisfactory conclusion.

Planning and finishing a series is a skill. You're not a beginning writer, and you should have the skill set to finish what you started.

But Jack thinks: Except I don't.

He says that he's not sure series work well in his genre anyway.

Luke says: which genre? You've written in four that I can see.

Yeah. That's right.

To make matters worse, Jack's had some other ideas. He wants to start on them, because, hey, shiny new idea! He could just take "Book 1" off the cover of his first books, but for at least one of those books, the ending makes it very clear that another book is planned. Jack confides that he's just not very good at this branding and series thing.

Luke writes out a long post about his approach to series, here paraphrased by Tom:

Starting a series

When you realise that a story is going to develop into a series, plan a number of exit points, at which you can rest or even abandon the series. The first exit point could be at the end of book 1, which means that book 1 is a standalone book with series potential. Plan other exit points at book 3 and 4 and 5.

If you really wanted to be meta, you could write three standalone book 1s and see which one sold best to decide which series you should complete.

People advocate dropping a series once the sales are lower than a predetermined number.

While that all sounds very businesslike and analytical, Luke thinks this is a dumb move for a number of reasons, especially for early-career writers who don't have a huge stable of finished series yet:

- Up until about three or four books, a series will generate more income when you add books.
- A completed series is a valuable advertising asset.
- There is no guarantee that a new series will sell any better. It may not, and then you have just discarded a lot of work for nothing.
- You can't control how well a series will sell. You can control how well you advertise it (Jack understands advertising). Advertising

is where you make money, but you need more books than one, and preferably, the series needs to be completed, or at least have three books, before you can do too much with it. So finish it and then we go and make some money with that puppy.

So Luke would never discontinue a series?

He would and he has, but only if the sell-through is really poor. He writes fantasy and doesn't worry terribly much about the sell-through between book 1 and 2. After all, you're going to advertise the living daylights out of book 1, and might give it away for free. Lots of people are going to get the book who have no intention of reading it. We know that free books languish on a lot of reading devices, and we're not going worry about the books that aren't read. We worry about the ones that are.

But if the sell-through between book 2 and 3 is poor, Luke says he definitely wouldn't write any more books. That's great, because he planned an exit point at book 3 anyway.

What is poor sell-through?

By the time you get to the end of book 2 in a series, people should be hooked. At this stage, you should see sell-through percentages of over 80%. If your series sell-through from book 2 to 3 is 50%, can it after book 3. Because by the time you get to book 4, you've lost too many people and making a profit on your ads becomes increasingly harder.

But that doesn't mean you should discard the series. It's worth more if your sell-through is higher, so you might want to see if you can do something about that first.

Have a look at the reviews of book 2. Do they state a couple of clear issues why people don't read on after book 2? If so, you might want to employ a beta reader and ask them to look at the book with those comments in mind. And then, if possible, fix them.

Let's make money with this puppy!

A completed series of three books is an asset that you can use to create more sales. When you hold a sale on the first book, or give the first book away for free, a certain percentage of people will buy the other books. The more books you sell cheaply or give away, the more you will sell. The numbers may not be stellar, but as long as your sell-through is good, add them up over time and your series becomes a constant source of income.

It could be that the first book responds quite well to pay-per-click advertising, or that when given the book for free, quite a high percentage of people enjoy it and are prepared to pay for the next books. The success of the first book in the series when you first launched it doesn't always align with the sell-through to the rest of the series. You can use a series with a high sell-through rate to great effect, even if book 1 never sold terribly well on its own.

But you can't do this as effectively when the series doesn't at least have three books in total and the ending is left hanging.

Series design

Planning a series is no different from planning a novel, except on a larger scale. Except now you would expand the story's sections or chapters into individual volumes. Each of the volumes needs to tell a separate story. If the volumes are more open-ended, keep the release of all volumes tight, or release all the books at the same time.

Luke says he tends to plan series in lots of three. This is not because he thinks that by three books you should be able to tell whether or not a series is going to be a bestseller. You can probably tell this by the first book.

You can't plan for fluke bestsellers, but you can plan for a three-part asset that you'll use to generate a steady income.

How do you design a series?

There are several ways. You can make it so that each volume tells its own story and the books can be read in any order, or so the books follow one another and can't stand alone.

The first requires a protagonist who never changes and who faces a different, unrelated, problem each time. Examples of this format are the famous detective series where the focus is on solving the crime, and developments in the life of the main characters are non-existent.

Most series need to be read in some sort of order because, even if they deal with individual issues, there is a larger story arc, even if it's only that the main characters learn and age.

Then there is the trilogy.

A lot of antagonism exists in the author community against series that are "just a very big story chopped into three parts", but it's very common in fantasy.

You know one of the most famous books that did just that?

It's called *The Lord of the Rings.*

Yeah. That.

If you happen to write fantasy, as Luke does, planning a very large story and dividing it into three sections is a very good way of designing a series that will both earn you money and is easy to abandon once you decide it didn't work as well as you hoped. After all, it's done after three books.

If it sold well, then you can decide to write more books. If you weren't happy with sales, then it's still a completed series that you can use in advertising.

If you write a series, you should look ahead. Keep a notebook with the major events you are going to cover in each volume and how they are going to end. It is best if you cover a distinct event in each volume. If you have a large story arc that needs to be completed, make sure you plan where you are going from the beginning. Start with a story arc spanning three books. Plan for a further story arc that could take the series to five or six books. Make sure that after three books enough plot threads have been resolved that you can leave the series if necessary.

That's easier said than done, however. Jack thanks Luke for this and contemplates his mess of books. His most popular series has two books. Writing the third book in the series, which readers are forever asking him to do, might be the easiest option. With a few of the other books, he might get away with taking "Book 1" off the cover. He does know how to do graphic design.

While he's at it, he might change a few of the covers so that it's clear the books are all by the same author. That's the next best thing to having a completed series.

CHAPTER 130
TIME MANAGEMENT

Lucy is worried about her upcoming release. If only she could find some extra time.

She asks in the group: how do you guys manage to find time to write?

Tom has recently bought a tablet so that he can take it when he goes with his wife to her health appointments. He often writes in little snatches of time. He's not employed full-time, but he might as well have a job.

Jack works at home. He tries to write for an hour every morning after he's gone for a run. The rest of the day is taken up with marketing activities until his partner comes home.

Emily lives alone. She chose to get a cat instead of a dog, because she doesn't have to walk it. Emily has lots of time. The question is spending it wisely.

Lucy has two children. They go to school, so the day is free, but on weekends, they need to go to soccer and drama, and her husband won't do any of this.

When Lucy is not doing the team's snack duty, she goes for a walk. (*Psst!* Don't tell her husband that the soccer game was not that far away and she could have come home while her daughter was playing.) She uses her phone to dictate a chapter or two.

Jack posts a link in the group to a talk about this subject. This is the gist of it:

Writers talk about the troubles finding the time to write, especially those who are just beginning.

This is a big subject with some people, as if they expect there to be an easy fix.

For some people, there isn't one solution. They have other commitments that they can't or don't want to drop. They might enjoy the day job. They may not make enough money from their writing to quit the day job yet. They may be looking after relatives, either small children or elderly parents, who require varying amounts of attention.

Time management is never going to be easy, because no matter how much you talk about it, there are only twenty-four hours in the day. If you take up one thing, the flipside is that you must spend less time on another thing.

If you have a day job, you are quite lucky. Most likely, your job will involve time spent getting to and from work. A commute in a train or bus can be ideal for getting some words in. You will also have the necessary finances to buy equipment to allow you to do this. You can write on your phone with the aid of Scrivener for iOS. You can use dictation while walking, or get an iPad to take places where you may need to wait for a while, such as watching kids at swimming.

If you have a day job, you are also reasonably likely to be blessed with something called lunchtime.

This is a luxury to some of us, especially those with small children.

Many day jobs are highly structured, which allows you to structure your writing around them. You get to work at the same time, you have lunch at the same time, you leave at the same time, and spend roughly the same amount of time getting there. This allows you many different snippets of your day where, given the right mind frame and technology, you can get some words in. Even if you only write 100 extra words a day this could amount to one novel in a year.

That is, assuming that all you ever get to write is 100 words on the bus.

If you're caring for relatives, it's going to be much harder, because often the nature of your other activities is going to be erratic, and you need to be able to put things away at the drop of a hat.

In this case, having something with you where you can write in the little snatches of time you do get is very valuable. Again the trick is training yourself to think in small snippets of time and in paragraphs.

The writers discuss it in the group, and this is the summary of their conclusions:

News flash: it is very hard to stay focused for long stretches of time on a daily basis anyway. There are only very few writers who can do this successfully for long stretches of time.

As a writer whose primary activity during the day is not writing, you have a certain advantage. You learn to focus very clearly from the word go.

If you have little time, your time must be wisely spent. You will know that the most important thing you can do is to write more fiction.

You probably feel that other people are writing far more fiction than you, and that you could write so much if only you had the time.

You will probably spend less time marketing, and therefore probably waste less time on it.

You day job gives you things to write about. Hate your colleague? Make him a villain. Going on a work trip? Raunchy Christmas party? Use them in your fiction.

If you're caring for someone, it is highly likely that this situation is temporary. Kids grow up, elderly folk unfortunately die, and it is best to spend as much time with either as you can. It's not going to last forever.

Quite often, the fiction of people who have cared for a relative can be very emotional or full of black humour. You can use this to great effect. Recognise that your situation is not the same as everyone else's. Make sure that you differentiate yourself according to the experience that you have. If you're a writer, but you also have an interesting job, you will bring something to your fiction that a full-time writer doesn't have. If you are caring for relatives you will understand things that many writers won't. You will know how to connect with people in similar situations, and there are many of those.

If you're a student, you're probably studying with the aim of getting a degree and a better job. In that case, studying should probably be your first priority (especially if your parents are paying for it!).

Most of these interruptions are temporary in nature. Examine your priorities and act accordingly. Next year, the situation may be very different.

If, however, you have the tendency to fritter away time on Facebook or slump in front of the television at night or lose hours in gaming, you may need to restructure your day if you want to get anything done.

Time spent at home not doing anything that you absolutely need to do is time you could spend writing.

So carve out one hour a day—it could be in the morning, if you're a morning person, or it could be after dinner or just before going to bed. Whatever takes your fancy, take that hour, and make sure there are no interruptions. Make sure that the children are in bed and that your adult relatives understand that this is your writing time.

If you have small children, putting on a movie is a great thing.

If you have a large and boisterous family and live in a small apartment, you may need to learn to become less insistent on silence while writing. Learning to write anywhere and shutting yourself off from distractions is a skill we can all learn.

In the end it is all about how badly you want it.

If you can't come up with any time to write, you may not want it badly enough. If your job is so busy that you don't have any time whatsoever, you're probably quite well paid. You may be able to take an extended period of leave to write a book or two.

You may need to look for a different job.

How badly do you want it? Make sure that your excuse of not having time is genuine and that you're not looking for an excuse to do nothing.

CHAPTER 131
FOCUS ON STORY

Tom makes a decision.

At this time, he neither has the will or energy to write book 2 of the series that didn't sell.

He's been told his first series sold better than average, so maybe he can make it better. Some of the comments from group members have gotten under his skin, especially the ones suggesting that his style was quaint and old and the insinuation that this is to be expected from an old author. Just the previous day, someone in the hospital called Helena, at 61, "quite young". He's not ready to face the scrap heap. Or if that's his lot, he's going to go down fighting.

So he writes to one of the bestselling authors in the group, and true to the spirit of the community, the author, whose name is Luke, engages Tom in a pretty comprehensive discussion. Here is the gist of it:

Story alignment issues

Tom wrote from his heart. He wrote the type of fiction that he might have been reading thirty years ago. Surprise, surprise—in the meantime the world has changed. There is probably still an audience for his stories, an audience which looks much like him, but it's likely that the audience is quite small and easily exhausted. Also, like himself, they are probably quite cynical about things like advertising, and prefer to stick to the classics in the genre.

Tom needs to focus on his content. He needs to look at the way of modern storytelling and align his fiction with the tastes of modern readers. You remember how Tom said that he didn't like much of the fiction in this current genre?

Oh dear.

This presents a problem indeed.

The fact that he wrote a book like those that were famous thirty years ago or more doesn't necessarily mean that new readers will enjoy his fiction as much as earlier generations did. The type of fiction may not be very popular any more and may not have aged well. It's likely that the type of fiction still exists, but Tom needs to go and find where it hangs out, and what the new tropes are.

But, Tom says, people still read the old classics. I don't see why I can't write like that.

Totally, he can, but he was complaining about sales, right?

Luke says that the bottom line is that he is not one of those famous authors that he thought to emulate. Readers these days are attracted by different elements in their fiction.

Tom has a choice: he can adapt his fiction, or he can adapt his expectations. Or, before he does any of this, he can try some advertising, but he's already said he doesn't like running ads and he's pretty emotionally tied up with his wife's illness right now, so Luke won't suggest that to him.

Tom grumbles a bit that fiction now is supposed to be more politically correct, whatever that is supposed to mean. Maybe in this case it means: I'm an old fogey who can't be bothered to find out what audiences these days like. Maybe it means: I can't even be bothered to find out who I'd like to read my books, other than "people like me and people I want to be like me".

Luke says: Mate, that is a valid audience, but if it doesn't turn out to be very large, and you want to sell better, something needs to give.

Story structure issues

Luke then goes on to say that Tom's way of storytelling is slightly stale.

Not just the subject matter and presentation of fiction changes over time. Also the style of storytelling has changed.

When people didn't have much option to watch movies in the genre, a lot of the scenery needed to be described in exquisite detail. You rarely see this in fiction any more. People tend to get bored by it. You don't have to tell anyone what Paris looks like. A lot of readers will have been there themselves.

Modern audiences are far less tolerant of wooden characters, long sections of description, dialogue that exists only to show a certain plot point, or fiction that is unnecessarily emotionally distant.

Readers want to connect with a character who is engaging, possibly sympathetic, and definitely takes an active role in the story and has an interesting personal story to tell.

Many of the older books, especially in the traditionally male genres, were quite distant. They were about the plot much more than about the characters. They were about nifty ideas and clever plot twists.

It's not just the characterisation that has changed.

The style of storytelling has changed on a sentence level.

Stories in a lot of genre fiction are told in a tight prose, with few flowery passages or clever turns of phrase. It could be that Tom's writing and interests align more closely with literary fiction.

If this is so, and he wants to go in that direction, he would also have to adjust his expectations. Literary fiction can sell quite well, but it is harder to sell, and harder to market. For one, you are competing with a lot of very well-known writers who are backed by the big publishers.

* * *

Tom says: so, basically, my writing sucks?

Luke replies:

If you want to see it that way, it's up to you. I'm only saying that in order to sell better, something needs to change. Your style and subject matter comes across to me as old-fashioned. That's where I'd start to make changes.

You've already said you're not going to do big ad campaigns, and to be honest, I think that would be a waste of money. For those campaigns to be successful, you need to be a bit closer to the market, otherwise you'll just burn through your budget with that pretty cover. Man, those covers are really awesome. Who did them?

So Tom asks: What should I do?

Luke says: if you're prepared to do the work, I would find a developmental editor to see if you can work on style and story craft. Personally, I wouldn't touch your existing books, but write something new.

Except Tom only has his existing books.

CHAPTER 132
BUT YOU WILL KILL YOUR CAREER!

MEANWHILE, LUCY IS STILL UPSET OVER THAT ONE-STAR REVIEW. AMAZON won't take it down. The people in the author group tell her to ignore it, but then the same person gives another one-star review to another of her books. This is a fairly new book that doesn't have so many reviews, and it drops her average to 4 stars.

Again, the other writers tell her to ignore it, but she can't. This nasty person obviously has it in for her, and it's all her own fault.

She has been told numerous times that writers can't be involved in anything remotely political, but Lucy likes that sort of thing. Animal protection isn't related to writing, but it's just that it is causing her a tremendous amount of heartache.

Should she stop being political on social media?

She doesn't know who to ask about this. Her husband will probably just tell her to quit writing if it bothers her so much, and he would be happier for it. At least he would get her undivided attention.

Then she remembers Jack.

Jack is very different from her. He's so sure of himself, so good with his ads, he knows so much. But Jack is gay and he makes no secret of being gay. She is a Facebook friend of his, and he often reposts political pro-gay posts.

She asks him: should I stop posting about animal rights?

Jack says (in the time he should be writing):

Writers are often advised that "it will kill your career" if you utter as much as a word that could be interpreted as political. I want to stop that sentiment in the bud.

There is nothing that will kill your career unless you stop writing.

We all know that famous writer who flies off the handle at reviewers who dare to post negative reviews on her books. We know the old fogey writer who insists that the best place for women is in the kitchen. We know the literary writer who delights in rubbishing every other writer, especially those of genre fiction.

We know the writer who is generally a dick online all around.

People say they won't read these writers anymore, and indeed some people don't.

But many more people won't even know that this is going on. They're not in the places where these people have misbehaved or sprouted their unpalatable political views. They're looking for a book to read.

So if being a general dick doesn't harm the career of famous writers who spend a fair amount of time in the spotlight, why should it harm you?

I'm not advocating that you should be a dick online, because there are other ways in which it may harm you, but in your sales, it won't.

Even if a huge online argument breaks out, the collective memory of the internet is about twenty-four hours and after that, everyone has moved on and the vast majority of people can't even remember the name of the writer who said all these stupid things online. Never mind the things that were highly partisan but by no means stupid, or the writers who simply said something of a political nature.

Being political does NOT hurt your sales. In fact, it can attract people of a similar bent, and those who don't share your view probably wouldn't have enjoyed your fiction anyway.

Saying something stupid online, or getting into a public argument also does NOT harm your career.

The only thing that will harm your career is if you stop writing.

Lucy has no intention of doing that, although she very much doubts that her new book is going to be well received. It's about a woman who rescues dogs. It will probably give the trolls more ammunition to one-star her.

Jack goes on: That said, being a dick online will absolutely harm the opportunities other writers are willing to give you. If you're known to be hard to work with, this will go around to the organisers of promotions, to the owners of promotion sites, to the people looking for others to include in box sets.

Lucy says: I know that. I organise those sets. Some people are just horrible to work with.

Jack says: I didn't know that. You should advertise in the group. You might get some interest from other writers.

Lucy thinks: If only I were as self-assured and confident as you are.

CHAPTER 133
YOU HAVE TO BE PROFESSIONAL

When Emily first started writing, she didn't have two cents to rub together. It was just after her divorce and she couldn't afford any of the things that the well-meaning "they" said she should have. Yet, she feels that those books she wrote back then, edited with the help of a friend and published with a—really substandard—cover she cobbled together herself, take a place in her career that will never be replaced by any other book with the slick production she has now. She has of course paid to edit those books and has put nice covers on them, but there is something about the raw emotion in those stories that captured a lot of readers despite the amateur presentation that she's having trouble reproducing in her other books.

She's questioning the whole mantra of slick professionalism.

There is such thing as spending too much money on books.

Tom knows better than most that there is a tremendous pressure in the self-publishing industry for writers to spend big on their books before they have earned the first dollar in sales. He's had a fair few people knock on his virtual door.

This is what a veteran writer said about it:

The advice goes that you have to invest if you want to be in business.

If you start a shop, that would be true. You would have to buy stock, you would have to refurbish the shop-front that you just signed an expensive lease for, and you would have to invest in employing someone even if it's only to do your accounts.

Starting like a writer does not need to be like that. It is in fact one of the beauties of the business.

Self-publishing is a very democratic movement. Anyone with an internet account and text editor can do it. You can make use of free resources to clean up your book and create a cover.

No, it wouldn't look "professional", but there is nothing to stop you doing this, to check out if a project has legs before you invest more money into it.

For people who aren't sure if they want to do this writing gig, or people who don't have a lot of money to spend, the bootstrapping method is awesome, because another basic tenet of business, apart from having to invest funds in your business for it to be successful, is never to spend more than you earn.

In the beginning of someone's self-publishing career these two things are diametrically opposed.

On the one hand we have bestseller writers pressuring new writers to spend big on the covers and their editing, and on the other hand we have people who advise writers to work their way up and upgrade from the proceeds of sales.

I am quite wary of writers who advise others to get professional straight off the bat.

I don't see a problem with the actual advice. It is good advice. The cover does sell a book, and editing is extremely important. Both could make or break a book.

The problem lies in the fact that when you are new, you're unlikely to know how to pick a good cover, or good cover designer, or how to pick the right editor for you.

I have seen more than one writer spend thousands on a really beautiful cover that was totally inappropriate for the book, or made by an artist who had absolutely no clue about typography.

It just makes me sad to see this happen to people who have spent cash they probably couldn't afford to lose and wasted it because they felt this great urge to "be professional".

As far as I'm concerned, bootstrapping your way to better covers and better editing is completely professional. Never spending more than you earn is utterly professional.

You only spend big whenever you can afford to gamble, or you are pretty sure that you are going to make that money back. Spend when you're a bit more experienced.

The advice that "you have to be professional" usually comes with a price tag for a product or service we should be willing to buy because "you have to be professional".

Jack agrees. He says he recently went through all his expenses and was quite horrified with the number of auto-renews coming out of his credit card for services he barely used. So he cancelled a few. So many of these services sell themselves with the promise that it's "only" $10 a month, but a handful of these subscriptions can really add up.

If you really want to be professional, you need to evaluate what you're spending and whether those services are still useful to you. Some of them will be worth it to you, absolutely.

"Being professional" is not about using the services or not, it's about evaluating whether you do, or would, get your money's worth out of them.

CHAPTER 134
FIND NEW AUDIENCES

Emily has been working through her list of things to do. She made a note to check her Facebook page for messages once a day, and see if anything needs to be replied to.

She does eventually reply to the woman with the missing daughter, explaining that she's been in a difficult position herself. The woman writes back saying that she can understand. Emily is not sure she deserves forgiveness.

She also connected with a reader called Chris, who is also recently divorced and trying to find work while looking after a five-year-old girl.

Emily pays for a writer from the author group to set up a website and sets up a mailing list signup. She's dismayed that three people sign up on the first day, and five on the second day.

She also plans to use her KDP Select free days for the first time ever, and she books some promo sites to go with it.

But after doing that, she's stuck. What else is she supposed to be doing?

Jack seems to know a lot about advertising, so she asks him.

Jack says that because Emily wasn't doing any marketing, all her new books would have appealed to the same people who already know her. For marketing, she would have relied solely on the algorithms that kept recommending her books to other people on the retailer sites. These algorithms favour churn: new books, new authors, at an ever-increasing rate.

This is especially true on Amazon, and Emily's books are all in Kindle Unlimited.

Her books might have fallen out of favour with the algorithms. It could have been because some programmer at 2 a.m. in the bowels of Amazon changed a line of code. It could have been because a new author launched a series of very successful books which took the recommendation slots Emily's books used to take up.

The pool of readers might have been on the move anyway, to another, new genre. She will never know.

Since writing more and more books is not going to be a solution for her, she probably needs to cut down on her writing and work out who her audience is and how to increase it.

There are several ways of doing this. If Emily doesn't already have a mailing list, she should start one, and start talking to those people. (She can respond with a tick on that one). She could look at the other books that retailers suggest people buy at the same time as buying hers. This will give her valuable information about where she can find an additional audience.

If she had an active Facebook page it would have valuable information on the location, age and other demographics of her audience. Unless she paid for Facebook likes, which she hasn't, this will represent a good section of her audience and their characteristics. Are they male or female, what country are they in, what age are they? With these characteristics, Emily can find authors who make a good target in advertising or who she can collaborate with. She might discover that her fiction is popular in certain countries. She could try to concentrate on those countries by selecting other people who have big audiences there and whose audience she can use.

But she has only twelve likes on her page.

Jack suggests that she should put her Facebook page in the back of all her books and ask her readers to "like" it.

Emily feels like she's finally starting to understand this. There is a lot more to having a website or Facebook page than meets the eye. It's not always about the blatantly commercial stuff you do there, says Jack, but if you engage people there, you can find out other things about them, such as which other writers they like. And that can be very helpful.

FIND NEW AUDIENCES 449

She doesn't need to write any new fiction for this, since she will be looking for new audiences who are not familiar with her fiction. She could try giving books away for free to the mailing lists of other authors. She could set up swap requests with authors in those genres: she gets to mention books by other writers to her readers, and those writers will do the same for her.

Jack is pleased to hear that Emily has already set up a free promotion.

With the information about her audience and their popular books, Emily will be in a much better place to target future projects she wants to write.

CHAPTER 135
SOME POSSIBILITIES

A few discussions in the group are initiated by other people, and some apply to our writers.

Should you start a new genre?

In an ideal world, you should stick to a narrow brand and focus on its audience only.

But, as Emily has experienced, there are two risks attached to this.

The first is burnout. You just get too jaded, too tired of the same things. You run out of ideas and stories no longer feel fresh. You lose enthusiasm and your writing output and quality suffers.

The second risk, as Emily also experienced, is that the audience shifts elsewhere. This can happen quite abruptly, or very slowly over time.

Writing in another genre spreads the risk of this happening.

But beware of excessive fragmentation. This is a problem that Jack faces, which also means that he needs to spend such a lot on advertising, because the books in his catalogue don't neatly feed into each other. He's got little bits of unfinished series and incomplete catalogues floating about everywhere.

What he really needs to do is finish some of his unfinished stuff and tidy up some other unfinished series.

While he's working on that—and it's not a quick project—how can he mitigate the problems?

In the first place, by branding well. He should design all his covers in a similar style, for example, with a similar font for his name. While he's at it, he should get the cover designer to make him covers for the books that aren't yet written, but need to be written to complete the series. When Jack says he's a graphic artist, people wonder why he hasn't done this yet.

Good question.

If his branding is the same across all his books, readers will know that the books are written by him, and the image on the cover will help the readers understand which genre they are. He will need to have a strong website which lists all his books. He will need to have links to all his books in the back of each book. He will probably need to work his mailing list pretty extensively.

Multiple pen names

If you start another genre, should you be using another pen name?

Emily has toyed with the creation of new pen names but has pretty much abandoned it because it was too much work to keep all the profiles and "careers" of both writers alive.

Lucy has a successful pen name, and she publishes a book or two per year in that name. It's not a secret to her fan group that she has this name, but she uses it as a genre delineation. Her pen name books are more explicit in nature.

Jack started a new pen name when he started self-publishing in case any stigma from this activity tarnished his traditional publishing career. He then found it didn't, so he merged everything under one name. Since he only used his initials instead of this first name, that was easy. (Tip: you can just change the name on a book as long as it's only an ebook without an ISBN. Once your book is in print, you need to publish a new version).

Whether to use a pen name will depend on a number of factors. In the first place, you want to make sure you do it for the right reasons. If your pen name is to experiment with a new genre and that genre is very much unlike your current genre and attracts audiences that are incompatible with your current genre, it is probably a good idea to start another pen name.

Examples often cited are children's book authors writing racy fiction, or distinguishing between fiction and non-fiction.

There are some genres where you may easily use the same pen name for both genres. Science Fiction and Fantasy are very much alike and unless you want to micro target your audience—and are prepared to do the additional work—there probably isn't much point or need for a new pen name. It just creates a lot of work for you.

If you write children's fiction and adult fiction, of the sexually explicit type, the situation is pretty clear-cut. And this highlights the reason why I think a pen name is useful: when the audiences for each genre are clearly separate.

Young children and adult readers are obviously very different people. If you write for children, you can't swear and a number of subjects won't interest them. But if you write crime and science fiction, the difference isn't going to be so great. Your readers are adults in both cases, and things like sex and swearing are going to be acceptable to both audiences in the same amount. If your science fiction is of the mystery or crime-solving type, I can see no reason to separate out real world crime fiction under a new name.

Another way of subdividing your audiences is through their reading behaviour. You could have a pen name that is 100% in Kindle Unlimited, whereas fiction under another name is not.

Your pen name doesn't need to be a secret. It could merely be a shortcut for a different type of fiction.

However, having another pen name has the potential to create a lot of extra work.

What are you going to do about a mailing list, a website and social media presence for your pen name? If you don't want this to become onerous, you need to think carefully about how you're going to manage this.

Here are some things you can do to reduce the amount of work required:

- Keep the same mailing list and make it clear to your audience who the pen name is and what it's for.
- Separate the mailing list, but keep it under the same account and cross-pollinate both.
- Forego a website and have a Facebook page only.

- Use a secondary service, like Draft2Digital, to display your pen name books on a single page as you would on a website.

CHAPTER 136
BROADEN YOUR HORIZON

Following her discussion with Jack, Emily has a looked at some ad possibilities, including the Facebook ad portal, but it all feels foreign to her, and it feels like mastering it will take a long time.

She asks about this in the group: how soon can I see results from this?

The replies vary from "I faffed around and spent money for no return for a year before something clicked and the ads started working," to "They worked for me straight away." There were also people who'd spent a lot of money on ads without anything to show for it.

Then Tom said: I don't want to state the obvious, but why don't you take some of your books out of Kindle Unlimited?

To which some other writers replied that was a terrible idea, because the vast majority of books that sell well in Emily's cosy mystery genre are in Kindle Unlimited.

But Tom is adamant. He says: I'm in the same boat. My genre is all Kindle Unlimited. I have only three books that sell anything worth squat, and my sales are a few hundred a month. A bit over half those sales are not on Amazon. I know it's not much, but I don't do any marketing and the sales are pretty constant. With all the books you have, you should be able to make at least ten times what I get.

Emily likes the sound of that. She doesn't live expensively—the notion of having a lot of money is still novel to her—and has some reserve. Because she and her cat don't spend much, it's worth a try. She doesn't like being beholden to one retailer anyway.

But it's a lot of work. She now needs EPUB files of all her books, wants to update the back matter while she's at it—she needs to put her new mailing list signup there!—needs to open accounts at other retailers, decide which ones to go direct and which ones to access through an aggregator. Initially she thinks to just use an aggregator for everything, but Lucy points out, rightly, that their 10% cut can add up to quite a bit of money once you start selling well.

She sends Tom a private message to ask about any pitfalls she needs to consider.

Tom, thorough fellow that he is, has kept a check sheet for the publishing process on all retailers, and he sends Emily a copy.

It's amazing (note to the reader: if you want to know about this, read *Going Wide Unboxed*).

He says: If you have any questions, let me know. I'll reply tonight when I'm home from the hospital.

And then they talk a bit about Helena, who has gone into surgery, and Emily's dad who died of cancer last year.

In the middle of going through Tom's instructions, she gets a random email from a fan who asks her if she's ever thought of putting her books on Apple, and when Emily says "Guess what I'm doing?" the woman is very happy.

Meanwhile, Tom rushes home to get a new set of pyjamas for Helena when she wakes up out of her surgery, and he does the shopping. He talks to his daughter and then Helena's brother rings from Greece. Should he and his wife visit after Helena recovers? Implied is that it might well be the last time he will talk to his sister. So then there is the visit for Tom to arrange, beds to take down from the attic and put together in the spare bedroom.

And while he's doing all this, it dawns on him that when you go to the Amazon chart of science fiction, you will notice that almost everyone has their books in Kindle Unlimited. There is a bit of bias going on, because the charts favour books that are in Kindle Unlimited, but the fact remains that a number of science fiction writers do very well in the program.

Since Tom is not getting a lot of sales on his new series, he might take book 1 down, then write the others and then release the lot quickly in Kindle Unlimited. He doesn't have much of an audience elsewhere, and there is much potential for growth for him. If his type of book is going to be popular, this will be where it's at. He can always later remove the books and place them wide. Right now, he doesn't have any mental space to think about this.

This is how he has come to see it: KU is an easy, short-term strategy that can be successful for launching series. However, it cannibalises more of your sales the longer you stay in it. Being wide is a long-term strategy that should probably be the long-term default for all books.

CHAPTER 137
SACRIFICES AND FAMILY

ONE DAY, UNANNOUNCED, LUCY'S HUSBAND COMES HOME EARLY FROM WORK. He's never early, so it's clear that something is up.

He says that they had a work meeting, that there will be changes in the company and management wanted to give older workers a chance to step out by offering them packages.

They explained everything, and then sent everyone home to discuss it with their families. He's thinking about it.

Lucy's mind goes into panic mode. He's only 51, and what's he going to do, sit at home?

He says they can do things that they always wanted. Lucy can't think of anything more claustrophobic. He never wanted to do anything when the kids were small, leaving her to do all the work, and now he expects her to drop everything?

The girls need to go to school, she says, and I have my work, too.

But you're only writing stuff. You can do that whenever you want.

No, she can't, because he will complain about it. He will complain about how much time she spends, and how much money, and will ask questions about the people she interacts with, and will continuously butt in and distract her, and then he will say that it's all "stuff for women" anyway as if that somehow makes it less important.

And it's not as if he will offer to get the girls from school, or do the cooking or the washing.

What on earth is she going to do?

She has an idea: she will tell him that since her business now supports the family, she wants to set it up as a business, with her own bank account and everything so that she can pay a monthly amount towards household expenses.

But is that the right thing to do? Of course she should have done this long ago, but she dislikes everything to do with money, and it was much easier to just let him handle it. But if he's going to sit at home, he's going to obsess over the money.

At the first opportunity, she goes to the author group, and asks: does your partner support you?

The answers are quite interesting.

Tom says his wife has zero interest in his writing, but he started writing when he took time off from his work to look after her in her illness. She also understands that he needs something stimulating in his life. They are financially OK, but could use the money. Ultimately, his first priority will always be his wife and her deteriorating health.

Emily feels kind of trapped, because she started writing after an acrimonious divorce, and she hasn't been able to find a partner who understands her life. She really wants a bit more free time so she can rediscover other activities and find another partner in the first place, never mind whether he supports her.

Jack and Tony could use a bit more money. Tony works in a low-paying job and he would dearly like to go back to university but, at the moment, Jack's income isn't quite secure enough.

But it really depends on what sort of support you're talking about, Jack says.

And he continues:

As someone who has a fairly supportive family, and who did not have to make any major sacrifices in terms of work time, because I was self-employed anyway, I feel I'm not entirely qualified to talk about how to handle the lack of support by your family, and balancing their demands on your time.

But I have seen many of my friends struggle with this.

I also believe that support from a partner is a function of your overall love relationship dynamic, and your expectations of it.

My partner doesn't read anything of what I write. He is a reader of non-fiction, and does not read fiction at all. So it would be kind of torture for me to require him to read all my books. I'm not going to.

Yet I hear people finding it disturbing and disappointing that their partner doesn't read their books.

I don't believe that support by a partner means forcing them to read all the books I write. I believe that support by a partner is allowing the partner to do something they love, giving them the time and not subjecting them to emotional blackmail over time spent doing that thing.

Support is not standing by the sidelines and cheering. Frankly, that can be a little creepy. If that is your requirement in your life, that your partner cheers you all the way, then you really need to take a step back and consider what you would do if your partner forced you to do something they loved and you have no interest in.

At this point, Lucy remarks that she's not expecting that at all.

Tom says: I agree with Jack. Support is giving your partner the opportunities, not whining when they spend time doing the thing they love, not blackmailing them with conditions that have to be met before they can do this thing they love, not treating this thing that they love as something that is somehow going to stand in the way of the relationship, or holding financial conditions over their head.

At this point, Lucy starts feeling something bad in her bones. It has been there for a long time. Not only does her husband not really support her, but he's actively trying to blackmail her in subtle ways. If he's going to spend so much time at home, it's going to get infinitely worse to the point she's not sure she wants to be in that situation.

And it scares the pants off her.

Jack says to the group, not Lucy in particular:

Partner support and writing are going to be infinitely harder when you are struggling financially, or both of you have really busy jobs.

If you come up against a conflict, you may have to examine where your priorities lie for the time being. If you're both studying or working sixty-hour-per-week jobs so that you can get ahead and build a future together, demanding to take out a chunk of time to do something just for the love of it would sound selfish to the other partner. If you have really young children, there just may not be any time and emotional space to write. But children have a habit of growing up.

Many situations are temporary. It may not be the right time for you to be a writer.

If you want a writing career, you have to write. That's your job, and your partner should understand that.

Tom says that he agrees and that he expects writing to take a back seat for him for a little while.

Lucy says nothing. She is planning to go to the bank tomorrow morning.

CHAPTER 138
GET YOUR SH*T TOGETHER

It's a coincidence that while everyone is talking about future-proofing their business, a new writer in the large Facebook group asks: I recently inherited a bit of money, and want to spend $10,000 on promoting my book, what do you all suggest?

The reaction from other writers is interesting, to say the least.

Many suggest ads, but it's really hard to spend that kind of money on ads that are also effective. Luke, who sells the best of all writers in the group, says: sure, you could blow money on Facebook or Google ads, or buy expensive PR packages, but to be honest, you'd only be feathering the nests of the ad executives and PR people. Presuming you'd like to spend that money to make back more, there isn't a huge lot you can do. Get new covers, maybe, but don't go overboard.

Other people suggest hiring developmental editors, but other people yet again say that they spent lots on editors and are yet to make a profit.

At this point, Tom makes a short and blunt comment: mate, put it in a bank account or some investment that pays a return.

The conversation at this point has bled into little indecisive discussions where no one can really suggest anything major to spend the money on.

But Tom gets together with our group in private and tells them something.

When I was in my twenties and finished my masters degree in chemistry, the bottom had fallen out of the labour market. It was next to impossible to get a job in the field, so I did random temporary work in the building industry. I lived with my parents. I wasn't spending much, because the money could dry up overnight. And then my grandmother died, her house was sold and I inherited some money. It wasn't huge because it had to be shared with many people: she had six children and I have a sister and a brother. My brother bought a new car. I was already used to being the loser in the family, so I didn't need to fight those opinions of me. The money was so precious to me that I put it away. First in a bank account with interest, because the rates were good. But when they fell, I invested it in other things, mostly boring old bank shares that pay me an income every year. I also made the decision to keep paying into the account every year. That has been the single best decision I made in my life. Since I get money from my redundancy, I've even paid my tiny writing income into it.

And he shows them the account, and can almost hear the cries of surprise.

Even Luke, who out-earns all of them combined, is impressed. Mate, you have it made, he says.

Tom suspects that Luke, in his fifties, doesn't have his money sorted.

Yes, the power of compound interest. And it applies not just to money, but also the compound interest on having, and having control over, a large catalogue of books. When you have a lot, you can play with some of it. Sales beget more sales. People will buy more if there is something for them to buy.

Tom says, especially to Emily, if you have some good times with good sales, get your shit together and put whatever you don't need away in some form of investment that gets you an income. Over time, that income will develop into a secondary source of payment that's 100% independent of your writing.

This hits Emily in the gut. She's got more than $50,000 sitting in a bank account that doesn't even pay interest. She doesn't feel confident about money.

Do I need to get a financial advisor? She asks.

You could, but I wouldn't, since they're expensive. It's not that hard. Just open an account that pays decent interest, put the money in there, keep adding to it and maybe later branch out to some additional boring but safe investment.

CHAPTER 139
USING A DEVELOPMENTAL EDITOR

Tom felt he wasn't getting anywhere. He had hoped that in addition to some extras in life, his writing would fund a trip to see his wife's brother, but he doesn't yet have enough money, his wife is not any getting better and her brother and his wife came to visit them instead.

Note for Tom: Priorities, mate!

It was a great week, in which his brother-in-law surprised him by saying how cool he thought it was that Tom was an author. He had read some of Tom's books—bought them, no less—and recommended them to his friends. Tom had noticed a flurry of sales in Greece on Google Play.

He was a bit embarrassed, because if Giorgios had told him, he'd have given him the books.

To make a long story short, now Tom has a little bit of money left over that he wants to use for his fiction.

He started publishing really set in his ways, but he's become convinced that some people he's been talking to may have a point. After all, he *did* model his books off some 1950s classics and he can see that modern fiction is different. Besides, he's had an idea to use his life experience of dealing with a sick relative in a new book. Not all space captains or hard-nosed detectives come without personal lives after all. He wants to make his fiction more real and less pew-pew.

He has also seen that his current books have some plotting and writing deficiencies. He never learned to write properly, and one doesn't rock up to a symphony orchestra expecting a job after two music lessons either. So at the very least he wants to do his best to fix his writing.

And prove that 62 is not old.

He scouts around for recommendations and hires Priya who lives in Sweden, but we won't hold that against her. She has a degree in Creative Writing, worked a bit for a big publisher until she married, moved to Sweden with her husband and had twins.

Note for writers like Tom: check prospective editors' credentials. What qualifies them for the job?

Priya has a special interest in story structure and works mostly while the twins sleep. She also writes, but has put this on hold while the kids are little.

She uses Skype, which is something that Tom knows well, although he's never used it for anything to do with writing.

What does she tell Tom?

Potentially, there may be some hard truths for him to hear.

She says:

The writer's job

As a writer, when you're trying to persuade people to buy a book, you have a few things to play with. These are your cover, your blurb, and retailer specific things like categories and price point, and one of the most important ones, your sample.

Readers often look at the sample of the book that is available for free to check if they are likely to enjoy the rest of the book.

There are definite things that you can do that turn the reader away. This is not about the rules of writing, but it is about what makes people likely not to want to continue reading.

If your control of storytelling is poor, the reader will be confused. The reader might not know why they don't like the story, but it is not the reader's task to point this out to you. The reader only knows that they would prefer to read something else.

These are things in your style that may stop your readers:

• • •

Unengaging, stodgy prose

This is especially common to writers who have a fairly high level of education, and consider themselves professionals. (Tom falls squarely in that territory.)

In a lot of areas of work, like academia, wordiness is rewarded. Or, maybe I should rephrase that, wordiness is expected. If you are terribly wordy in your communication, you will look important. (Tom can totally relate to that.)

Whether people actually read your communication is another question. I wager that they probably don't. But much work, especially in larger organisations, relies on looking important. On selling yourself. It does not rely so much on whether people actually read your stuff.

When you start writing fiction, this will work against you. Readers are merciless, and will ditch any book that takes too much space to get to the point. Lean prose is always better than wordy prose.

Learn to cut out the flab. Look at your sentences to see which words are needed. You may need to ask an editor to guide you with this if you are doing this for the first time. And, yes, it may hurt, because the editor may tell you to get rid of words and phrase constructions that you have fallen in love with.

This brings us to another problem. There is a fair bit of repetition. If you fall in love with a type of sentence, your prose becomes monotonous, sometimes even to a ridiculous level. Variety is king. You should never fall into the trap of doing the same thing over and over again.

Throat clearing clauses

"In the beginning, there was a book. Now you must know that this was a very bad book. When writing it, the author had forgotten that he was not writing a technical manual."

Each of those three sentences includes a piece of throat clearing. We could clean this up by saying: "There was a book. It was a very bad book. The writer had forgotten he was not writing a technical manual."

The example above may seem a little sparse. If you cut out flabby words, you're likely to create a kind of staccato style that still has to be cleaned up. In the example above, I would probably choose to keep one of the short sentences. But I hope I've explained how a lot of extra words don't mean anything and just bog the reader down.

That was what it was verbiage

The phrase "that was what it was" is the ultimate string of empty words. Some writers of course will advise you to get rid of every instance of the word *that*. Try it, then give your piece to an editor, and you will find that the editor will put half of them back in. Words exist in the English language because they have a function. This means you will sometimes need them. But words like *that* and *was* and *what* easily become crutches for lazy writers who don't bother to find more specific terms. Be specific. Don't say "it" when you can mention what it is.

Poor point-of-view control

Modern books are almost all told in some form of "close" point-of-view. This can be third person or first person. It means the reader is in the head of a character throughout the story. A break of viewpoint happens when the reader is shown something that the character can't possibly see, or hear, or know. The reader gets confused and starts wondering whose story this is anyway. Do it too often, and you've lost them, and they can't even tell you why, just that they found reading too much hard work.

After the talk, Tom contemplates that he's never had as much of a dressing-down from someone as nice, young and dark eyed and dark skinned as Priya. He thinks about the latter and concludes that it's important that Priya is totally not like him, because his readers are not like him, and in order to sell, he needs to think less like him and more like the readers.

He reads through the first chapter of his first book and finds so many of the things that she pointed out. He might as well toss the entire chapter and start over.

He really is a hack.

CHAPTER 140
WHERE TO BEGIN

During the next meeting Priya goes on:

Beginning your book

Most beginning writers start their stories in the wrong place.

When I was reading for the publisher, I made a tally of all the submissions reviewed, and the reason I didn't think they were suitable for publication. You would expect a lot of the submissions to be badly written and full of mistakes, but that was only a very small percentage of them.

The biggest reason submissions were rejected was because the story was uninteresting. Specifically, the beginning was uninteresting.

The beginning of your book is extremely important. You have to start it in the right place, preferably where something happens that makes the reader take notice. It doesn't have to be "action" like a fight. Beginning writers also often make that mistake of inserting action before the reader knows—and recognises—the characters and cares about them. I'm not saying categorically that it *can't* be a fight or a long description of the scenery, but there has to be *something* in it that makes the reader want to read on. If anything, readers are less forgiving than they used to be, because there are thousands of other books they could read.

The other day I was listening to the Writing Excuses podcast. This is a show of short episodes that is very traditionally focused, but they also talk a lot about craft, especially story structure. This aspect is often overlooked by a lot of creative writing advice, which focuses on sentence structure.

One of the hosts asked: how do you make stories memorable? This is the Holy Grail. We want to write stories that people will remember, because if they do, they'll remember the author, they'll remember to check that author out, and they'll recommend the author to their friends.

There is a sad tendency in the self-publishing writer space to be copycats. Well, I think it's sad anyway. The advice goes that you read bestselling books in your genre, write down the common plot elements, and use those in your book. If this is all you do, and it is indeed all a lot of people are doing, it will result in bland, cookie-cutter fiction that may sell reasonably well for a short period of time, but will otherwise be completely forgettable.

At the time Harry Potter came out there were already many books about young wizards who learned the craft of magic. In fact, it is entirely possible that some publishers were already saying "no more of this."

But the one thing Harry Potter did that none of the other books did was to add so much incredible detail to the world and how the characters interacted with that world. It made the concept *school for young magicians* its own.

The author took a concept that was beaten to death, and turned it into something so specific that it became alive to people. "Muggles" has become an accepted word in everyday vocabulary.

The fact that she did this with a concept that was already tired shows that it doesn't really matter what setting you choose, but you have to own it and add something to it that's unique, and you have to do this from the beginning. Own it.

With that in mind, how should you structure the beginning of the story? One of the main problems with a lot of the submitted fiction I saw in my time as slush reader was that the story did not begin at the point where the plot began. We saw many stories with characters waking up and going about their daily business, and it took at least one scene to get into the reason for the story. The Look Inside on Amazon is a chapter at most. When you have only a few thousand words to play with, putting boring, everyday stuff there is a huge waste of space. The beginning of your book is the most important real estate that you have. Don't waste it with mundane things.

Deciding where to begin your story is the most important thing you can do.

* * *

Tom writes back: So you don't think I started the story in the right place?

Priya says: No, I don't think so. I think the story starts at the end of chapter three, because this is where the dramatic event occurs that changes the characters.

Tom is horrified. He says: but I need the stuff before that to explain how the world works.

And Priya says: You don't. Take it from me. I want you to take chapter three. Don't cut out the scene where he gets robbed. Rewrite it. Start the novel with the scene where the main character walks into the street and gets robbed. If the reader needs to know anything about the character, that he is half-robot and that the city is a metropolitan space station, this will come out in the scene or future scenes. Write the story so that you offer as little pre-explanation as possible, and offer it only when the reader absolutely needs to know it to understand the character's predicament.

Well, that's kind of annoying. Tom has spent the previous night cleaning up chapter one. And now it turns out he may not need it anymore, because he sees Priya's point. The story really does start at the end of chapter three.

CHAPTER 141
THE SIDE HUSTLE

Jack is facing a problem.

This morning, their washing machine broke. It was already on its last legs and fixing it would be a waste of money for a small benefit. It's fifteen years old and would just break again.

They need to buy a new one.

But he also has a couple of expensive writing bills coming up. What can he do?

Piling some money on ads and selling more books is not the answer. That will just widen the financial hole. It's at least two months before the retailers pay, and the ad bill is due at the end of each month.

And to be honest, he's quite sick of the irregular and fickle nature of his writing income. One thing about Tony's shelf-stacking job is that the income is poor; the other is that it comes regularly.

Jack is seriously considering reviving his graphic design career.

He asks in the group: do you have a side hustle?

According to the replies, quite a few people do.

This is the consensus:

A side hustle could solve some problems.

It may take a while to get your career off the ground. Maybe you are not a particularly fast writer. Maybe you hate marketing so much that it becomes an impediment to your sales. Maybe your career is taking too long to develop, and you need money more immediately. Maybe you want to use this money to buy better covers and better editing. Maybe you're plain bored of only writing.

Jack thinks: yes to all those things.

He asks: what sort of things do people do?

The obvious ones are editing and cover design if you have any qualifications in those areas. Good cover designers are always in high demand. Cover design goes through phases and fashion, and if you can catch a wave and do it well, you can supplement your writing income in this way.

Things like speaking engagements and courses are more suitable to writers of non-fiction. But then again, maybe you have a specific field of knowledge from your previous job that you can use to write non-fiction. Non-fiction books are usually shorter and require less emotional energy to write.

Writers are hungry for knowledge, so if you can quickly write an informational guide on "The Writer's Guide To Airline Pilots", "Medical Terms For Writers", "What Writers Get Wrong About Farming" or something of that nature, go ahead and do it.

You could do website design for your fellow authors.

Quite a few people can do their own WordPress design, but there are others who lack the confidence or have additional money to pay someone to do it.

Commercial website design companies often charge too much, because their designs are tailored towards higher-end customers. Most writers just want a website that lists their books and has a form to sign up for their mailing list and maybe some information about themselves. These types of sites are hardly worth the effort of a full-fledged website design company.

If you write a lot and quickly, but you don't like plotting, you might find a second career as a ghostwriter. Many writers will pay well for those services.

If you have any training in audio production, you might find some money in becoming a narrator for audiobooks. Especially if you are not in the top tier of charging narrators, there will be quite a steady market.

And you could become a personal or virtual assistant to other authors. Many of them will ask for someone to run their promotions, submit their books to promotion sites, run the Amazon and Facebook ads, run their mailing list and all kinds of things.

Since these are often well-selling authors, it is your opportunity to learn how to do these things. I don't need to tell you that this can be very beneficial.

All of these ideas for making extra income involve you trading off some of your time for a fixed income. This means that you will have less time for writing but, since it is nearly impossible to write all the time effectively for eight hours a day, it may be a worthwhile trade-off while you find your feet.

Having a side hustle is a little bit like having a day job. You need to carve out time for it, and this could force you to become more efficient in your writing. But since you will be working with other authors, it may also be beneficial for your writing career.

Jack is not the only one listening in on the discussion. He has already decided to put a selection of pre-made book covers on his website and is reasonably confident that he can find the audience who will buy enough to give him a little extra cash this month.

But Emily is also watching. She likes the option of becoming a ghostwriter. How easy would it be to receive a plot, write the book in a week or two and be handed a few thousand dollars guaranteed? No marketing skill required.

Even Tom is thinking that he might be able to turn his knowledge about science into a book that helps writers get things right.

CHAPTER 142
WHAT IF I'M NOT GOOD ENOUGH?

LUCY IS PREPARING FOR THE LAUNCH OF HER NEW SERIES. IT'S ANOTHER historical romance, but she has started to have serious doubts about whether it will do well. That troll who left one-star reviews on her books is still out there. Amazon hasn't taken down the reviews. What if she returns and dumps a one-star review on the new book? Lucy has been a bit late completing the book and there isn't the time to send the book off to readers before it goes live. All this stress with the group and then the situation with her husband just makes her want to crawl into a hole.

She asks a question in the group: do you ever feel you're not good enough?

The replies blow her away.

Even the most accomplished, best-selling writers in the group admit that they often feel this way. That someone will come along, pierce their bubble and say: look, you were a fraud after all. Now go back to your office cubicle.

It's astonishing.

Not even getting a traditional publishing deal does anything to alleviate it. Jack says he started his publishing career by landing a deal with a traditional publisher. Reflecting on why he signed the deal—knowing it wasn't going to make him a lot of money—was that he needed validation.

But validation is a trap, says another group member known for hard-hitting replies. The need for validation can also be labelled "self-doubt".

If being rejected by agents and publishers makes you feel like a bad writer, then I have some news for you: the fact that some of your books are ranked in the millions on Amazon will also make you feel like a bad writer. Not only that, but you will continue to feel this way, because there will always be people who do better than you, there will always be bad reviews, and rankings go up and down naturally.

If your happiness depends on external factors, whether they be a publisher's nod, an agent's accolades, a good review in *Publishers Weekly*, 500 five-star reviews on Amazon, or whatever else you can dream up then you will be set up for a lot of disappointment.

This is the truth: external validation is a fallacy.

It may exist for short periods of time, but supposing you landed a really good deal, and the publisher paid you six figures for the book you haven't yet written and hasn't hit the shelves, you will just replace it by the next validation parameter that your overactive mind dreams up.

What if I can't make my deadline? What if I can't get the book to be as I want? What if I don't like the editor of the publishing house? What if they give you a horrible cover? What if the book doesn't sell? What if the industry magazines give it horrible reviews?

It is not hard to see that this process goes on and on.

Then you self-publish and similar types of doubts bubble to the surface: what if no one buys the book; what if my reviews are bad; what if my readers hate it?

If you're going to wait for these kinds of external parameters to prove whether or not you're good enough, you are going to wait forever. Validation is rubbish, and you should forget about it right now.

Well, Lucy scoffs. She finds the response a bit rude, to be honest. It's not like she can turn off a feeling that she has.

No you can't, the writer agrees.

But you should manage it so it doesn't destroy you. You should undertake all the steps that you feel are necessary to put out a book of decent quality. Then you should quit looking for validation.

It means taking some hard steps. It may mean dropping out of that community of writers who judge others by the size of their publishing deals. It may mean not looking at your reviews for a while, or ignoring your sales dashboard at times when you know sales are going to be slow. It may mean not interacting with certain people who make you feel bad about yourself.

This will be hard when those people are close to you, but in some way you have to carve out some space for yourself. If you can't find the space, you may need to assess who you associate with.

It is really hard to talk about these kinds of things. It's common, for almost every writer, to be worried about how the new long-planned release will do. If it does poorly then you have just wasted a couple of months of your life writing this book. That really sucks.

But ultimately, you can't control the reaction to your books. If you're looking at your reviews for validation, you will not find it, because there will always be bad reviews.

Some writers with self-doubt find it therapeutic to go to the page of a very successful book in their genre. Have a look at the 1-star reviews. Read what people have said about those books that have sold millions of copies. Not everyone will like everything. You can do nothing about it.

Lucy knows full well that the need to be liked, to get good reviews, to quell disunity in her groups, is destroying her, because she can't do and be everything. People jokingly call her a mother hen, and that's what she is: making sure that none of her babies—her real life ones or her book babies—suffer any bad experiences.

And now her husband is throwing a spanner into the works by giving her less time and looking over her shoulder. He wants to be another baby she needs to mind.

It's late at night when she's reading this, and she's crying at the computer. Maybe she should give the whole thing up and go be a dutiful housewife.

What is most distressful to her is that she knows what she has to do, and that she has a tendency to take far too many things too personally, but still the despair surfaces at the most inopportune moments, such as just before a new release.

CHAPTER 143
REFRESH YOUR WORK

Tom has spent a few weeks rewriting his three books.

Self-publishing gives you the freedom to change anything about your book at any time. A lot of writers try different covers, and some even edit and re-edit their books several times.

Is this worth doing?

He's about to find out.

Lucy feels quite uncertain about those first books that she wrote. She has learned much as a writer and every time she looks at those first books she cringes and wishes to unpublish them. To make matters worse, they're still selling. Or does that really make matters worse?

To Lucy, it's an embarrassment. To the readers, it's obviously not.

A number of Lucy's friends have rebranded their books. Is it a good idea for her to do this?

In the author group, Luke says:

Rebranding a book can be a good idea for a number of reasons. First, to make sure that all books in the series look similar and that you can easily tell that it is a series. This is very important and always worth doing.

Second, when you have a feeling that the covers currently on your books mislead people about the genre or the type of content. This may be worth doing, but it carries the risk that you're wrong. It wouldn't be the first time that I have seen this happen to people.

People also rebrand their books because they feel that the old versions of the book were not up to scratch. Since this is so highly subjective, I don't think it is worth doing, especially in Lucy's case, where the books are still selling. I've seen many writers ruin reasonably respectable sales figures by pulling the books, rewriting and republishing them.

Since it is hard to determine what attracts readers to a particular book, it may be that your rejigging of the content upsets something and you may lose your sales. If you have any kind of sales, don't touch existing work. Yes, it's likely that if you are doing all the right things and you're learning about your fiction, you will learn a lot and your earlier books will make you cringe. But this doesn't mean that by supposedly fixing them with things you have learned you will necessarily improve their sales. I have almost never seen this happen. If you have done the right thing and have learned to write better books, then use that knowledge to write more and better books, but don't touch your existing books.

If you're really so embarrassed by a book you have published that you don't want to see it any more, simply unpublish it. But I would advocate very much against doing so unless the book also doesn't sell at all. As long as the book is selling it means that people enjoy it and they don't see all the things that you see wrong with it. You don't know what attracts readers to a book, so don't try to second-guess because you will get it wrong. Practice your new skills on a new book.

To sum up:

- Recover and refresh the presentation of your books if it brings them into line with their series or genre.
- Don't rewrite existing books. If they sell, it's likely to kill sales. If they don't sell, you just waste time.

But Tom goes ahead and tries anyway.

CHAPTER 144
THE UPS AND DOWNS

It's D-day.

Tom's newly rewritten series goes live.

Lucy also has a new release.

Jack has set up a page and his cover design business goes live.

Emily launches new books all the time, but today, her KDP Select term expires and she's going to start selling books wide.

Tom is using his mailing list to announce the revamped series. He knows that the people on the list are likely to already have read the book, so a friend in the author group has agreed to send a notification to his list as well. He's made the first book 99¢ and booked a few promotion sites.

Apart from using her list, Lucy is planning to put some notifications on her Facebook reader group, and she knows she will get a lot of sales from it, but oh dear, why is it that when she planned this release date, she didn't check the school calendar. It's school holidays! Her kids are at home.

It's around mid-morning and she has just made some coffee when she hears a crash outside, followed by crying. A moment later, her oldest comes running into the house. Her sister has fallen off her bike and hurt herself. Lucy rushes outside to find her girl—and bike—at the bottom of the patio steps, clutching her arm. One look, and it's clear: it's obviously broken.

Lucy jumps in the car and takes both girls to the hospital, where a long cycle of waiting ensues. She worries about her release. She rings her husband, but when she asks if he can come home earlier from work—that he still hasn't notified about his interest in taking the exit package—he's evasive and talks about meetings. What about her release and the emails she needs to send?

So much for wanting to spend more time at home.

In the group, Luke says:

Writing is a very fickle business. You can be selling gangbusters one day and then all of a sudden for some reason not clear, the wheels fall off, sales drop and you have to do something to rescue your career. It could be something simple, or it could be something you don't even know how to begin to diagnose.

Many writers can be hit hard when Amazon changes certain things, I have seen them get burnt out, I have seen people have great hopes for a new series which flopped, and I have seen people simply wanting to do something else.

The fact is that if you sell at a certain level, there is absolutely no guarantee that this will continue. Writing is a creative career, and it is fraught with ups and downs. The sooner you realise this, the better.

There is only one foolproof prediction of sales, and this is zero: your book will always get at least . . . zero sales. If you've been around for a bit and people know you, there will be at least some sales, but beyond that, no one can predict sales, especially not for a new project.

This is quite discomfiting to a lot of people. New writers may even get angry. What do you mean all of a sudden my audience will just pack up and leave and my sales will be back down to the same levels as when I began?

It happens. The best way to deal with it is to be prepared. Or, should I say, don't ever expect it never to happen.

Emily can feel that uncertainty right now. In between uploading her books to other retailers, she's checking her sales, and there aren't many to speak of. She's been told that sales on other retailers will take a bit longer to show up.

She did get an email from her fan Chris, who said that she's very happy that she can finally buy Emily's books on Apple, and that she has done so.

The sale takes more than a day to show up, and then there is only one. Emily is not calling this a great success. Yes, she needs to have patience. She's budgeted six months for this. No need to get anxious yet, right? Right?

Jack is doing better. His site launch has resulted in four cover orders, and it looks like he won't have to forego anything in order to buy a new washing machine.

Considering the circumstances, Tom is reasonably happy with his relaunch. No, it didn't smash any records, but he's sold more than he has for a long time, even if most of the sales were at 99¢. He's also still a long way in the hole after paying Priya, but he feels he's getting somewhere. He accepts Luke's point that the best place to show off his new skills is in the next book. He quietly unpublishes the fourth book, because he can see that if that series is ever going to be successful, he needs to gut it, but he wants to think about starting something else. He doesn't know what it's going to be yet. At the moment, his mind is occupied. After a brief period at home, Helena is back in the hospital, and he fears she may not come out again.

And Lucy?

Her daughter is fine.

But when she comes home at six, her launch emails still unsent and her phone buzzing with "where are you?" messages from her readers, she finds that her husband has been home but has gone again. To the gym probably. The milk is sitting out on the table, everything she needs to cook is still solid frozen and the back door is wide open.

She's fuming.

CHAPTER 145
CHANGE DIRECTION

Enough faffing.

Emily has finished uploading all her books to all retailers. She's watching her sales like a hawk, and it's discouraging, because after a little flurry of sales, things have dried up again, and to make matters worse, she's received an email from a reader asking why she can no longer read the books in Kindle Unlimited. Emily resists snapping back with: because I got bills to pay.

But it wouldn't be the truth. She's got money saved and thanks to Tom, it's now in an account where she gets interest. It's just that all this doing nothing stresses her out. She's going to start on a new project. Also, she clearly needs a plan to increase her sales on other retailers.

Even if Jack's brief foray into cover design had the desired result, the effect is short-lived, and he still has to face the fact that his catalogue is scattered and that his ad costs keep increasing. The effect is masked briefly because he has one ad that's particularly successful, but it addresses none of the underlying issues: he needs to get his act together and write the books that need to be written. But the ultimate issue is that he's not a fast writer. He needs to do research and he needs a few weeks' worth of zero-stress time so that he can get a first draft done.

While Tom drives to and from the hospital and sits in waiting rooms, he thinks about future projects. How about he writes a book about a space captain with an elderly mother on board? Or someone with a serious health issue? In a spacefaring future, not everyone is going to be healthy.

But he can already hear Priya's voice: that sounds like a for-the-love project. You shouldn't stop writing them, but they probably won't help your bank balance.

Then what?

Lucy is trying to salvage her disastrous launch.

She explains the situation to her readers, and they're all very sympathetic. The book is a bit slow off the mark, but sales pick up soon enough.

Her writing is fine. Her marketing is fine. The underlying issue that she needs to address is: she has to stop freaking out about everything.

And somehow she needs to make her husband understand that there are four people in the family. If he wants to work less, he's going to have to pick up some slack at home. After all, she's done that for years.

She needs a plan.

She asks in the group: how many writers here are full-time and how are you doing?

There are some heartwarming and spectacular stories going around of writers who walked into their boss' office and told them where to stick their crappy jobs and never looked back. Those are awesome stories.

However, the reality is, that "going full-time" looks much more mundane for most writers:

- They gradually transition into full-time writing, for example teachers scaling back hours
- They are retired and don't need to work
- They lost their jobs
- They haven't worked for a long time because they've been caring for relatives, or because they live in a job-poor area, or because they've got health issues which make them near-unemployable
- They're supported by partners
- They have alternate income

A writer named Debra says: going fulltime is a chicken-and-egg situation. And I have to—unabashedly gleefully—admit that it's just about the only career where the traditionally disadvantaged are at an advantage: if you're old, unemployed or unemployable, this world really is your oyster. (Debra uses a wheelchair)

Luke adds:

If you're the main breadwinner for a family of four, two dogs and a healthy mortgage, then, yep, you're going to have to pee your pants about going full-time. You want a big buffer. You want a family member picking up the slack, if at all possible. You can make a trade off: how about you spend a few years furthering your career full-time in the workforce while I drop off and pick up the kids, drive them to soccer, do the washing, go to the post office and do the shopping. Oh, wait. I'm meant to write.

You could downsize. Get rid of the mortgage. Move to a cheaper area. Move to a cheaper country. For Americans: move to a country where healthcare is universal and cheap or free.

Another writer says: For many beginning writers going full-time as an author is the big dream. For quite a few, having reached that lofty goal, they find that they don't like it and go back to some form of paid employment.

There are a few things about writing full-time that you must know.

It is a terribly lonely existence. You spend a lot of time by yourself with your computer, looking at your screen. You can go to a cafe or some other place where you are surrounded by people, but this won't mitigate that you are not talking to people, or that your productive time is spent alone. You may not be the right type of person to do this.

Some people do collaborations with other writers. This may work.

As soon as you spend a significant amount of time at home, all the other people who live in your house will start dumping domestic tasks on you. Because you are at home, you wouldn't mind going to the post office, doing the shopping, staying at home so that a parcel can be delivered, talking to the lawn-mowing guy, and making sure that the pool is free of leaves.

Because you're at home anyway and have nothing to do, right?

Yes, that's the issue Lucy needs to address, besides a few others. She has done a poor job of managing her finances, because she's had her husband to rely on. She's recently opened her own bank account, but there is more to be done. Because even if Lucy has written full-time for a while, she plans to go full-time financially. What shape that will take will depend on her husband.

CHAPTER 146
MAKE A PLAN

The dreaded p-word. Jack hates it.

He's never had a plan and he sucks at plans and, even right now, he's being pulled in two directions. It would make excellent sense to finish those series, and he will do that. Eventually.

But he's recently received an email from a company that wants to put his best-selling book out in audio. He's been hearing a lot of good things about audio books. In his many half-arsed careers, he used to work for a radio station, and he reckons he can record audio books. His own audio books, because he's not going to go into any deals with other people. The last time he handed his books to someone else, it didn't end so well, so he prefers to record his own.

Well, that's a plan, of sorts. Record his books in audio. Finish the damn series.

Tom's plan is to do something with what he has learned about writing engaging fiction.

Because his mental space was so crowded with hospitals and doctors, he has no ideas of anything else to write, so he plots a story about the space captain with the elderly ill mother. But a little voice in his head that sounds like Priya tells him that this kind of thing is not going to appeal to a lot of people.

But something else happens.

He is waiting somewhere, leafing through books to buy on his tablet when a book comes up in the science fiction list that is so ridiculous, the description makes him laugh out loud. He buys the book—by an author he'd never heard of—and laughs his way through it. Not only that, when he finishes, his first thought is: I could totally write something like this. He knows about science and chemical reactions. It will be a story about space scientific officer goofballs who stuff up everything in science labs. Of course, when you're in space, unexpected chemical reactions have even more impact. Out in space, no one can smell your rotten eggs.

Tom doesn't quite know what's going to be the main plot of the story yet —a major departure from his usual way of thinking—but he knows a number of the funny scenes that happen.

Emily's plan involves figuring out how to get people on other retailers to start buying her books. She's already lost a month worth of sales and she's getting antsy. Her mailing list is growing, and they appear to like it that the books are everywhere, so maybe she should work harder on that. She also figures that if she continues to write a book every 6–8 weeks, there will be no need to send chatty emails. She can just announce the books to her list.

She has also decided to launch new books in KU for three or six months, since she knows how to give them a good headstart, and she sees many other writers doing this.

But meanwhile, she has been replying to at least one fan each day, and she's added a few features to her website.

Her cat has obtained a section in her newsletters. With every announcement, she posts a picture of something silly she has caught him doing (yes, cats really do drink out of the toilet). People seem to like it.

Her plan also involves taking at least one night per week off and doing something non-writing related with her time. She always enjoyed plays, so she's joined the drama society. It's actually fun looking at a story in another way. She might learn something new she can use in her fiction. And, you know, talk to normal people.

Lucy is almost done setting up her business. She's managed to salvage most of her ruined release, and found that, although it can be fun, a Facebook release party doesn't really add that much in terms of sales. Her husband hasn't mentioned taking up an exit offer again. She hopes he realises she's busy.

There is a lot of discussion about publishing plans in the author group. Some new writers are planning twelve-book series, and Tom feels proud to say that he was once planning a very long series, but now he understands why designing a series like this might not be a good idea (if it sells and it grows that way, that's another matter).

Luke says:

It is important to have a plan. The plan may be that you write a series in one genre, then write another series in a slightly different sub genre and make the first books free to advertise them. The plan may be that you write a book a month in a particular genre and the only advertising you will do is writing another book.

You may need to think about what you will do when your chosen strategy doesn't work out as well as you hoped.

You may need to think about a number of alternative directions you could take. Another genre, preferably one that is fairly closely related, or one that is really close to your heart.

You could try another pen name, hopefully attracting a different audience.

You could try advertising and cross-promotion. You should always have a mailing list, but you can put more emphasis on it, or you can go in a different direction altogether.

If you still have a day job, this will be easier for you, because you will have less time to play with, so you have to make hard choices. Since, if you have less time, those choices will be towards writing more books, it is natural that for the amount of time spent writing, you will have more books than someone who does it full time and has to contend with all the marketing.

Then Lucy asks Luke: what is your plan? Because Luke earns more money writing than all of them could ever attain combined.

He says: I plan to retire early, buy a boat and marry the mother of my stepson.

An admirable goal, they all agree. There is no point to being a writer if you can't also be happy.

The next subject: How much time should your plan include for doing marketing?

The group concludes: this will depend on a number of things. Your writing speed for one, but also how well your books normally sell.

If you sell well, the temptation is not to do any marketing. But the danger is that at some point your sales are going to plummet. It always happens unexpectedly, and usually it's not a gradual process. Once the retailer sites stop showing your book to prospective buyers, sales drop off very quickly. If you have never spent any time thinking about or practising the various ways you can market your books, you are going to be at a significant disadvantage to people who might have sold much less than you, but who have had to market for every single book sale.

The advantage you will have, if you use it well, is that you already have a style or subject matter that people like. But by changing tack and writing yet another series, there is also a chance that you throw this advantage out the window.

No matter how much success you have currently, you should always keep your eye on the future. What if your sales start declining?

If your books never sold that well, at least you don't have this problem. You have always had to market for every single sale.

It's funny that writers like to be given a percentage that they "should" spend marketing. They want to hear that it is 10% or 20% or 50% or whatever. The truth is that this will vary per person, it will vary depending on your current situation. It goes without saying that around a new release you will spend a lot more time marketing than you will when you're writing something new.

But ultimately, marketing should never come at excessive cost to your production schedule.

If you're spending so much time marketing that you don't have time to write, something is wrong.

In that case, you may need to look at your audience, your fiction, and your targeting.

Marketing should not need to take over your entire life.

A book that hits the audience well and is well received shouldn't need a huge amount of marketing. If you feel your current series is constantly pushing sludge uphill, you're probably better off trying again with a different series.

Park your current series wide, make the first book free, use it to attract subscribers to your mailing list, but then stop all the other marketing and write something new. For most writers this is going to be the default course of action.

If however you find that the little marketing you do is very successful, do more of it.

If it feels like hard work for little reward, do less of it.

Those principles should be engraved on the writers' foreheads.

There is no norm.

Groups of well-connected writers often gravitate towards their "norm" of best practices. People in the group will tell newcomers that they "must" do this or that.

Luke cautions against this way of thinking.

He says: when I first started publishing, things were different; so I can tell someone what I did, but they wouldn't be successful by doing what I did, and it wouldn't be relevant. Sadly, a lot of people look up to certain people so much that they seem unable to think for themselves. Everyone in this group should know that circumstances change all the time and are absolutely not the same as last year. I know squat about making it as a new writer today.

Jack jokes: So we should all leave?

Luke says: You shouldn't take what I say as gospel. Or anything anyone else says. Think for yourself. Your path will not be the same as your neighbour's.

CHAPTER 147
WHERE ARE THEY NOW?

Where does this leave our writers? Where are they now?

After six years of illness and a month in a hospice, Helena passed away peacefully. Tom was devastated, but found solace in a small community of writers. This is also where he met Dave and Susan, a couple in exactly the same situation. He's helping them through hardship for when Susan will succumb to her illness.

It changed his outlook on life.

His work with Priya paid off. He wrote, in short succession, a series about romping space scientists that just took off—well, at least compared to his other books. He put it in Kindle Unlimited, made some good money, but he's now ready to take it out.

The money helped him sell his house and move closer to his daughter.

He then wrote his idea of a space captain who deals with his dying mother aboard his ship, and he cried every page of the book. In the end, the sales weren't terribly great, but the book earned out and he wanted to write it. He's convinced he can write another book and is planning to use some of his money to go travelling.

When Emily took her books out of Kindle Unlimited, it was terrible. But she persevered, and now she has a growing income that doesn't depend on her churning out a book every month. It's a long-term project, but it's going in the right direction. She has more time to do other things. The reader Chris has become a friend.

She met a nice guy at the drama society. Trouble is, he comes with two little girls and a dog that really doesn't like her cat. Fun times ahead!

Jack has been busy finishing some of his projects. It's a hard slog, but he's getting there.

But he's finding it hard to let go of his advertising addiction. He's set a time limit to how much time he's allowed to work on it over working on new books.

His completed series relaunch gives him reason for hope. That did better than he expected.

He recorded his books in audio, and they now give him some welcome extra income.

Unfortunately, Tony got laid off from work and they went through a hard couple of months. Jack tried to get Tony to do his ads, but that didn't work out, so he decided instead to cut down on his writing and take up more cover design work. He's done that before, and the income is a lot steadier. They moved to a cheaper apartment and he sent Tony to get the degree he always wanted.

On a romantic visit to the beach, he proposed to Tony, and they now have a wedding to plan.

They're moving ahead, even if there will be no money to get a dog for a while.

The day Lucy found out her husband was having an affair, she bundled the kids into the car and left for her mother. The next day, she went to the bank and changed the address on her accounts and took his name off them.

He begged her to come back, but for her, this was it.

She was so upset that she didn't write anything for six months. Her sales suffered, but fortunately, she still had her supportive communities.

She's started writing again. She cares less about what people think, because she no longer has someone who measures her worth by her sales. She'll be starting a new series, and she has great hopes for it.

What about you, author-reader?

If you've read all the way, you will know that there are no endlessly upward trajectories or perpetually happy endings. There are only happy people. Nothing is ever permanent. Both good and bad things happen all the time. The saying goes: if you're handed lemons, you make lemonade. It's about the journey, not the destination. I could go on and on, piling on clichés and mangling bad metaphors. However, the clichés wouldn't have become clichés if they weren't true.

These are the things that are true:

Be happy

You have to enjoy what you're doing now. Not some time in the future. You have to enjoy the process, the learning, trying new things. There is no easy button. There is no reward for hard work if you hate the work. That's just not worth it.

Keep learning

Always do this. It doesn't matter what shape it takes, but don't get stale. Don't keep doing the same thing over and over and expect different results. Keep an open mind.

Try stuff...

Always try new things. A new writing process, new advertising, a new genre or pen name, heck, even going back to basics. Try it.

...even if people say it won't work

If you really like to do it, try it anyway. Don't listen to the naysayers. If you have a plan, it may just work. Or it may not, and you may learn something else that turns out to be valuable. The naysayers are not you. They know nothing about you and your circumstances.

Remember the economics

This is vitally important: always spend less than you earn. If you suddenly have a few good months, invest the money. Don't just go and spend it all. Save up for the future.

Do more of what works

This should be obvious, but it's amazing how many writers spend huge amounts of effort and time chasing sales for books that have a hard time getting off the ground, or series with poor sell-through rates. If you want to invest, pick the part of your business that works best and invest in that.

Do less of what doesn't

This should also be obvious, but writers need a reminder that it's OK not to do stuff that doesn't work for them at that point in time. "Stuff that doesn't work" includes stuff you hate.

Consider the needs of others

Like those in your family. There may be times that they are more important than writing. That's OK. There may be times that you need money and it's easier to do some work-for-hire project that delivers a fixed income. Nothing wrong with that either.

. . .

Don't forget to enjoy yourself

Ultimately, you got into writing because you wanted to. If it starts feeling too much like the cubicle desk job that you hated, something is off. You are your own boss. You get to make the rules.

―――

That's pretty much it. Now go forth and write.

ABOUT THE AUTHOR

Patty Jansen lives in Sydney, Australia, where she spends most of her time writing Science Fiction and Fantasy.

Her career started in earnest when her story *This Peaceful State of War* placed first in the second quarter of the Writers of the Future contest and was published in their 27th anthology. She has also sold fiction to genre magazines such as Analog Science Fiction and Fact, Redstone SF and Aurealis, before making the move to independent publishing.

Patty has written over fifty novels in both Science Fiction and Fantasy, including the *Icefire Trilogy* and the *Ambassador* series.

pattyjansen.com

BOOKS BY PATTY JANSEN

More information:
pattyjansen.com

For a complete list of books, scan the image below with your phone.

BOOKS BY PATTY JANSEN

www.ingramcontent.com/pod-product-compliance
Lightning Source LLC
Chambersburg PA
CBHW070454120526
44590CB00013B/646